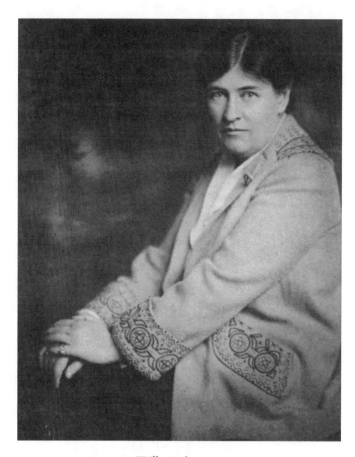

Willa Cather

Photograph courtesy of the Cather family.

Richard Giannone

Music in
WILLA
CATHER'S
Fiction

Introduction to the Bison Books Edition by
Philip Kennicott

UNIVERSITY OF NEBRASKA PRESS
LINCOLN AND LONDON

⊗

First Bison Books printing: 2001

Library of Congress Cataloging-in-Publication Data
Giannone, Richard.
Music in Willa Cather's fiction / Richard Giannone.
p. cm.
Originally published: Lincoln: University of Nebraska Press, 1968. With new introd.
Includes bibliographical references (p.   ) and index.
ISBN 0-8032-7099-2 (pbk.: alk. paper)
1. Cather, Willa, 1873–1947—Knowledge—Music. 2. Women and literature—
United States—History—20th century. 3. Music in literature. I. Title.
ML80.C32 G5 2001
813'.52—dc21
00-069049

Portions of the discussion of the following works have appeared in different form in
the indicated outlets: *Death Comes for the Archbishop* in the *Arizona Quarterly; The
Professor's House* in *Colby Library Quarterly; The Professor's House* in *College English*,
March, 1965, reprinted by permission of the National Council of Teachers of English;
My Mortal Enemy in *Die Neuren Sprachen; My Ántonia* in *Prairie Schooner; One of Ours* in
South Atlantic Quarterly; O Pioneers! in *South Dakota Review*; and "A Wagner Matinee"
in *The Modern Talent*, edited by John Edward Hardy and published by Holt, Rinehart

For Frank D'Andrea

Introduction

Philip Kennicott

"Seen from a balloon, Moonstone would have looked like a Noah's ark town."
Willa Cather's description of the town of Moonstone in *The Song of the Lark*, the
hometown of Thea Kronborg, the most sophisticated of the musician characters
that inhabit her fiction, doesn't convey much visual information. What exactly
does an ark look like? But that's not the point. With this odd image Cather
connects Moonstone, its people, and their habits to a familiar Old Testament
story, and we understand immediately that it is a town filled with just enough of
the Old World to propagate a new one. It also suggests that between there and
here, between the remembered civilization of Europe and the newly forming
"civilization" of America, something catastrophic has happened; something is
always lost in these projects of transplantation. Something always darkens our
imagination of new and better worlds.

Of all the old habits transported on that ark, music is perhaps the most precious to Cather. Few authors write so consistently about musicians, and none
writes with greater sensitivity to the power of music to nurture and destroy.
Cather's musicians are very much *American* musicians, and this native quality
distinguishes them from all others. Music is almost always a foreign place that
they make their own; some seek out this world elsewhere for refuge, others for
escape and yet others for growth and transcendence. The closest metaphorical
cousin to music in Cather's writing is the garden: a space set against the wilderness, created yet bounded by cultivation, an ambiguous space that is both an act
of defiance and an act of love.

There is a very odd character who wanders through James Fenimore Cooper's
The Last of the Mohicans (1826), a musician with the Old Testament name of
David. He is one of the prototypes of the musician in American fiction, a psalmist who trusts absolutely, if a bit foolishly, in the power of music to protect him.
He lives both an enchanted and a dangerous life: music brings him into peril, and
it rescues him. There is something utterly foolish and incongruous about his
singing in the middle of the wilds, yet he is one of the first of Cooper's Europe-
ans to make contact with the primeval forest. For Cooper, music is the advance
guard of civilization. For Cather, many generations later, the musician is still out
in front of the American project, a little exposed and a little foolhardy but still a
prerequisite to the making of a new world.

In the more than three decades since Richard Giannone's *Music in Willa Cather's
Fiction* was first published, Cather studies have grown immeasurably in depth and

breadth. But if anything, the understanding of the role music plays in her fiction may well have contracted, especially among casual readers. The kind of music that was fundamental to Cather's cultural life—music of the opera house and concert hall—is not so fundamental to the experience of readers today. Things that she took for granted—the cultural context of nineteenth-century composers, for instance—can't be taken for granted anymore. Giannone's book is an invaluable guide to an increasingly obscure cultural landscape.

Cather drops musical references with great fluency, and these references function as a kind of shorthand and counterpoint within her fiction. That Gluck's *Orpheus and Eurydice* is the favorite opera of Thea Kronborg's hometown music teacher, Wunsch, is a very broad brushstroke in the painting of his character. If he believes Gluck's opera "the most beautiful opera ever made" we can be sure that he is a purist and a classicist and more than a bit crusty. That the character of Aunt Georgiana, the prairie exile who hears Wagner again for the first time in decades in the short story "A Wagner Matinee," knew the composer's early works from her days as an apprentice musician tells us that she is extraordinary. Do the math: this old woman, almost spent by her hardscrabble years in Nebraska, must have done her training in the 1860s; to have saved a score of Wagner's *The Flying Dutchman* from those years—indeed, to have acquired it at all—tells us immediately that she was an adventurous musician, perhaps even a firebrand of the avant garde.

Both of these examples, elucidated by Giannone, concern composers whose works remain central to the canon. But for every Gluck and Wagner that appears in a Cather story, there is also a Balfe and a Nevin, composers whose music is known today only as a historical curiosity. Giannone is equally invaluable as a guide to the footnotes of music history. Cather was mostly catholic in her tastes, but she had her quirks and inexplicable enthusiasms. Every listener does.

But to map out an author's use of something as overdetermined as music is a very difficult project, especially when the author is as knowledgeable about music as Cather is. Music as metaphor isn't easily pinned down in Cather's writing. It shifts in meaning in very broad ways from her early fiction to her later works, and it can shift in meaning even within a novel or story. In 1892 a violin became one of the three protagonists of her first published story, "Peter." This early usage of music is straightforward. From Cather's newspaper writing, and from stories such as "Peter" and "Eric Hermannson's Soul," one senses an unprocessed enthusiasm for music, an amateur's first blush of love. Music takes one to a better place, connects one to cherished memories, releases one from the crushing forces of work and social conformity. The usual things.

By the time Cather publishes *Lucy Gayheart* in 1935, it seems as if music has changed its function entirely. Lucy is a promising though not brilliant pianist. Music, as it was for Thea Kronborg, has been her means of escape from small-town life. But she escapes into a world almost as oppressive as the one she has left. Working as the accompanist to a great lieder singer, she experiences the inexplicable pleasure of wordless communication with a serious artist. But she attracts both envy and erotic desire, and discovers through slow and painful revelation that the world of professional music making has little ennobling about it. Her beloved singer drowns, dragged down by one of Cather's creepiest and most unfortunately stereotypical creations, a fellow pianist who may well harbor a murderous sexual and professional jealousy. Music has become a claustrophobic endeavor; it gives and it takes away.

As Giannone points out, in the early stories music functions as "a counter-image" of enclosure. Silence and imprisonment, both real and metaphorical, are conjoined; growth, aspiration, and a kind of contrarian life-force are linked with musical expression. By 1915, when Cather published *The Song of the Lark*, the author was seriously questioning this neatly constructed antinomy. Long exposure to music, years of critical listening, the experience of friendship with professional musicians, and a greater understanding of the demands and sacrifices of the creative life, had made it impossible for her to maintain such a clean link between music and personal fulfillment.

Indeed, a small catalog of artistic pathologies could be derived from Cather's fiction. "The Prodigies," from 1897, is a study in exploitation and remains as relevant to the commercialism of today's music world as it was a prescient study in the warping of talent when it was written. Music is experienced only as a regimen of discipline and performance for two young singers, still children, who perform songs that demand an emotional maturity they are incapable of developing. It has an uncanny edge to it, a Hawthornesque edge; but it also shows the author's awareness of the simple but easily overlooked fact that music, more than most other arts, demands repetition and study, detachment and isolation. And these things can be debilitating. It is Cather's great strength as a writer about musicians that even when she uses music most metaphorically, her stories remain grounded in the reality of practical music making. Cather's stories about lonely people playing their precious instruments in the God-forsaken wilderness have particular power because she knows exactly what an organ or violin cost—to buy, to transport, to maintain.

Music and madness was a well worked-over romantic trope by Cather's day. In her hands, the association shifts from the madness of genius and untrammeled self-expression and becomes more pathetic, more a study in the febrile qualities of self-destructive artistic solipsism. One of the last works in which she makes substantial reference to Richard Wagner—her greatest musical idol—is the 1925 "Uncle Valentine." It is a study in musical disappointment, failure, alcoholism, and mental illness. These are still the very real and very substantial dangers of attempting a musical career. It is astonishing that a writer who could celebrate music so unambiguously in her early stories could treat it with such clear-sighted realism in her later ones.

It's easy to forget the simple fact that our knowledge and love of music evolve over time. We are not born sophisticated listeners. What we like when we are new to music, and the intensity with which we like it, very often changes over the course of a lifetime. Cather was very much a listener of her time, a listener who had prejudices, who discarded some of them, kept others, and grew throughout her lifetime in ways that reflect the capacities of a very knowledgeable amateur who kept a mostly open mind. It's worth sorting through what we know of her taste, because some of her enthusiasms offer more traction on understanding her fiction than others.

She would probably regret many of her earliest statements on music. There is a lot of juvenilia in the pieces that the Pittsburgh-based Cather sent back to the *Lincoln Courier*. She liked a big performance, a dramatic presentation; she had the usual American distaste for mannerism and pretension. We know that she admired the music of Mascagni and found Rossini tedious. But it's tempting to believe that both of these opinions would not sit well with her now. At the time, Mascagni seemed a radical figure, almost expressionistic in the violence of his verismo style, a style the composer believed was a realistic presentation of the earthiest, peasant passions. Mascagni's *Cavalleria Rusticana* remains a favorite in the opera house, but today its supposed realism seems just a brand of sentimentality, a class-bound romanticizing of a fictionalized rural culture. What Cather responded to at the time—the uncompromising lyrical insistence—would quickly be overtaken by yet more daring forms of musical expression.

Her dislike of Rossini is equally a reflection of the times. Throughout her lifetime, exposure to Rossini was severely limited. *The Barber of Seville* was about all that made it regularly to the stage. The bel canto singing style, based on length of line and a highly developed technique for light and rapid figuration, was dying out. That style was essential to appreciating Rossini, as was exposure to his darker, more serious works. Cather had little opportunity for that and it's not surprising that she found his music mannered and superficial. Again, it's tempting to imagine that today she would happily applaud the dramatically rich discoveries of the Rossini revival.

It is Cather's love of Wagner that gives the safest and most sound insight into her musical personality. Cather's access to the music of Wagner was extraordinary, especially given that throughout much of her lifetime there were few adequate recordings of his music. The years at the end of the nineteenth century were a boom period for Wagner's music in America. In February 1898, when Cather spent a week in New York City attending the opera and theater, the Metropolitan Opera had productions of Wagner's *Tristan and Isolde*, *Das Rheingold*, *Die Walküre*, *Siegfried*, *Tannhäuser*, and *Lohengrin* all running the same month. These productions were star-studded: Ernestine Schumann-Heink, Lillian Nordica, Jean and Edouard De Reszke, and Anton Von Rooy all sang in New York that February, all of them legendary singers even at the time. The Metropolitan also performed in Pittsburgh during Cather's years there. Her reviews suggest an immediate and total capitulation to the music.

Wagner remains a consistent theme in Cather's writing, from *The Troll Garden* stories through *One of Ours*. Or rather the stories of Wagner's operas remain a consistent theme for Cather. Her response to the music itself, the stream of constant modulation, the chromatically restless and lyrically distended open forms of his musical style, is manifested most clearly in an enthusiasm for singers. Wagner was a divisive character in the history of music, not just because of the force of his megalomaniac personality and the cult loyalty it inspired. The demands of his music required special vocalists, artists of uncommon physical and mental stamina. Cather was enthralled with these artists. Her contact with Olive Fremstad, one of the greatest and most profound of Wagnerian interpreters, eventually provided more than ample material to flesh out the character of Thea Kronborg. Cather, always concerned with hierarchies of moral, spiritual, and artistic development, found in the Wagnerian voice an ideal of expression: intelligence and discipline wedded to something terrifying and primitive.

Even from the days of her early criticism, Cather was inclined to translate her musical experience in distinctly visual terms. As a critic, this led to some embarrassing flights of fancy; as a novelist, it inspired some of her most thrilling prose. The music of Wagner was especially fertile as a source of imagery. In "A Wagner Matinee," she describes a character's memories jogged by the conflict of motives in the overture to Wagner's *Tannhäuser*: "And I saw again the tall, naked house on the prairie, black and grim as a wooden fortress; the black pond where I had learned to swim, its margin pitted with sun-dried cattle tracks; the rain gullied clay banks about the naked house, the four dwarf ash seedlings where the dish cloths were always hung to dry before the kitchen door." There is an immediacy of visual response, an access through the ears to the eye of memory that colors many of her best descriptions of music, whether it is Fremstad's Wagner reminding her of "the ranges of the Pyrenees" or visions of *Die Meistersinger* coming to her while vacationing in the Southwest.

The music of Wagner is always a special case for Cather. As it did to many contemporary listeners, Wagner's music suggests boundless spaces, and that boundlessness is often a metaphor for the dissolution of the boundaries between oneself and something larger and potentially engulfing. It is music that leaves the listener raw, defenseless, yet refreshingly susceptible to memory and the pain that memory brings with it.

The opera house is a very strange place to go if one is looking for an experience of the sublime in nature, and this oddity—this identification with Wagner's music on a specifically scenic level—set Cather apart from the wider body of Wagnerian appreciation. European writers who take up Wagner as a subject for fictional treatment (Thomas Mann most prominent among them) are concerned with the composer as a political figure, or a sociological problem, or even a psychological illness. For Mann, Wagner is a pathology—an inspiring one to be sure—but a pathology that needs, in the end, to be exorcised both from the author's mind and from German culture.

Cather is happy to appropriate Wagner to her own fictional needs, to use his music idiosyncratically to articulate a response to landscape, and to borrow from his texts a mythology that suited her needs. With her 1922 *One of Ours* she had reached a watershed in her use of the composer. Without making explicit reference to Wagner, she built up layers of reference to his *Parsifal*, and even more profoundly to the Ring Cycle, incorporating in her most subtle way a profound sense of pessimism about the world and its ideals of heroism. But Wagner had also gone underground in her writing: it was there as a kind of silent substratum to her story, guiding it but no longer a part of the action. When she turned again to music, in her penultimate novel, *Lucy Gayheart,* she was more concerned with the song repertoire, with smaller, more chiseled forms of expression; the larger mythology of Wagner was gone and so too the pure exultation in the glory of the voice.

Cather's love of music never left her. She remained an avid listener throughout her life, and several of her late friendships—with Myra Hess and the Menuhin family—were with musicians of the first rank. But her fiction turns elsewhere, to other subjects in which music plays a lesser role. Throughout her career, she prized the ability of writers to depict the unnamed thing, to create the sense of an event, an emotion, a meaning, without undue elaboration, without overt statement or crude explication. Music was a fundamental aid to her efforts to realize the ideal explicated in her statement of creative purpose, the brief 1922 essay "The Novel Démeublé." She sought "the emotional aura of the fact or the thing or the deed, that gives high quality to the novel or the drama, as well as to poetry itself."

In the same essay, Cather uses a telling musical metaphor. The unnamed thing is compared to "the overtone divined by the ear but not heard by it." Overtones are part of the sonic composite that gives richness and depth to every fundamental musical tone. Cather imagines a fiction composed more of what musicians call the "upper partials" than the fundamental tones. The use of music literally as a subject and strategy to create stories becomes less important; but the overtones remain through the last of her novels. Music had been subsumed completely into her fiction.

Contents

✾　✾　✾

Acknowledgments

My first debt of gratitude is to Professor Joseph X. Brennan for suggesting the topic of this book and directing the initial version with more than customary generosity. In later stages of my work several former colleagues at the University of Notre Dame provided encouragement of the most valuable kind. I thank Professor John Edward Hardy, who helped me at every turn (and return), and Professors James Walton and Peter Michelson, who criticized portions of the study. Professor Bernice Slote of the University of Nebraska read the manuscript more than once and each time brought me to a fuller understanding of the subject.

A grant from the American Philosophical Society made possible a trip to Red Cloud and to Lincoln, Nebraska, to study the early, uncollected materials; and a stipend from the Committee on Grants for the Humanities at the University of Notre Dame allowed me to spend a summer at the Newberry Library. Also, two students, Michael George Ryan and James Liebherr, cheerfully helped prepare the manuscript for press.

Sections of this work have appeared in different form in *Arizona Quarterly*, *Colby Library Quarterly*, *College English*, *Die Neueren Sprachen*, *Prairie Schooner*, *South Atlantic Quarterly*, *South Dakota Review*, and John Edward Hardy's *The Modern Talent* (New York: Holt, Rinehart & Winston, Inc., 1964). I am grateful to the editors of these journals and to Professor Hardy for permission to revise and reprint. Also, thanks are due Alfred A. Knopf, Inc., the Houghton Mifflin Company, and the University of Nebraska Press for allowing me to quote from Willa Cather's essays and fiction.

My debt to Professor Robert Turley goes beyond the formal limits of acknowledgment.

RICHARD GIANNONE

MUSIC IN WILLA CATHER'S FICTION

Prologue

"I must have music!"
Willa Cather to a friend

My main purpose in this book is to present the uses of music in Willa Cather's fiction. Initially I was fascinated by the prominence which music and musicians acquired in the stories and novels; and eventually, as I thought about the masterly way music is made to vivify so much of what Willa Cather had to say, and as I reconsidered her total work in view of this engagement with music, I realized that music is not accidental to technique, not simply an extension of personal interest in musical art, not merely ornamental to her achievement. Music is a distinctive quality of Willa Cather's mind and creation; and it is a univocal index to her loyalties.

Others have observed the impress of music on Willa Cather's art. Edith Lewis, a close friend of the novelist, emphasizes the need to study the importance of music to appreciate Willa Cather's artistry.

Music, for Willa Cather, was hardly at all, I think, an intellectual interest. It was an emotional experience that had a potent influence on her own imaginative processes—quickening the flow of her ideas, suggesting new forms and associations, translating itself into parallel movements of thought and feeling. I think no critic has sufficiently emphasized, or possibly recognized, how much musical forms influenced her composition,

[1]

and how her style, her beauty of cadence and rhythm, were the result of a sort of transposed musical feeling, and were arrived at almost unconsciously, instead of being a conscious effort to produce definite effects with words. All this quite apart from the fact that music and musicians were so often the chief subject of her books, as in *The Song of the Lark, Lucy Gayheart*, and *Youth and the Bright Medusa*, and as a minor theme in *One of Ours* and *My Mortal Enemy*.[1]

In his reminiscence of the novelist's Pittsburgh years, George Seibel describes the excitement Willa Cather derived from mingling with people who took music as a natural prerogative and how this pleasure shows up in her stories about that city.[2] Elizabeth Shepley Sergeant's *Willa Cather: A Memoir* establishes many connections between the musical interest and the fiction. In addition to informing us that attending the Metropolitan Opera twice a week made all the difference to Willa Cather when she worked for *McClure's* magazine,[3] Miss Sergeant states, for example, that the 1925 novel, *The Professor's House*, was conceived of as a sonata. She even specifies *molto appassionata* as the intended notation for the middle portion, "Tom Outland's Story."[4] This memoir, however, interprets Willa Cather's work from a psychological perspective, and so the opera finally holds more interest for the escape it offered the novelist than for its possible fictive uses. E. K. Brown's critical biography assures us that "music remained a passion to the last," that recordings of Beethoven's quartets and the great singers were Willa Cather's unique concessions to machines,[5] and that in her final secluded years musical intimates like the Menuhins and Myra Hess were among her cherished friends. Occasionally Brown offers a suggestive insight into the writer's use of music, as when he remarks that a clue to the artistic growth between *The Song of the Lark*, published in 1915, and *Lucy Gayheart*, published in 1935, lies in the author's change in musical taste from Wagnerian opera to the songs of Franz Schubert.[6]

1. Edith Lewis, *Willa Cather Living: A Personal Record* (New York: Alfred A. Knopf, 1953), pp. 47–48.

2. George Seibel, "Miss Willa Cather from Nebraska," *New Colophon*, II, Part 7 (1949), 195–208.

3. Elizabeth Shepley Sergeant, *Willa Cather: A Memoir* (Lincoln: University of Nebraska Press, 1963), p. 48.

4. *Ibid.*, pp. 203–204.

5. E. K. Brown, completed by Leon Edel, *Willa Cather: A Critical Biography* (New York: Alfred A. Knopf, 1953), p. 325.

6. *Ibid.*, p. 301. One reader has tried to define the impact of music on Willa Cather's art. Joseph X. Brennan's "Willa Cather and Music," appearing in the 1965 Spring and

One need do no more than adduce a few widely known, representative facts to show that music counted throughout Willa Cather's life. We know from Mildred R. Bennett's book on the novelist's early years that the young Willa Cather was deeply appreciative of music. On that lonely stretch of prairie between the Little Blue and Republican Rivers in south-central Nebraska music was a beautiful relief.[7] It brought the warmth of community and a feeling of belonging to something larger than Webster County. The most influential people, those most prominent to the mature artist looking back on her native land, were those who had a musical identity, like her Aunt Frank, who promoted singing groups and thereby taught the frontiersmen self-expression, and like Peorianna Bogardus Sill, who taught painting and music and who simply by being in Red Cloud, the county seat, after having studied under the famed Russian pianist-composer Anton Rubinstein in Europe, related the province to the elegant world beyond. During Willa Cather's years at the University of Nebraska in Lincoln and for a short time after graduation, from 1890 to 1895, she became part of a lively cultural scene which featured, after drama, a number of local and traveling musical offerings. And as a critic and columnist for the *Nebraska State Journal* and the Lincoln *Courier* she developed certain ideas about music. By June, 1896, when Willa Cather at the age of twenty-three left Nebraska to pursue a writing career, her inveterate love of music had been complemented by a seasoned knowledge of musical performance.

She ventured eastward, of course, and the move provided access to a quality of music and to established musicians whose style of life and dedication the young writer was disposed to admire. In Pittsburgh, where she first worked for the *Home Monthly*, a family magazine, then for the *Daily Leader*, and eventually taught in high school for five years, there were the regular concerts of the symphony orchestra at Carnegie Hall. As her circle of friendship grew, Willa Cather's appreciation for music drew her toward other musical people, and she began steadily to attend

---

Summer issues of *The University Review* (pp. 175–183, 257–264), distinguishes among three kinds of music—music of nature, music which rises spontaneously from human passion, and a more formal and classical music. He suggests several structural and symbolic patterns the novelist develops through music. Music, he says, serves "as a yardsitck for both humanity and civilization," measuring "the moral worth of individuals and the human values of a society." The essay is selective but sensitive; it concludes that much more remains to be said about the subject.

7. Mildred R. Bennett, *The World of Willa Cather* (New edition with notes and index; Lincoln: University of Nebraska Press, 1961), p. 14.

private chamber recitals. Being on cordial terms with musical artists like Ethelbert Nevin came naturally to Willa Cather.

The next move east was to New York City, where Willa Cather went in 1906 to write for *McClure's*, which was then an influential national magazine. For a music lover, New York is home. At the time Cather arrived, the opera bade an especially warm welcome. Magnificent voices, those which are myths for us now, were routine expectation at the Metropolitan—Nordica, Melba, Calvé, Chaliapin, Fremstad, Mary Garden, Farrar, Sembrich, the de Reszkes, Amato, Tetrazzini. Willa Cather became a part of it all. As she found in Pittsburgh a cultural freedom denied in Nebraska, so in New York she came upon a world elevated by the human voice to a scale commensurate with what she had long before believed could be.

The supremacy which music gained above Cather's other cultural interests was not grounded in technical knowledge. She was not a musician herself. As a child she had taken piano lessons, but she was more interested in what her teacher could tell about other things, especially his European past, than she was in playing.[8] Speaking of Willa Cather's lifelong involvement with music, Edith Lewis writes: "She recognized fully her own limitations where music was concerned—her lack of technical knowledge, which so far as I know, she made no effort to extend. But she had a very sure intuition of the qualities of music—both its aesthetic and, so to speak, its moral qualities; its sincerity, or the lack of it, its elevation or vulgarity."[9] Willa Cather was devoted to music but as a member of the laity. She listened to music to add to her dreams. She was an enlightened amateur, in the sense of amateur as lover; and a nonprofessional attitude was all to the good because it left her free of those formal demands music places on composers and singers, which finally would hinder a fictionist from exploring the more personal associations of mood and picture. For Willa Cather's fiction, music was a matter not of technical excellence, but of imaginative choice.

This involvement with music manifests itself as soon as Willa Cather starts to write. Music appears in her first story, "Peter" (1892), and in her nonfiction prose. The journalistic writings actually provide a full statement of Cather's initial concern with music. The first comments on music (in the Lincoln years, 1893–1896) were made when Cather was in her early twenties, so they are tentative. Even up to 1900, though her ideas

8. *Ibid.*, p. 153.
9. Lewis, *Willa Cather Living*, p. 48.

[4]

about music were well formed, the *Journal* and *Courier* columns which
carried her views were not overseen by anyone so formidable as a music
critic, so in general the statements are impressionistic. To the mature
artist many of those impressions seemed platitudinous and over-exuberant,
as indeed some are, especially the salutes to art's ineffabilities. And as we
consider the essays we must keep in mind that drama and literature, about
which she had important things to say, most fully engaged the young
Willa Cather. Music is a minor topic. The casual tone in the title of her
Courier column, "The Passing Show," suggests the kind of impromptu
notice she gave music. But if the observations were impromptu, they
were nevertheless serious. Singers and musical performances held a
special fascination for Willa Cather. In her later years, while visiting Mrs.
Charles Weisz, a childhood friend with whom she felt free to speak openly,
Willa Cather is remembered to have said, particularly when she was
fatigued and distressed, "I must have music!" [10] The pronouncement
comes as no surprise. Nor does it exaggerate her need for music. That
music would come to dominate her cultural and psychic life is predictable
from the special attention it receives when she first expresses herself.

II

Art for Willa Cather is a mystery.

> Art is not thought or emotion, but expression, expression, always expression. To keep an idea living, intact, tinged with all its original feeling, its
> original mood, preserving in it all the ecstacy which attended its birth, to
> keep it so all the way from the brain to the hand and transfer it on paper
> a living thing with color, odor, sound, life all in it, that is what art means,
> that is the greatest of all the gifts of the gods. [11]

Willa Cather's journalistic discussions of this process amount to a celebration of mystery. She employs music to express her belief in the vital
feeling which is born through art and to preserve the mystery of creativity. Music appears in the newspaper pieces as metaphor of, or ideal
analogy to, the excellence Willa Cather felt in all great art. Music

10. Brown, *Willa Cather*, p. 301.

11 *Nebraska State Journal* (hereafter cited as *Journal*), March 1, 1896, p. 9; collected in
The Kingdom of Art: Willa Cather's First Principles and Critical Statements, 1 8 9 3–1 8 9 6, selected
and edited with two essays and a commentary by Bernice Slote (Lincoln: University of
Nebraska Press, 1966), p. 417. Hereafter cited as *KA*.

becomes a strategy, a way of treating qualities of art which are repeatedly asserted as being beyond the very words one is using. And this strategy is a clue to her assumption that music is the pre-eminent art, the condition toward which other significant forms aspire.

Her praise for Sarah Bernhardt illustrates Willa Cather's equating the rarest quality of artistic genius with music. Bernhardt's stagecraft is found impeccable; and the young journalist can specify many features which make up so admirable a style: passion, technical control, emotional poise, regard for details of the part, and exact diction. But as much as she enumerates the discernible strengths of Sarah Bernhardt, Cather feels that she still has not accounted for the strongest power behind such acting. "It is all these things plus the most perfect voice that ever spoke through a human throat and something else beside, for which language has no name." The endowment of "that voice of gold" is variously associated with music in the several pieces on Bernhardt. The particular essay noting the "something else" in her acting ends by relating the inner verve of Bernhardt's performance to the indefinable, *felt* coherence of musical harmony. "She never fails or disappoints you because under all those thousand little things that seem so spontaneous there is a system as fixed and definite as the laws of musical composition. Her very enunciation, which baffles all the artists of her country in its perfections, is the work of years of labor, her every tone is not only beautiful, but correct."[12] The control is so complete, and yet so natural, that it suggests melodic unity. "That's just what Bernhardt does . . . , she phrases her lines as if they were music."[13] Willa Cather describes both the rhythmic effect and the mental power creating the effect as music.

Willa Cather believes that all art shares in a fundamental passion which communicates itself above literal content. That appeal, the expressed passion of a work, is also music for Cather. The identification of the universality of art with music provides the basis for her metaphorical descriptions. One need not know the vocabulary of a foreign play, for instance, to respond to it. "It is true," she says, "that great actors can overcome the obstacle of speaking in a foreign tongue—that we can feel the fire and pathos of Bernhardt's French, or the majesty of Salvini's Italian."[14] The judgment implies a distinction between literal and emotional meaning, semantics and beauty. It is a common distinction, one

12. *Journal*, January 26, 1896, p. 9; *KA*, pp. 120–121.
13. *Journal*, August 11, 1895, p. 9; *KA*, p. 216.
14. *Journal*, February 25, 1894, p. 9; *KA*, pp. 220–221.

most people make when attending an opera. In opera it is the music, not the libretto, which carries the higher excitement. Willa Cather stands in that relation to all art. The essential appeal of a play or poem she freely calls the music of a work. Writing on several student presentations of *Antigone* and *Elektra* in the original Greek, she says that "the real beauty of the Greek play lay in two things; the music one heard and the colors one saw." The music in turn was of two kinds, instrumental and "the speech itself, the 'vowelled Greek,'" which was "none the less beautiful" for being spoken—and beautiful, Cather holds, to those in the audience who are ignorant of Greek.[15] Reviewing the work of Paul Verlaine after his death in 1896, Cather again celebrates verbal music, this one capturing a "sensation" or "mood." "His verses are like music, they are made up of harmony and feeling, they are as indefinite and barren of facts as a nocturne. They tell only of a mood. He called one of his greatest volumes *Romances Without Words*, and indeed they are almost that. He created a new verbal art of communicating sensations not only by the meaning of words, but of their relation, harmony and sound."[16] Music figures the total propriety of medium and emotion in art.

Music, then, represents the spiritual bond between creator and receiver. Verlaine's poetic harmony, the vowelled Greek of classical tragedy, and Bernhardt's exquisite tones in their direct appeal to man's noblest nature link soul with soul. Art strives toward an unalloyed relationship. Where she finds that art fails to lift out of meaning into emotional immediacy, Willa Cather invokes her standard of spiritual form. Zola's prose is so burdened with relentless detailing that it does not awaken "the living soul within." "Only a diamond can cut a diamond," she continues, "only can a soul touch a soul."[17] Music, a medium which exists above fact and therefore communicates directly, stands for the discourse of the soul. It is in the nature of such discourse that cause and effect should coexist and that pleasure should not survive sound; and so music also serves Willa Cather as a figure for the precious transience of the performing arts and the special living relationship with the audience the performing arts involve. "Poets can die trusting their work to the appreciation of the future," she explains, "but an actor's greatness dies in him, as music dies in a broken lute."[18]

15. *Journal*, February 24, 1894, p. 6; *KA*, p. 216.
16. *Journal*, February 2, 1896, p. 9; *KA*, pp. 393–397.
17. *Journal*, February 16, 1896, p. 9; *KA*, p. 371.
18. *Journal*, April 8, 1894, p. 13; *KA*, p. 216.

So far I have spoken of musical analogues in non-musical arts. For these, Willa Cather uses music unambiguously as the symbol of transcendence. In her discussions of music itself, however, the figure for the ideal condition of art assumes other forms. She still looks for a "something else" in music, that nameless power which transports listeners to "the stainless heights of art." But music itself being unavailable as an analogue to the purity that the art of music must achieve, Willa Cather either settles for an indefinite "higher thing" or she draws upon words like "soul" and "emotion." Whatever the expression, the aesthetic imperative of sublimity which brought Willa Cather to use music as metaphor when treating the non-musical arts is also at work in her commentary on music. "When a singer can feel strongly and make others feel, then her voice is merely an instrument upon which a higher thing than even melody does its will."[19] Reporting the opening of the 1900 Pittsburgh opera season to her Lincoln readers, Willa Cather takes the occasion to elaborate a preference for *Cavalleria Rusticana* over *The Barber of Seville*, the two works which made up the double-bill gala. Rossini's style is artificial, mannered, lacking in "dramatic coherency," and therefore does not reach the lofty rapport expected of art. Mascagni's music is something else. *Cavalleria* is passionate and frankly so. It is all that music should be. "Here is music that means something more than pleasing sound, here is music that becomes a notable emotional language, the speech of the soul."[20]

Soul is Willa Cather's standard for expression and communication. As applied to music, which is the metaphor for purity of form in the other arts, soul implies several virtues. For one thing, it expresses Willa Cather's predilection for the elemental, primitive resources of music; for another, it implies the successful release of music's intuitive appeal. An admonition to Lillian Nordica, a singer whom the journalist thought "proficient" but spiritless, illumines Willa Cather's appreciation of music as the speech for the soul.

> Yet, forget it not, music first came to us many a century ago, before we had concerned ourselves with science, when we were but creatures of desire and before we had quite parted with our hairy coats, indeed; and then it comes to us as a religious chant and a love song. I believe that

19. *Journal*, December 9, 1894, p. 4; *KA*, p. 132.
20. *Courier*, May 12, 1900, p. 11. This article will appear in *The World and the Parish: Willa Cather's Articles and Reviews, 1893–1903*, selected and edited with an introduction and commentary by William M. Curtin, to be published by the University of Nebraska Press in 1968. I am indebted to Mr. Curtin for allowing me to use his materials during the preparation of this book.

through all its evolutions it should always express those two cardinal needs of humanity, carrying the echo of those yearnings which first broke the silence of the world.[21]

The concept of soul is dualistic. It connotes elevation and includes origins, implies both artistic transcendence and transient human blood. Willa Cather will call Sarah Bernhardt's acting musical and she will remind a musician that "singing is idealized speech."[22]

The dualistic idea of soul derives from Willa Cather's view of the human personality. Man is divided. As the speech of the soul, music becomes the medium of man's higher nature. The account of Blind Tom, the astonishing Negro pianist who could accurately reproduce whatever he heard, presupposes a belief that music is a medium of the spirit. "It was as if the soul of a Beethoven had slipped into the body of an idiot."[23] The music of Beethoven reveals a certain grotesque beauty behind Tom's "queer actions." What stays hidden, what lies dormant or secret or lost, this is one's higher self—and this hitherto unshared life is what music frees and makes known to others.

As there are two selves, there are two voices. One is the physical organ, trainable and powerful when properly used. The other is a spiritual instrument, elusive as the breath which bears it, and chromatic, capable of conveying the shaded essence of an idea. Willa Cather admires the sheer mastery of a physical organ, but she always looks for a voice within a voice. Marveling at Jean de Reszke's Lohengrin, she is at a loss to explain the rich "emotional resources" of his singing. Physical power itself does not account for his vivid reading of the knight. It is his second voice which vitalizes the role. "The organ itself is purely accidental";[24] De Reszke's taste and intelligence, these are what make him "the prince of tenors." The spiritual instrument generates "magnetism." "A concert singer must have voice and magnetism, an opera singer must have voice and magnetism and a powerful dramatic instinct and must be altogether an artist."[25]

Willa Cather's fascination with the voice and with singers reveals her idea of the literary artist. Given her love of music and a burgeoning

21. *Courier*, December 16, 1899, p. 3. The comment about Lillian Nordica's proficiency appears in the *Courier*, June 10, 1899, p. 3.

22. *Journal*, September 30, 1894, p. 13; *KA*, p. 217.

23. *Journal*, May 18, 1894, p. 6; reprinted in *Prairie Schooner*, 38 (Winter 1964/65), 343–344.

24. *Courier*, June 10, 1899, p. 3.

25. *Journal*, September 30, 1894, p. 13; *KA*, p. 216.

desire to write, one would expect the composer, who creates, and not the singer, who interprets, to offer insights into her creative choices. But clearly she feels closer to the interpretive artist, and that is because Willa Cather does not conceive of the writer as an inventor. He brings nothing into existence. "The first drama," she says, "was not drama at all, but life."[26] In writing, just as in singing, one's voice becomes the shaping receptacle for the fleeting substance, life, thereby raising words themselves to the height of Verlaine's song. Moreover, the literary process of molding life through words resembles interpretive singing in the necessity to subordinate oneself to the material. Impersonality in art lifts vocal talent to genius. Where the artist does not become a medium for art but uses art as a vehicle of self, Willa Cather finds an offensive egotism. Where she finds great art, she recognizes a great sacrifice of self, as with Calvé's Santuzza. "Surely Emma Calvé is the singer of singers to speak this lofty language, the greatest singing actress of her time, whose inimitable art so far subordinates its medium that the mere beauty of her voice is well nigh forgotten. Yet what a splendid organ it is, what richness and color and throbbing vitality in her every tone!"[27] The artist must have so much technique and control that skill does not show through and mar the lofty language.

This lofty language requires a balance between emotion and thought. Intelligence is the complement of physical endowment for musical genius. So Clara Butt, though she is vocally impressive, does not satisfy Willa Cather. "It is perhaps the most wonderful contralto voice in the world, but there is no mind to direct it."[28] Without a shaping idea, music does not speak to the soul. The journalist is equally critical of those musicians, like Mark Hambourg, who skillfully control their performance and work toward the idea behind the melody but slight feeling. He is all intelligence, all technique.[29] Where Hambourg is cold and intellectual, Clara Butt is cold and unaware. Either approach denies art the compound genius Cather looks for. There is a suggestion that Ethelbert Nevin, the Pittsburgh song composer, comes near fusing feeling and idea in his art; but Willa Cather's remarks on his work are only critical pencilings.[30] In the newspaper pieces she is more likely to honor that balance than to analyze it.

26. *Courier*, January 7, 1899, p. 11.
27. *Courier*, May 12, 1900, p. 11.
28. *Courier*, January 6, 1900, pp. 2–3.
29. *Courier*, January 17, 1900, p. 3.
30. See especially the comments in *Courier*, February 5, 1898, pp. 3–4.

Though not given to theorizing on how a poised tension between emotion and thought creates a speech of the soul, Willa Cather does describe from time to time what such a speech says to her. Her habit is to transpose that "something else" in music into picture. An account of Anton Dvořák's Ninth Symphony, *From the New World*, for example, reconstructs the work scenically. The opening movement calls to mind "those wordless, minor melodies echoing through the silver silence of the Virginia moonlight." The second movement "is placed," Willa Cather puts it, "in an altogether different atmosphere." It presents "the empty, hungry plains of the Middle West." The endless prairie is so vividly felt that "it seems as though from each of those far scattered lights that at night mark the dwellings . . . , there comes the song of a homesick heart." The picture is vivified through action, a drama of Willa Cather's devising. "The largo closes with [a] little staccato melody, begun by the oboe and taken up by one instrument after another until it masters the orchestra, as though morning was come, and the times for dreams was over, and the peasant was hurrying to his plow to master a strange soil and make the new world his own." And the last high note from the wind section "is like the flight of the dove over the waste of waters."[31] In a notice of Massenet's oratorio *Eve*, Willa Cather visualizes in the music "those sacred pictures of the contemporary French school that works the characters of sacred literature in with modern conditions and surroundings . . . ."[32] The aesthetic correctness of turning sound into picture and then supplying action is not at all an issue for Willa Cather. Subjective programing gives that "something else" dynamic and communicable form. And rendering melody into *tableau vivant* is a clue to her fictive approach in the early stories.

A taste for music replete with story and scene predisposes Willa Cather to opera, which provides what she imaginatively supplies for instrumental music. Opera for her is heightened drama, and the standard is "dramatic coherency." Wagner, who constructed elaborate theories and techniques on this principle, is naturally the young writer's master-composer. Wagner "has stung the palate so that all other styles seem insipid."[33] His art unites form with feeling, song with scene; and his operas variously commemorate the two cardinal needs of humanity that

31. *Courier*, December 25, 1897, p. 2; reprinted in *Prairie Schooner*, 38 (Winter 1964/65), 344–345.
32. *Journal*, December 6, 1896, p. 13.
33. *Courier*, May 12, 1900, p. 11.

music, in the Catherian view, issues from. In Wagner's music Willa Cather encounters an art which not only draws on these two cardinal needs of love and religion but which is totally structured on the tensions between the two. And he is anything but trivial or artificial, to borrow Willa Cather's disapproving description of Rossini's style. This early admiration never tapers off; it increases. His music both pleased and taught her. The economy and suggestiveness of the writer's early manner perhaps derive in part from the Wagnerian *leitmotif*; and her fiction shows, sometimes in theme and sometimes through allusion, a familiarity with the German composer. Richard Wagner of course wrote the music of the future, and it is indicative of Willa Cather's sensitivity to music that she found his advanced style sympathetic.

III

A passage from one of Willa Cather's first idols, Carlyle, is helpful in summarizing her early relationship to music.

> Musical: how much lies in that! A *musical* thought is one spoken by a mind that has penetrated into the inmost heart of the thing; detected the inmost mystery of it, namely the *melody* that lies hidden in it; the inward harmony of coherence which is its soul, whereby it exists, and has a right to be, here in this world. All inmost things, we may say, are melodious; naturally utter themselves in Song. The meaning of Song goes deep. Who is there that, in logical words, can express the effect music has on us? A kind of inarticulate unfathomable speech, which leads us to the edge of the Infinite, and lets us for moments gaze into that![34]

Willa Cather too believes in the power of music to penetrate the inmost heart of things and to provide an unfathomable speech to express the best in man. The imagistic alpha and omega of music are primitivistic and cultural, with the initial breaking of silence in earth and sky and then extending to a historical fullness. Music is even the discourse between God and man, as "the Lord has so revealed himself to man through music."[35] A speech of the soul can do this.

It also can create a world of its own. Like the Greeks, and for pretty much the same reason, Willa Cather conceives of a world patterned on musical harmonies. It is a way of reconciling cosmic nature with human

34. Thomas Carlyle, *Heroes and Hero-Worship*, Vol. V of the Centenary Edition (New York: Charles Scribner's Sons, 1897), p. 83.
35. *Journal*, October 7, 1894, p. 13; *KA*, pp. 177–178.

nature. The universe, when understood as musically ordered, takes on a rhythm actuated by man's feelings and therefore is sympathetic. Music connects the slight to the immense and gives man a central place in a vast balance of parts. It gives the highest possible status to human emotion. In fact, music creates an environment for feeling; it builds a world elsewhere.[36] As used in this book, the word *music* refers to all the materials Willa Cather uses to create this environment: aural appeals in general, like those of animal and geological nature, if they express the melody of life; musicians of all kinds; and allusions to musical compositions. The word *music* also refers to forms as traditional as the sonata or as subjective as a suave scale of impression, and to Willa Cather's various techniques of expanding meaning through musical allusion. The emphasis in surveying the kinds and uses of music will be to show their richness, then the bearing of that richness on individual stories and novels, and finally the cumulative relation of music to vision. "Good music is just a little above anything else that ever honors any stage, and everyone owes it a certain respect." In fact, the young writer reminds the 1894 Lincoln audience, "Music calls for the best of everything . . . ."[37] In the fiction, music is just a little above anything else Willa Cather chooses to honor. It receives the best of everything because that is what it signifies: Willa Cather's intuition of human happiness derived from a harmony between man and his place and his time.

If I am right about the centrality of music in Willa Cather's fiction, then a study of music should offer a way into the evolution of her art. To test the truth of this approach, it is necessary to go beyond the four or five novels and dozen stories which are generally taken as the enduring part of her work. In covering the entire body of Willa Cather's writing, I do try to hold a balance between artistic merit and length of treatment, mindful that what is memorable in her work is what justifies such a study in the first place; but I want also to be comprehensive and to take my own critical stand. Naturally the balance tips from time to time. The early stories which do not come up to the later fiction are analyzed because

36. The phrase is taken from Richard Poirier's recent *A World Elsewhere: The Place of Style in American Literature* (New York: Oxford University Press, 1966). It is a measure of the richness of Mr. Poirier's study that, though he does not mention Willa Cather, his thesis that American writers build through language a special environment congenial to their imaginative determinants suggests many parallels between Cather and the whole of American literature.

37. *Journal*, October 21, 1894, p. 13; *KA*, pp. 176–177.

they provide a basis for surveying the continuity of music in the art and because they disclose ways of handling music which clarify the more complicated uses of it in the later works. Occasionally the balance goes the other way. I have permitted myself to discuss thematic relationships between novels if such relationships gloss the use of music; and I consider other formal aspects, like the pictorial manner of the three stories comprising *Obscure Destinies*, which subordinate the importance of music. I am, then, concerned with the incremental contribution of music to the fiction. This accounts for the chronological scheme of the book. Where I depart from chronology, as with the stories about the lyric artist following *The Song of the Lark*, my purpose is to examine the development of a fictive character especially important to the study of music. But while showing the coherence of music in large, I am interested as well in its service to the meaning and unity of a particular work. This emphasis explains my considering the novels singly.

CHAPTER ONE

The
Kingdom
of the Soul
Without music, life would be a mistake.
Nietzsche

Willa Cather's conception of music as the speech of the soul and as belonging to an imaginative order built to honor man's higher impulses not only shapes her early judgment of the arts but also informs the early practice of her own art. The twenty-five apprentice stories written between 1892 and 1902 dramatize attempts to utter a fine feeling within and to find a world in which the spirit can be at home. In fourteen of the twenty-five, music serves a central symbolic purpose in Willa Cather's treatment of that yearning. It does so in three large ways. First, music characterizes the sensitivity of the protagonists, who are artists manqués, men with a rich spiritual potentiality held in check by an alien environment. These early heroes are "kings in exile"; and music becomes an anthem for the special empire from which they are cast out. Finally, in its high service as discourse of emotion, music constructs a "bridge into the kingdom of the soul."

Significantly, the first appearance of music in Willa Cather's fiction coincides with her first appearance as a fictionist. "Peter,"[1] an undergraduate piece published in 1892, illustrates the use of music as spiritual communication. The conflict in "Peter" announces the central paradox in

1. *Willa Cather's Collected Short Fiction, 1892–1912*, with an introduction by Mildred R. Bennett (Lincoln: University of Nebraska Press, 1965), pp. 541–543. Hereafter cited as

all of Willa Cather's prairie dramas. The land has a pastoral, untouched vitality which promotes strength and freedom, but its rawness can break and imprison man. There are men on the prairie who reflect the worst features of the land, and they compound the hostility of nature with meanness of mind. In her first story Willa Cather uses music to represent man's effort to free himself from the double harassment of nature and society, and reach a condition supported by beauty rather than economics.

"Peter" contrasts music with greed. Peter Sadelack immigrated to southwestern Nebraska from Prague, but emotionally he never crossed the Atlantic. The five years he has spent on the prairie have only deepened his attachment to the European capital. Life there was rather fancy. He was "second violinist in a great theatre" and knew "all the great singers" and actresses of the world. He wore a dress coat every day and went to parties after the play. Such a style with its touch of the debonair, which Peter had cultivated from early youth, could hardly accommodate itself to homesteading in one of the dreariest corners of the world. In Nebraska Peter is a misfit. He cannot even support himself. His compensations take the forms of a pipe, music, and daydreaming of Prague. The measure of Peter's alienation is the animosity of his son, Antone, who has adjusted to the new life by going nature's hardness one better. He blends ambition with filial cruelty. Where Peter turns everything into romantic illusion, Antone melts everything down into coin. Each habit of mind is disabling, but Antone's, being materialistically sound, is more powerful. Most of all, Antone wants to sell his father's violin, a useless plaything, for the fifty dollars it will fetch.

What is a commodity to Antone is a sacred object to Peter. Besides having provided a livelihood, the violin is an entrée into a magical realm Willa Cather called "the kingdom of the unattainable" which is "right beyond that line of [stage] lights . . . where the grand passions die not and the great forces still work."[2] Peter's attachment to music derives from a pleasure in its transporting power. "He could never read the notes well, so he did not play first; but his touch, he had a touch indeed." . . . Music acts as metaphor in the root sense, *to transfer*. In Nebraska, fiddling recalls his proximity to those lights dividing the worlds of fact and fancy. Even in the Prague theatre, music transferred Peter to another world. Inter-

---

CSF. Page numbers will be given in the text for quotations from the novels and novellas, but not for quotations from the short stories.

2. *Courier*, September 28, 1895, p. 8; *KA*, p. 282.

estingly, Willa Cather describes his reaction to Sarah Bernhardt in terms comparable to her own. Peter forgot the actress's name and face, did not know French, and yet he still felt the beauty of Bernhardt's presence because "it seemed to him that she must be talking the music of Chopin."

Peter has the power and hunger of soul Willa Cather admires, but the power has gone wild and the hunger has intensified into rapacity. He is so given to total surrender to enchantment that he forgets the kingdom is *un*attainable and believes it to be within reach. His pietism and superstition, which equate "his violin and the holy Mary," stress the recklessness of Peter's fantasy. The imagination erases the line dividing the double nature of the world. Trapped on the solid material side, Peter naturally tries to go to the other extreme. Unable to live in fact and therefore without music, he kills himself in the stable, a sardonic counterimage of the great theatre in Prague where he lived fully. Before he shoots himself, he plays the "Ave Maria" with his nearly paralyzed hand, then breaks his fiddle. Suicide actually gives final form to the way Peter Sadelack's fancy has worked all his life. One of the plays he saw in Prague required that Sarah Bernhardt stab a man after he touched her arm; and Peter, captivated by the music of her voice, yearned to be stabbed. He would go all the way to preserve an ecstacy. In the great Prague theatre he died many times traveling into the bright realm across the footlights. In Nebraska the only death available is the irreversible one. There is nothing to intoxicate him on the prairie except religion which, lacking the sensuous delight of music and drama, does not cheat effectively. Physical labor threatens the fancy because it minimizes freedom. It is understandable, then, that Peter should cling to the violin bow after he shoots himself. ("'I can play thee no more, but they shall not part us.'") The bow is talismanic. It will admit him into the empyrean of the fancy and it will provide for him there.

There is another side to Willa Cather's use of the violin in "Peter." As we have seen, it reveals an excess of spirit in the father and solicits sympathy for the beautiful madness he dies from. Music moves in a negative direction, as well, to expose an unfathomable spiritual void in the son. Antone demands of his father: "'But I need money; what good is that old fiddle to thee?'" There are so many instances in Willa Cather's fiction of tyrannical unfeeling attacked through music that we might reserve attention for a more complex sort than that of Antone Sadelack, whose emotional size is measured in his final gesture: never one to miss a deal, he peddles the violin bow which his father neglected to destroy, and he completes the transaction before the funeral.

"Eric Hermannson's Soul,"[3] published in 1900 when Willa Cather was a more skillful writer than when she published "Peter," most amply illustrates the early use of music as a span between man and the outer world. In "Eric Hermannson's Soul" music vies with puritanical belief and moralistic self-righteousness. Religion which binds is shown as a more subtle corruption than Antone Sadelack's materialism, because such a religion raises inhibition to virtue by equating pleasure with "all forbidden things." To the Free Gospellers in the story, "the violin is an object of particular abhorrence . . ."; and the violinist, Eric, a Norwegian rough known as "the wildest lad on all the Divide," is singled out for conversion as though his submission would bring with it a triumph over all the evil in the world, which seems epitomized in his untamed exuberance. Willa Cather's scorn for the Free Gospellers is unequivocal. Asa Skinner, a converted train gambler, has the prudery and malice expected of a reformed sinner; and his face, especially his eyes shining with "a terrible earnestness, an almost prophetic flame," projects the vengeance of God which he preaches. When Eric has finally been brought to his knees and crushes his instrument to splinters, "the sound was like the shackles of sin broken audibly asunder" to the evangelist's ears.

The violin created very different sounds for Eric before his conversion. It was a touch of beauty in the ugly world around him. "It stood . . . for all the manifestations of art; it was his only bridge into the kingdom of the soul." Music elevates Eric. It brings him in touch with the exotic while he is living amid the prosaic. Lena Hanson, who, like Peter Sadelack, knows the ways of big city life, embodies the bright associations Eric derives from music. She has a perky manner, touches of elegance, like her silk stockings, and a fair throat. Just as it is Bernhardt's voice that holds magic for Peter, so Lena's voice is the source of her power over Eric. Lena accompanies her singing on a battered guitar, and the combination of voice and plinking, though crude, captures Eric. But his mother and her Gospellism turn every pleasure into guilt, and the conflict tortures him. Even so simple a person as this Norwegian boy who does not question the categories of his seniors cannot understand how mirth and music are evil. Gospellism succeeds in persuading Eric. Without a force in the world more lasting than Lena's occasional song, he cannot continue to believe in his natural impulse. Gospellism reaches him where he is most vulnerable—in

3. *CSF*, pp. 359–379.

his feelings—and it does so through the emotion which it condemns. Caught in a revivalist frenzy of "shouts and hallelujahs," the simple Norwegian impulsively wrecks his violin. The bridge into the soul is razed. The fineness which humanizes the world is gone. Music, Eric's soul-right, is surrendered; and a heavy gloom settles on him.

Music marks Eric for abuse but it also saves him. After two years of living by this hard faith he accidentally meets Margaret Elliot who has come to Rattlesnake Creek on a last jaunt across the country before her approaching marriage. Margaret is a musician, and her talent restores Eric's psychic bridge. He first hears her playing a parlor organ at the Lockhart place where he is helping with the threshing. In his inarticulate way he makes Margaret understand that he wants her to sing. She responds generously. "'I sang just the old things,'" she tells her brother Wyllis, with whom she is traveling. But for Eric they are new things, hints of a large, beautiful place where he feels welcome. It is Lena's world again. The cumulative effect of his encounter with the old/new things is almost excruciating. He twists and shuffles as though fighting off a strong force let loose inside. Two years of deprivation have sharpened his need for music, and the silence of the heart, when it breaks, breaks traumatically. The soul has a voice. "'It gave him speech, he became alive,'" and in his voice "'were tears.'" Margaret continues to Wyllis: "'Think of it, to care for music as he does and never to hear it, never to know that it exists on earth! To long for it as we long for other perfect experiences that never come. I can't tell you what music means to that man.'"

Margaret's music dispels the dark curse put on Eric. Where the "gospel of maceration" seeks to save the soul through starvation, music saves man's spirit by nourishing it. Eric's first response is to recall a lost love. One arc of the musical bridge is to the past. He tells Margaret of a crippled younger brother whom he carried in his arms until death. Willa Cather specifies the music which unlocked Eric's memory. "'And of course I played the intermezzo from *Cavalleria Rusticana* for him,'" Margaret explains. It is inviting to read "Eric Hermannson's Soul" as Mascagni's opera in reverse—as a resuscitation of the searing passions of strong, peasant blood rather than a destruction by them. But Willa Cather's story treats rustic vitality, not rustic chivalry, and a rustic strength as a life suggesting first things. "'I think if one lived here long enough one would quite forget how to be trivial, and would read only the great books . . . , and would remember only the great music . . . .'" In one of Willa Cather's *Courier* pieces on Mascagni she describes the Intermezzo with an awe comparable to Margaret's when she sees the breaking of new life on the plains. And Willa Cather's appreciation of the Intermezzo, marked by a sense of tension within man's double nature, suggests the function of the allusion in the story. There is "its bass that labors and fails and struggles, that suffers and protests in its black despair; its treble that never yields, never falters, dips sometimes toward the lower octaves like a bird that is faint with its death wound, and then flies on, flies on."[4] The Intermezzo is Eric's struggle in musical terms.

Eric's awakening, the unyielding high melody of his soul asserting itself, is confirmed when he once again plays the violin. This time he plays at a dance Margaret has arranged for the villagers. The dance is Margaret's musical gift to Rattlesnake Creek, and it is the counterforce to Skinner's strident prayer sessions. The dance is universally restorative. Mirth becomes "irresistibly infectious." Music briefly liberates these settlers from the dullness and isolation they have endured for a long time. "Something seemed struggling for freedom in them tonight, something of the joyous childhood of the nations which exile had not killed." Toil, irritation, denial, all dissolve in musical air. "Tonight Eric Hermannson had renewed his youth," and so have the others. Even Margaret, jaded somewhat by New York life, feels a primitive stirring within herself. "For the first time in her life her heart held something stronger than herself, was not this worth while?"

The question is not rhetorical because the awakening of the spirit leads man to expect rare things which he shall not find. Twice in the story Cather warns that a blessing is also a burden. Wyllis answers his sister's explanation of Eric's excitement: "'Poor devil . . . and so you've given him a new woe. Now he'll go on wanting Grieg and Schubert the rest of his days and never getting them.'" And Margaret herself wonders at the dance, "But was it a curse, this awakening, this wealth before undiscovered, this music set free?" For the innocent like Eric there is the curse of wanting what is rarely available and having to defend a soul-right against arrogance like Skinner's question, "'Certainly you did not dance, Eric?'" Certainly he did. For a moment he is at home in the world and becomes something larger than himself: he becomes Siegfried—a northern god who lives without fear. But only for a moment. He is a marked man living among enemies. His fate is suggested in the Intermezzo, in what the Intermezzo meant to Cather at least. In the *Courier* piece cited earlier, she writes of "that treble that knows and sees the hopelessness of all things and yet never wavers; love betrayed that still loves on, hope deferred

4. *Courier*, September 7, 1895, p. 7; *KA*, p. 162.

that still hopes on; it is the despair which passes despair, despair sublime, impersonal, and full of awe as though it comprehended universal futility and universal doom."[5]

II

In a number of the early stories no unyielding treble rises from darkness to assert itself, however tentatively, over a dominant bass. There is doom without hope. Freedom, harmony, communication, and pleasure are absent. There is silence. The stories of silence show how desperate and unbalanced life is without a treble emerging even faintly.

"On the Divide,"[6] published in 1896, typifies the stories without music. Here as in the others the outer darkness of a hostile world invades man's spirit and puts out his bright center. Canute Canuteson, "the wreck of ten winters on the Divide," never smiles and hardly ever speaks. A giant of a man, he has taken to raw white alcohol and manages to avoid the common alternatives of insanity and suicide. Though he lives alone, he yearns for human companionship; and in seeking it, Canute deals with people in the same manner that the Divide has dealt with him: caveman-like he carries Lena Yensen from her house and forces a Norwegian minister to marry them. For all its brutality, Canute's act seems more pathetic than cruel because it is an attempt to escape an incredible loneliness. For years Canute morosely tolerated isolation; now he has Lena. That is the best his spirit could do. "For ever and anon the soul becomes weary of the conventions that are not of it, and with a single stroke shatters the civilized lies with which it is unable to cope . . . ."

Like Lou in "Lou, the Prophet" (1892),[7] who lives in the apocalyptic atmosphere of his belief, and Serge Povolitchky in "The Clemency of the Court" (1893),[8] who endures a subhuman life without a single amenity, Canute has fine feelings which conditions suppress. "He was a man who knew no joy, a man who toiled in silence and bitterness." There are two references to music in the story. Music is associated with life beyond the Norwegian settlement, referred to but never experienced. Mary Lee startles her friend Lena with tales of "ten cent theatres, firemen's dances, and all the other esthetic delights of metropolitan life." Lena shares in such

5. *Ibid.*; *KA*, pp. 162–163.
6. *CSF*, pp. 493–504.
7. *CSF*, pp. 535–540.
8. *CSF*, pp. 515–522.

pleasures imaginatively. She prizes a town beau, and while performing tiresome kitchen chores, she sings loudly. Her rather boisterous joy, her bit of music, strikes a responsive chord in the seemingly insensitive giant, Canute. Though it occurs to no one around him, Canute too searches for music, a delicacy, a love. Every night after working, he gropes for a more hospitable world. He drinks staggering quantities of liquor, and while drinking, he either carves on the window sills with his jacknife or plays away on a mouth harp. The delicate instrument is no match for the alcohol which sinks him back farther into himself, to a dark corner of his nature where "all the hells of Dante" lurk. That neighbors fear Canute, who rejoiced when the first men settled close enough to be called neighbors, exacerbates his loneliness. A love unshared, like a sound unheard, dies.

Where the soft treble in man does not reach sympathetic ears, where mercenary values take precedence over aesthetic values, where religion restrains and intimidates, where the commonweal does not provide for creative impulses, there is no music. Its presence signifies man's success in breaking the silence of the world and thereby warming to life's rich possibilities or man's striving but succumbing and honoring those possibilities in defeat. Such nobility of struggle is what the stories of silence do not treat, and the absence of heroic undertaking partially accounts for the limited use of music in them.

III

An 1896 story, "The Count of Crow's Nest,"[9] illustrates the way music broadens out from a definition of the contrary needs in man to make moral distinctions among several characters and to establish values. It is a tale of manners, money, and mystery. Crow's Nest is a west side Chicago boarding house with an "atmosphere of failure" pervading furnishings and inhabitants. Downstairs is the "old grand piano, with the worn yellow keys that clicked like castanets as they gave out their wavering, tinny treble notes in an ineffectual staccato"; upstairs is a "thin, pale, unhappy-looking" prima donna "with dark rings under her eyes, whose strength and salary were spent in endeavoring to force her voice up to a note which forever eluded her." Amid this wilted gentility is the Count de Koch with his "calm patrician face" and natural dignity. His taste in music corresponds to his moral integrity. Just as he lives by a high code which demands that he sacrifice personal fortune to repay the debts of his prodigal family, so he prizes the best in traditional music and speaks out

9. *CSF*, pp. 449–471.

against the emptiness of modern light opera. He is "'not fond'" of frivolity like Arditti's waltz song or anything of "'that style of music.'" He prefers Haydn, Mendelssohn, and "'the modern classics'"; and among a public which demands more accessible music his preference is singular.

Cather uses artistic awareness as an index to moral responsibility. The Count does not confuse art with cash; nor does he feel that aristocratic privilege places his family's debts outside ordinary obligations. His grubby circumstances do not force him to betray a loyalty any more than popular taste makes him compromise his high idea of art. In resisting the vulgar alternative of meeting the world on its terms he becomes, by his own admission, "'a sort of survival of the unfit,'" "'the last of one's kind.'"

Opportunism is characterized by a decadent taste in music. A singer, Helena de Koch, the Count's daughter, shamelessly accommodates her art to vulgar expectation. "'You must give the people what they want,'" is her motto. Something of a cultural as well as a familial embarrassment to the Count, Helena "sang floridly and with that peculiar confidence which always seems to attend uncertain execution." Buchanan, a young tenant at Crow's Nest, feels that "her singing was rather the worst feature about her" because "to sing badly and not to have perception enough to know it was such a bad index of one's mental and aesthetic constitution." The Count has in his possession compromising letters belonging to certain European nobles, and their contents make them a marketable commodity. Helena's theft of the letters shows that her moral sense squares with her musical sense. In trying to bring Buchanan into the scheme with her lackey, Tony, "the silent tenor," we see that Helena has even more tricks in manners than she has in her singing, and they are not few. Cather uses Helena's musical talent, estimable only in pecuniary value, to indicate her betrayal of father and art. As in morals, so in music.

Other stories use music to suggest the moral course of life. In "El Dorado: A Kansas Recessional" (1901)[10] Colonel Josiah Bywaters, sitting amid the useless stock of a drygoods store he was duped into opening in the middle of nowhere, dreams of the sound of Virginia rivers, and the river music recalls the old values he lived by. In his mind he hears "that rhythmic song of deathless devotion . . . which the Potomac and Shenandoah sing to the Virginia shore." The sound, with its strong ethical message to keep his honor clean, marks the end of a noble code; El Dorado, the ghost town, represents the start of the new moral style of corrupt speculation. A more positive course is suggested in

10. *CSF*, pp. 293–310.

"A Resurrection" (1897),[11] in which a resumption of music attends the rescue of Margie Pierson, by nature a woman destined for a full life, from the poverty and pettiness in Brownville, Nebraska. Her rescuer, Martin Dempster, will take her to St. Louis where she will have singing lessons again. As in "The Count of Crow's Nest," music characterizes and under-scores the larger meaning of the stories.

IV

In three stories—"Nanette: An Aside" (1897), "The Prodigies" (1897), and "A Singer's Romance" (1900)—which concern professional singers, Willa Cather's treatment of the need for expression receives special emphasis. She romanticizes the singer's position in her newspaper columns, seeing in the lyric artist, with his prerogatives, a life she felt proper for art; but in the fictive accounts Cather shows the hazard as well as the reward of talent. Like his lost cousins Peter Sadelack and Eric Hermannson, the performing musician must struggle to release what is within. He does not have to combat savagery; but he must deal with a public and he must cope with the weaknesses of his own nature. Because his life is dedicated to those "'perfect experiences that never come'" yet which we must still hope for, the artist's frustration holds great interest for us. We learn that the rarefied "atmosphere of great emotions that are forbidden in our [ordinary] lives,"[12] as Cather once described the kingdom of art, can suffocate.

Strangest of all the failures is that of Adrienne and Hermann Massey, "The Prodigies."[13] In fact, it is something of a horror tale with art work-ing as peculiar an evil as does the prairie in "Eric Hermannson's Soul." At fourteen and fifteen, two children had already been consecrated by their mother to music so fully that they are permitted no life apart from it. Art determines every move. They have no friends, and though they are trained to give pleasure with their voices, Hermann and Adrienne are not allowed to enjoy anything. So routine a diversion as throwing snowballs is forbidden because it might harm their voices. Cut off from life, they endure a depletion of vitality and because their genius matures precipi-tantly, the loss is rapid. Adrienne, a family friend observes, has been trained to the point where life was "'drained . . . out of her veins.'" Music ener-vates her; the girl collapses while singing. As though the burden of one talent so

11. *CSF*, pp. 425-439.
12. *Courier*, September 28, 1895, p. 8; *KA*, p. 282.
13. *CSF*, pp. 411-423.

hastily ripened were not enough, Hermann, after his sister's breakdown, is told by his possessive mother that he must carry " 'not one destiny' " in his throat " 'but two.' "

The cruelty and terror of these final remarks have been prepared for through the music references. Music ironically comments on the absolute, hence destructive, autocracy of art as it is imposed on two children. The selections which they perform at their mother's dinner party not only brutally reduce the young singers to exhibits but serve to emphasize the incongruity of young talents weighed down by mature art. So corrupt is the atmosphere that even in the Massey music room where art never requires defense, the artist is a stranger needing to express the self which art has hidden. In obverting the primitive conditions of "Eric Hermannson's Soul" and placing the artist in a temple of music, Willa Cather exposes two sides of his loneliness. For Eric Hermannson there is a need for music; for Hermann Massey there is the cardinal need of love. Willa Cather twists the paradox of children singing about romantic love and has the painfully inappropriate music voice the secrets of the children's souls. Through the songs they sing we can infer their need. Each performs a solo before dinner. When Adrienne sings Juliet's waltz song from Gounod's *Romeo and Juliet* the lyric speaks for her tender dream to live a life beyond the rigors of a studio. The dream is in the opening bars and gives us Adrienne's version of Peter Sadelack's phantom hope.

> I want to live
> In the dream which intoxicates me—
> This day still—Sweet flame—
> I preserve you in my soul
> Like a treasure.[14]

Hermann follows with Schubert's "Serenade." The story refers simply to "that matchless serenade of Schubert's, so familiar, yet so perennially new and strange; so old, yet so immortally young." Of Schubert's two serenades, the more familiar is to a text by Ludwig Rellstab (the other is from *Cymbeline*). The celebrated "*Ständchen*" echoes the same yearning heard in Juliet's "Ariette."

> Softly my songs
> cry to you through the night;
> come down to me, my love,
> into the silent grove!

14. *The Authentic Librettos of the French and German Operas* (New York: Crown Publishers, 1939), p. 110. The translation is mine.

Slender tree-tops rustle
and whisper in the moonlight;
you need not, my darling,
fear lurking treason.

Do you hear the nightingales sing?
They are crying to you,
with their sweet plaints
they beg favour for me.

They know the heart's yearning
and the pain of love;
with their silver tones
they touch every tender heart.

Let your heart too be moved—
hear me, my love!
Trembling I wait for you;
come: make me happy![15]

After dinner "'those babies'" conclude with the finale of *Romeo and Juliet*, lamenting the lovers' death. The line between art and life which for the prodigies has always been a very fine one now vanishes altogether. Life appears momentarily absorbed into art. The operatic duet serves as a sad reverie between Hermann and Adrienne. The young girl falls as she lived—in music, which even offers her epitaph. She is "the little Juliet." The music room where she sacrificed time and strength for art literally entombs Juliet. Operatic setting is actualized. "*Saint, tombeau sombre et silencieux!*"

Not even a mature artist can live entirely in the atmosphere of great emotions. Madame Tradutorri in "Nanette: An Aside"[16] brings an audience to the stainless heights of pleasure but cannot lift her private affairs above disaster. She, like the prodigies, is "'loveless,'" as her maid Nanette rightly says. Her husband squanders his life away in Monte Carlo, and her crippled daughter remains secluded in an Italian convent. No artistic success makes up for her human losses. Music may go back to the cardinal needs of man, but it does not answer them for the musician. Ironically, a need unfulfilled brings about the very suffering that creates art, and the soprano's awareness of this one-sided relationship between art and life makes her loneliness sharper. Bidding farewell to Nanette, who

15. *The Penguin Book of Lieder*, edited and translated by S. S. Prawer (Baltimore: Penguin Books, 1964), p. 64. All quotations used by permission of the publisher.

16. *CSF*, pp. 405–410.

has known enough of her mistress' sacrifice to realize that marriage is preferable to art, Tradutorri says:

"When I began life, between me and this [a score for a role she is to originate] lay everything dear in life—every love, every human hope. I have had to bury what lay between. It is the same thing florists do when they cut away all the buds that one flower may blossom with the strength of all. God is a very merciless artist, and when he works out his purposes in the flesh his chisel does not falter."

The severity of that blade's cut is revealed through an allusion to a role which made the singer famous, Santuzza in *Cavalleria Rusticana*. The reference functions as does the Gounod opera in "The Prodigies." It is as Santuzza that Tradutorri displays a capacity to sing "not merely with the emotions but with the soul," and the "peculiar soul-note" makes her "unique among the artists of her generation." What is also unique is the way Tradutorri is a Santuzza in life. That soul-note has deeper relevance to the singer's fate than an audience would know. But Willa Cather allows the note to reach us and explain a secret in Tradutorri's heart. When Nanette cries over having to leave New York and her fiancé, Arturo, the soprano, unaware that a departure for Europe means the separation of lovers, jests, "'One would think you had sung "Voi lo sapete" yourself last night.'" The aria, a hysterical confession of love betrayed, requires great emotional and vocal energy; and on the surface the woman chides the maid for crying by reminding her that she has no excuse for such weakness. The subtler purpose of the aria is to characterize Tradutorri herself. In "*Voi lo sapete*" Santuzza reveals to Lucia, the mother of her lover, Turridu, that he has betrayed her by returning to a former love. The aria ends feverishly with Santuzza outraged over being disgraced and forsaken. "Ah me! alone I weep, I weep!" "Nanette: An Aside" ends as does "*Voi lo sapete*." Tradutorri, like Santuzza, facing a life without love, weeps "lonely tears of utter wretchedness" and might well say with Santuzza, "*Io son dannata*," since she is cursed.

Willa Cather also uses her heroine's vocal method to represent ideal artistry. Tradutorri's balance between technique and emotion endows her Santuzza with intelligent shape. Her restraint checks any imposition of personality. On stage Tradutorri is all Santuzza: "She takes this great anguish of hers and lays it in a tomb and rolls a stone before the door and walls it up." She generates emotional power only to conserve it. The effect is "classical art, art exalted, art deified." The method described in "Nanette" is actually a restatement of her newspaper comments on the acting of Eleonora Duse. The actress too dies "of her own peculiar kind of emotion, the kind that has made her great and unique in art."[17] If drama brings Cather to articulate her idea of art, music provides the material congenial to her creativity.

In the 1900 story, "A Singer's Romance,"[18] music reveals a deeper disappointment than Tradutorri's. Music deprives Frau Selma Schumann of artistic honor as well as a satisfactory marriage. For years she skimped and practiced rigorously, but her talent does not improve beyond competence. With the merely competent, art is never generous. In fact, art is ruthless with adequacy, imposing on it a "thankless life of underpaid drudgery." "No one ever went to the opera solely because her name was on the bill." The result of her sacrifice is a double failure, because denial in behalf of art made her vulnerable in love to the lies of her voice teacher who, after marriage, gambles away his wife's hard-earned money. Behind the public glitter of operatic life is a humdrum existence known only to those who work in shadowed anonymity. Moreover, at forty-two she has lived "without ever having known an *affaire de coeur*." Though she is part of the world Eric seeks, like him Frau Schumann must wonder "what that other side of life was like."

We do know something of the other side. Tradutorri has an exquisite *affaire de l'âme* and is miserable. The greatest art brings a special death since it thrives on denial of personality and repression of suffering. Frau Schumann wants what Madame Tradutorri has; but Tradutorri would happily change places with Nanette. Full expression of the inner self is impossible. The divine "'merciless artist'" arranges it this way so that artists will struggle for the next higher excitement. He has also arranged it so that the artist is "'a stranger always.'"

V

Beauty, Willa Cather says in one of her many remarks on the subject, "is the product of man's most perfect work and God's divinest moods."[19] Two stories published in the last two years of this early phase treat one of those divine moods and one of man's most finished creations. Though not about musicians, the stories use music extensively; and they do so with poetic effect. "Jack-a-Boy" (1901) and "The Treasure of Far Island"

17. *Courier*, September 21, 1895, p. 6; *KA*, p. 119.
18. *CSF*, pp. 333–338.
19. *Journal*, January 12, 1896, p. 9; *KA*, p. 165.

(1902) foreshadow Cather's interweaving thematic and atmospheric associations with musical detail. And in these stories the bridge into the kingdom of the soul is lowered.

"Jack-a-Boy"[20] catches a divine mood by having one of the gods descend from Parnassus to the mortal world. A child bearing the gift of beauty touches three lives which are suddenly filled with excitement and then just as suddenly deprived of it. With Jack-a-Boy's arrival at Apartment 324, Windsor Terrace, the locale acquires an Arcadian gleam. When "one of the immortal children of Greek fable made flesh for a little while" appears, man behaves as he would in the kindgom of the soul. The Woman Nobody Called On in Number 328 warms to her neighbors; the "crabbed old spinster in Number 326" makes toys for the child; the hitherto unneighborly Professor lifts his head from Sanskrit and Greek syntax to read Homer to the boy; the narrator, a tired music teacher, becomes the mother she never has been. Though only a child—a frozen artistic vision—his life is as timeless as his origin. "'He rose . . . like Cupid out of Psyche's arms.'"

Jack-a-Boy is the personification of art. Psychologically, he has the personality of Narcissus whose story, the Professor tells the narrator, Jack-a-Boy knows well. Cather uses Narcissus to define Jack-a-Boy in the way she uses Santuzza to explain Tradutorri's life. The lad reflects the secret self. To the Professor he is antiquity incarnate; to the Woman Nobody Called On, Someone To Call On; to the narrator, the child she does not have. "'All gossamer and phantasy and melody,'" Jack-a-Boy is known through the imagination which endows him with personality.

Music in "Jack-a-Boy" serves as an adjunct to myth. It suggests the child's privileged ancestry, his wonder, and his life apart from transient Windsor Terrace. He is the spirit of music. Born, in a way, of song, and having lived with "the pipes of Pan," Jack-a-Boy tarries long enough among mortals "'to sing a little like Keats, or to draw like Beardsley, or to make music like Schubert.'" His voice too is so delicate that "a certain musical quality" seems to have crept into it, giving his phrases "a certain metrical cadence of their own." We are given man as music. So his glimmering life ends with the swiftness of song, leaving an impression recalled in song, "Thine Eyes So Blue and Tender."[21] When he dies of scarlet

20. *CSF*, pp. 311–322.

21. "Thine Eyes So Blue and Tender" is a song by Edward Lassen (1830–1904) to a poem of Heine's "*Mit deinen blauen Augen*." The text of the song does not add to the association Willa Cather provides in the story.

fever, clearly a physical manifestation of his fiery nature, his Greek spirit returns to Arcadia where his melody plays on, occasionally to be heard on earth. Until beauty returns, man must make do with the impermanent versions of his music: "In the course of time the Professor settled down to Greek prosody again, and I to the giving of music lessons."

"The Treasure of Far Island"[22] reads like a prose pastoral elegy, calmly reflecting not on the death of a beloved friend but on the death of a beloved moment between friends—a moment of "'the old enchantment'" when life was comprehended through the imagination. Orpheus, Miranda, Penelope, Anchises, and other citizens of Arcadia represent the world of imagination, a world which Margie Van Dyck and Douglass Burnham recall during a reunion in Empire City, Nebraska, after being separated for fifteen years. Douglass' ambition to be a playwright took him to New York where he enjoys success; Margie has stayed on in Nebraska. The conflict between the harmony of childhood and the complexity of adult life focuses when the friends revisit Far Island, their private retreat of the imagination, "No-Man's-Land."

Music serves as an obbligato to their crossing back into the kingdom of the soul. At the beginning of that high sojourn, Willa Cather introduces music. The first words of the story's second section are from Robert Louis Stevenson's "Where Go the Boats?" which Douglass sings as he begins to row across the river.

> "Green leaves a-floating
> Castles of the foam,
> Boats of mine a-boating
> When will all come home?"

The "enchanted river flowing peacefully out of Arcady with the Happy Isles somewhere in the distance" reaches from mythic time and place to the here and now. Its pastoral freshness has a music which also passes through the barriers of history. "The ripples were touched with silver and the sky was as blue as though it had just been made today; the cow bells sounded faintly from the meadows along the shore like the bells of fairy cities ringing on the day the prince errant brought home his bride . . . ." The bells proclaiming the prince's triumphal return locate the crossing to Far Island in the timeless order of experience—"long ago in the golden age." The voyage is redolent of eternal lovers' arrivals "with victorie and melodie," to borrow from Chaucer.

22. *CSF*, pp. 265–282.

As Margie and Douglass penetrate deeper into the old reality, their former speech is figured as song. Douglass says, "'We were artists in those days, creating for the day only; making epics sung once and then forgotten, building empires that set with the sun." Like the Hellenic poets, they were content to sing and be forgotten. A solar world is "Rich in the simple worship of a day." They know the golden moment has passed, "'passed in music out of sight.'" Time and inattention razed their empire. Estate lost, they "'are only kings in exile.'" Memory alone retains dominion over that country. They embrace, momentarily regain the imperious feeling, "become as the gods"; but both know such sovereignty is titular. The music has passed. Another empire has dissolved.

CHAPTER TWO

The Rialto and the Desert

"Twice-blessed day,
that dawned upon a poet's dream!
. . . .
I saw the morning sun arise,
I won the singer's highest prize:
Parnassus and Paradise!"

Die Meistersinger

The Troll Garden, published in 1905, is Willa Cather's first collection of short stories. It brings together seven pieces, three of which had appeared in magazines shortly before publication of the entire set. As in the preceding stories, the principal subject is art; and again like those earlier stories, the first book of fiction reveals Willa Cather's dualistic habit of mind. In fact, that dualism unifies *The Troll Garden*. The seven stories systematically assay the status of art by disclosing it in two contrary conditions, one of civility (urban culture) where art is warmly, perhaps too warmly, welcomed and the other of barbarism (the primitive frontier) where art is not welcomed at all. The reader is never in doubt about Cather's affirmation of art, but her views are frequently expressed through implication and negation. No one voice or view wholly reveals her position. Each view is slant, each statement qualified. Rather in the manner of Hawthorne who in his tales defines the possibility of love by showing the extremes of reason and feeling which preclude love, Willa Cather composes the seven stories into a dialectic examining art through the abuses by both its practitioners and admirers and its detractors. *The Troll Garden* attacks the preciosity of the aesthete, exposes the hardship of the artist's life, and indicts the fatuity of the vulgarian. The opposing qualities of mind are located at the familiar poles on the Catherian map. The Rialto of the East encourages the fine feeling which is left to die on the desert of the West. Music serves in *The Troll Garden* as the representative, though not exclusive, figurative vehicle for Cather's dialectic.

"Flavia and Her Artists" (1905),[1] the first story in the volume, opens the dialectic with a reproof of a world which institutionalizes art and ideas. In Tarrytown, just outside New York, Flavia Malcolm Hamilton sets herself up as duenna of the intelligentsia. Though neither intellectual nor artistic herself, it is with such "'interesting people'" that Flavia shares "her natural affinities." For assorted, curious types she offers a retreat on the historic Hudson. "Flavia had at last builded her house and hewn out her seven pillars; there could be no doubt, now, that the asylum for talent, the sanatorium of the arts, so long projected, was an accomplished fact." She collects artists as Orgons collect Tartuffes, and for pretty much the same purpose: self-flattery. But Flavia's needs run deeper than the customary patronage of art. She gathers artists together so that she can patronize them and in turn be patronized by them. The possessive in the title of the story is not too strongly suggestive of her attitude toward her "lawful prey." That she thinks of offering a "refuge where the shrinking soul, the sensitive brain, should be unconstrained" is misguided fatuity. But to shuffle her guests about like retarded children and then to dissociate herself from them betrays her inherent falseness. Flavia mingles condescension with benefaction, only to be baffled by the ingratitude of those she means both to help and to look down on as odd and artsy. Amid the "*aves rares*" the patroness can recognize her own normality and regularity. Yet when she wishes to indulge the fancy and the mind, there is opportunity to do so. Her vicarious participation in the life of her superiors does not go unnoticed. One guest, Miss Jemima Broadwood, a comedienne, puts it this way to Imogen Willard, a philologist: "'You must remember that she gets no feeling out of things herself, and she demands that you impart yours to her by some process of psychic transmission.'"

Cather makes the artist-hostages as cruel and culpable as Flavia—and more so, really. The guests are aware of Flavia's motives far beyond her own knowledge of them, and they exploit the advantage. They go out on the golf links or stay in bed, demanding breakfast in their rooms, as the capricious need dictates. The musicians in the circle add special touches of their own to Flavia's cultural festivities. They mix ugliness and coarse

1. *CSF*, pp. 149–172.

manners with bad music, all of which endow their presence with an abrasive hilarity. Schemetzkin, a Russian pianist, is a stubby sort, "with an apoplectic face and purplish skin" topped with the standard thick, long hair. His fellow musician, Donati, an Italian tenor, complements him very nicely with "soft, light hair, much in disorder, very red lips, and fingers yellowed by cigarettes." The promise of foolishness in their appearance is fulfilled in their music. When everyone retires to the music room for after-dinner coffee, "Schemetzkin sat down at the piano to drum rag-time, and give his celebrated imitation of the boarding-school girl's execution of Chopin. He flatly refused to play anything more serious, and would practise only in the morning, when he had the music-room to himself." After "Schemetzkin had grimaced and tortured the keyboard with malicious vulgarities for half an hour," Signor Donati agrees to sing in order to end the torture. One gathers that Donati's willingness to entertain is no guarantee of better music than the mockeries of Schemetzkin, because, before Flavia's husband consents to accompany the cigarette-smoking tenor, he has to be assured that Donati will sing "'something with a melody, Italian arias or ballads'"—and be reasonably brief.

The antics of Schemetzkin and Donati are broadly derisive. By reducing themselves to buffoons, they mock both artist and art; and in their reluctance to perform anything serious or agreeable they show contempt for their audience. Schemetzkin's silly rendition of a novice playing Chopin is one of his private jokes. Chopin's style has just the lyricism and melodic flourish to make a schoolgirl feel that she is really playing the piano; and a haughty professional like Schemetzkin would find such a pretension amusing. The joke is also on Flavia. There is enough of the determined, if bungling, patroness in Flavia Hamilton to suggest that Willa Cather may have based her portrait partly on George Sand, a personage who had long preoccupied her; and the Chopin number enforces that suggestion. Certainly Flavia has none of the brilliance or aplomb or power that would entitle her to be numbered with George Sand among "women who have tortured and ruined musicians";[2] but she does succeed in irritating quite a few and she is in the right business.

The musicale serves as prelude to a more public rebuke of Flavia. One of the guests, M. Roux, a French novelist and intellectual at large, repays her hospitality by insulting Flavia in print. A newspaper publishes his views on the Advanced American Woman, and "the entire interview

2. *Journal*, June 14, 1896, p. 13; collected in *KA*, p. 170.

was nothing more nor less than a satiric characterization of Flavia, a-quiver with irritation and vitriolic malice. No one could mistake it...." Flavia's other beneficiaries react to the interview with "barbaric glee."

The article and its artistic counterpart, the mock-recital, are Cather's exposé of that large area of the artist's life which is spent away from creative work and which can be vulgar and dreary. Though booty for assertive patronage, artists are frequently covetous, selfish, thoughtless, cruel, compromising—human, in short, though their work aspires beyond clay. The term used by Flavia's husband, Arthur Hamilton, "'the faciles,'" while meant to expose his suppressed bitterness, has ironic aptness for the artists it indicts. Everywhere in the story (and collection) the life of art is ambivalently regarded. In this House of Song, ... "'of shams and swollen vanities, where people stalk about with a sort of mad-house dignity'" nearly all the inhabitants seem deserving of the injury they receive. One exception is Arthur Hamilton, who asks for less than he gives and who, curiously, takes his limited musical ability more seriously than do the professional musicians. His music holds personal meaning for Imogen Willard, the controlling consciousness of the story, who has been infatuated by him since childhood; but neither the quality of his musicianship nor its evocative power is developed in any relevant way. "Flavia and Her Artists" is a sarcastic sketch of the *beau monde* which reduces art to chitchat and merchandise, the kind of maltreatment which never escape Cather's gibe.

"The Sculptor's Funeral" (1905)[3] follows "Flavia and Her Artists" and balances the denunciation of the metropolis with a bitter censure of the frontier. Cather's charge is made rather in the form of an artist's reminiscence about the future, a going to one's funeral. The body of a highly honored sculptor, Harvey Merrick, is returned from back east to Sand City, Kansas, for burial; and from the self-indulgent grief of his mother and the venality and stupor of the citizens one can calculate the odds against the attainment of "the yearning of a boy, cast ashore upon a desert of newness and ugliness and sordidness, for all that is chastened and old, and noble with traditions." Steavens, the sculptor's student who accompanied the body, serves as an accurate aerometer of the emotional pressure in the house where the boy lived. The window sash is stuck, the room "'close'" literally to the degree of nausea. Aridity is the unchanging psychic climate at Sand City. But Cather's argument is louder than a gasp for air. With unrelieved harshness she contrasts the "splendid" and "noble" head of the sculptor in the palm-decorated coffin with his

3. *CSF*, pp. 173–185.

judges—an emaciated minister, a "Grand Army man . . . fishing his quill toothpick from his waistcoat pocket," two bankers, one of whom is "trimming his nails with a pearl-handled pocket-knife," and miscellaneous dealers in real estate, cattle, and coal. They are incapable of grasping the "'repytation'" of a native son whose artistic distinction gave Sand City its single importance. Merrick is still ridiculed for "'trapesing to Paris and all such folly.'" The margins of the Sand City mind stop at practicality which doubles as their region of the ideal. Cather finishes her case against the "'borderland between ruffianism and civilization'" with a public arraignment of frontier "'knavery'" by Jim Laird, a local lawyer and childhood friend of the sculptor. No music attends "The Sculptor's Funeral." It is another story of silence on the plains.

The third story in *The Troll Garden* returns to the Rialto to observe another kind of funeral. The rites in "The Garden Lodge" (1905)[4] are for the end of Caroline Noble's lingering attraction to artistic life. A pianist of modest talent, Caroline feels that whatever claim art once made on her soul was settled when she married Howard Noble, a quiet, wealthy widower. Marriage, she believed, made final her rejection of the shabbiness she saw attending a life devoted to art. But to insist upon the finality of her action, as Caroline does, is to admit vulnerability; and Willa Cather makes "The Garden Lodge" a test of Caroline's resolution to avoid the call of an old enchantment.

Caroline does remain in touch with art, but her family's fate taught her to keep that touch discreet. She grew up with two ragtag artists and an idolater. Her father composed "orchestral compositions for which the world seemed to have no especial need." Her brother, a painter, did newspaper sketches, drugged himself with poetry and chloral, and eventually "shot himself in a frenzy," one consequence of his death being the shattering of their mother's health. Caroline's life in Brooklyn was a mixture of "poetic ideals and sordid realities," of art talk, "emotional pyrotechnics," and boiled mutton. Her sentence in "the shrine of idealism" served, she called a halt to her musical education and married Howard Noble, a paragon of respectability. "She wanted the luxury of being like other people . . . ." Her reaction is extreme because her experience is extreme.

For six years all went according to Caroline's plan for a secure and predictable life. Then Raymond d'Esquerré, a renowned tenor, spent a month with the Nobles in their garden lodge; and the equilibrium was

4. *CSF*, pp. 187–197.

upset. For Caroline the visit was to be a proof of her resistance to the emotional excitement d'Esquerré represented. She would share in his art and enjoy his presence, but she would preserve her detachment. Apparently she demonstrates her immunity, yet for two weeks after the tenor's departure she returns daily to the lodge "for a quiet hour" to savor the memory of his stay. The self-indulgence of that emotional tryst is brought home to Caroline in her response to her husband's casual suggestion that the lodge be replaced by a summer house. "'Why, that seems almost a shame, doesn't it, after d'Esquerré has used it?'" Surprised by a flare up of sentimentality she thought outgrown, and ashamed of exhibiting the enthusiasm of a matinee matron, she goes out to the lodge to sort out her feelings. As Caroline sits in the silent room on that rose-scented June night reviewing her relationship with the tenor, Willa Cather offers the reader a reenactment of her earlier decision to detach herself from art. "It seemed to her that ever since d'Esquerré first came into the house she had been haunted by an imploring little girlish ghost that followed her about, wringing its hands and entreating for an hour of life." The entreaty is made through Wagner, specifically the first act of *Die Walküre* which was the last music Caroline and d'Esquerré practiced together and which expresses the revival of an admiration for art that Caroline thought was laid to rest.

She starts out playing listlessly; by the time she comes to the end of the first act, however, Caroline is deeply involved in music and memories. She can hear d'Esquerré singing the final duet, and the lyric takes on personal importance for her. "'*Thou art the Spring for which I sighed in Winter's cold embraces*'" are the words which come back to her, and with them she feels again d'Esquerré tenderly putting his arm about her and lifting her right hand from the keyboard. The gesture transforms Caroline into Sieglinde. Willa Cather has not given us a woman whose destiny is linked with the vast affairs surrounding the strange gold ring, but she has given us a Sieglinde, nevertheless—a woman who finds her spiritual twin, her namesake, Siegmund. It is this limited theme of *Die Walküre* which suits Cather's fictive purpose. Caroline's recollection of the early delirious music at the end of the first act excites her to the point where she wonders if art is not, after all, worth the devotion it requires. Her confidence in a carefully chosen marriage is shaken. "It was not enough; this happy, useful, well-ordered life was not enough. It did not satisfy, it was not even real." For the moment, what so disarms her is the humanity beneath d'Esquerré's artistic perfection. For the moment, what is real is the fancy exalted by music. Several phrases from Sieglinde's part of the duet double for Caroline's sudden grief over a world without the romance of the imagination:

> Foreign seemed all until now;
> Friendless I, and forsaken;
> I counted strange and unknown
> Each and all that came near.[5]

The atmosphere of the story foretells the brevity of this renewed identification with art. Significantly, the weather duplicates that of *Die Walküre*. The opera's Prelude portrays a tempest, the howling chaos in which Siegmund is lost. Willa Cather makes of the Wagnerian storm a signal of Caroline's disaster and a motif of her spiritual commotion. "The storm had held off unconscionably long" on the night she returns to the lodge. When it does break, Caroline breaks with it and "began fighting over again the battles of other days." Toward morning the rumbling of thunder subsides, as does the storm within. She sleeps. The dream is over.

Die Walküre emphasizes the end of Caroline's dream in two additional ways. Willa Cather times the narrative so that the seasonal reference in the duet comments on the season in the story. The spring for which Caroline sighed has passed before she dreams of it. D'Esquerré's visit was in May, and the story begins in June. Also, the final scene between Caroline and her husband, during which she announces her intention to have the lodge razed, subtly recalls the end of the first act of *Die Walküre*. Both the act and the story end with laughter, but with this difference: the triumphant lovers laugh as they envision a house of spring, while the Nobles plan to tear down the lodge associated with spring and build a new summer house. The operatic pair walk into a world of revelation; the fictive couple is at a breakfast table. And the oppositions between the opera and the story are figured in the revelation that Caroline-Sieglinde's true Siegmund, her spiritual twin, is Howard Noble, financial titan, not Raymond d'Esquerré, tenor.

Another allusion, this one from *Parsifal*, continues the ironic parallel with Wagner and reveals the way the tenor's visit deepens Caroline's awareness of artistic life. D'Esquerré visited the Nobles because he "felt occasionally the need of getting out of Klingsor's garden." The association between the fevered life of art and the forbidding, magical habitat of Klingsor is reiterated near the end of the story when Caroline recalls the

5. *The Authentic Librettos of the Wagner Operas* (New York: Crown Publishers, 1938), p. 154.

benefits to her family of artistic illusions. The unsuccessful composer, the dissipated painter, even the idolater "were nearer happiness" than Caroline. "Her sure foundation was but made ground, after all, and the people in Klingsor's garden were more fortunate, however barren the sands from which they conjured their paradise." As d'Esquerré's gesture while singing Siegmund transfigures Caroline into Sieglinde, his presence converts the garden lodge into the exotic enclosure of Klingsor. Raymond d'Esquerré too is a necromancer who practices not dark arts but bright ones. That June night was "a night of sorcery." One outcome of the singer's wonderful presence is Caroline's realization that for all the luxury of a life in the magic garden there remains "the helplessness of the enchanter to at all enchant himself."

"'A Death in the Desert'" (1903)[6] confirms Caroline's suspicion that the enchanter is helpless to enchant himself. The story is about three musicians graded in talent from genius (Adriance Hilgarde), through very good (Katharine Gaylord), to amateur (Everett Hilgarde, Adriance's elder brother). The action focuses on the death of Katharine, a concert singer remanded by a lung sickness to die on a Wyoming desert; but the meaning of her final hour reaches out to include Adriance, who is in Europe riding the crest of a brilliant musical career. The growth of Adriance's musical style from a bright lyricism to something darker and pensive contrasts with the singer's more rapid physical decline. As in "The Garden Lodge," Willa Cather employs a nonprofessional artist, one who cannot step within the "circle of flame set about those splendid children of genius," to register surprise that the flame does not protect the artist from the effects of time.

In this story the musical compositions are of Cather's own imagining. Adriance's fame came about through a cantata, *Proserpine*, which immediately won public favor and was popular with college glee clubs and in variety theaters. Though *Proserpine* is not an embarrassment, it is not representative of the composer's real voice. Appropriately, the memorable and widely whistled portion of *Proserpine* is the Spring Song; the work itself is from the young season of Adriance's genius. As he matures, his music acquires shades and depth. *Souvenirs d'Automne* expresses more serenity than jubilation, more contentment than agitation. His most recent work, a sonata, marks a clear transition from a "purely lyric vein to a deeper and nobler style." "'He used to write only the tragedies of passion; but this is the tragedy of the soul, the shadow coexistent with the soul,'" Katharine Gaylord explains.

6. *CSF*, pp. 199–217.

Katharine's appreciation of her former teacher's maturing style gives a personal emphasis to the relationship between music and time. For the dying singer the tragedy of the soul is the inevitable futility of man's highest effort, artistic ambition, and the brevity of his most sustained achievement, art. She knows "'the tragedy of effort and failure'" because she incarnates it. Now she sits, after a brilliant musical life, "'listening to the feet of the runners as they pass me—ah, God! the swift feet of the runners!'" The shadows of the soul which she detects in the music surrounded its conception. Adriance started the sonata "'when the late autumn came on, and the paleness of the Adriatic oppressed him....'" Those shadows fall on the narrative as well: "The bright, windy days of the Wyoming autumn passed swiftly." Music symbolizes the breaking swiftness of time. For Katharine Gaylord time is running out; her season is winter. "'A Death in the Desert'" provides a Winter Song lamenting a singer's lonely final hour to match the tender Spring Song heralding a composer's birth. The Winter Song sings of the dying seasons which Proserpine spends in the underworld, or the desert.

The story that follows does not go to Paris and show the limitation placed on Adriance Hilgarde's aspiration, but it does make exactly that point by showing the ultimate failure of artistic effort. The scene of "The Marriage of Phaedra" (1905)[7] is London where Hugh Treffinger, a painter, made a stir with his experimentation in color technique. Three years after Treffinger's death another painter, MacMaster, makes a pilgrimage to the studio preparatory to writing a book on Sir Hugh which will restore his reputation as innovator. The painting which best expresses Treffinger's method is the unfinished *Marriage of Phaedra*, and although it is contrary to his dying wish, the artist's widow sells the work to an Australian art dealer. MacMaster sees that Lady Treffinger's disposition of the *Marriage* is a settlement of her own marriage, a gesture of revenge against the art which exacted more attention from her husband than she did. As in "The Sculptor's Funeral," Cather considers the life of art after the artist's death. What she has MacMaster learn about the life of an artist is a point Willa Cather makes repeatedly: work is the thing, nothing beyond it counts. Artistic work aspires toward the timeless but it is itself timed. MacMaster murmurs, "'Poor Treffinger; *sic transit gloria.*'"

The power of "A Wagner Matinee" (1904)[8] comes from Cather's bringing together a sense of loss and a deeper need that the loss of art creates. Georgiana Carpenter was raised in Boston, spent some time in

7. *CSF*, pp. 219–234.
8. *CSF*, pp. 235–242.

Paris, and eventually returned to Boston where she taught music at the Conservatory. At thirty, undoubtedly apprehensive about marital prospects, she had abandoned the opportunities of a musical career to marry a twenty-one-year-old Westerner, Howard Carpenter, and move to Red Willow County, Nebraska. At sixty, after three decades of exposure "to a pitiless wind and to the alkaline water" far off from the cultural world of desire, she returns to Boston to settle a relative's estate. She is looked after during her stay by her nephew Clark, whom she had once taught scales and exercises, and who is now studying music at the Conservatory. Back in the city of cultural possibilities, she attends a Wagner matinee. This sudden confrontation with music stirs her dormant desire for the art she gave up, and brings home the deprivation she has suffered these many years on the plains. At the same time, Clark, the narrator of the story, discovers what his aunt went through.

Aunt Georgiana's adjustment to prairie life, the reader learns, is of a special and brave sort. After fifteen years her husband buys her a "little parlour organ," and with it she teaches her nephew the rudiments of music. Though she encourages Clark's musical training, she "seldom talked . . . about music." What is her true vocation becomes an avocation, and she tries to instill the same sense of music as hobby in the boy. Her reasons, one can see, are noble even if they are self-protective: "'Don't love it so well, Clark, or it may be taken from you. Oh! dear boy, pray that whatever your sacrifice may be, it be not that.'" While not living the renunciatory life that art demands of its practitioners, she does speak on its behalf by acknowledging its great personal importance. And in losing what is most sacred to her, Georgiana Carpenter achieves a renunciation of her own. We are given a clue to what sustains her through the silent, prairie life: "She was a pious woman; she had the consolations of religion and, to her at least, her martyrdom was not wholly sordid." If her martyrdom *is* sordid, as Clark implies, it is because Aunt Georgiana was defeated in her struggle to preserve her music against the forces of the prairie. In the war between man's higher and lower instincts, the lower has won out.

At the concert hall the struggle is explained through music. Gradually Georgiana Carpenter realizes her condition and the consequences of her choice. When she arrives in Boston she is altogether unaware of the world around her, but as she enters the hall she becomes "a trifle less passive and inert." When the musicians come out and take their places, she gives a "stir of anticipation," and when they play the opening bars of the Wagner selection, the rediscovery begins and the nature of her struggle is disclosed. The explanation is suggested in the leading motifs of the overture to *Tannhäuser*, the first number on the program, in which Wagner sets the symbolic struggle between the sacred and the profane in man. Willa Cather incorporates in her narrative Wagner's opposing motifs of man's higher and lower yearnings and gives them a special fictive immediacy and significance of her own.

The overture begins with the solemn chant of the pilgrims: it rises to a mighty outpouring and finally passes away. In the operatic text this motif represents the ecstasy of sacred yearnings; in "A Wagner Matinee" it represents the higher impulses of Georgiana Carpenter and of music and all art, as well. The old woman intuitively apprehends Wagner's musical message though it has been many years since she thought of the composer: "When the horns drew out the first strain of the Pilgrim's chorus, my Aunt Georgiana clutched my coat sleeve. Then it was I first realized that for her this broke a silence of thirty years; the inconceivable silence of the plains." Then there rises the seductive spell of the Venusberg motif, the whirlings of the frightening, tempting world created of man's profane desires. In the abstract, Willa Cather applies the Venusberg motif to the hostile world in which the artist must assert his higher drives and to which he occasionally succumbs. In the concrete, the profane world is the arid plains of Red Willow County, Nebraska, which destroyed Aunt Georgiana. The Venusberg motif also suggests her impetuous pursuit of physical love. In the tug between "the inconceivable silence of the plains" and "the little parlour organ," silence won. Clark's associations with the Venusberg motif run:

With the battle between the two motives, with the frenzy of the Venusberg theme and its ripping of strings, there came to me an overwhelming sense of the waste and wear we are so powerless to combat; and I saw again the tall, naked house on the prairie, black and grim as a wooden fortress; the black pond where I had learned to swim, its margin pitted with sun-dried cattle tracks; the rain gullied clay banks about the naked house, the four dwarf ash seedlings where the dish-cloths were always hung to dry before the kitchen door. The world there was the flat world of the ancients; to the east, a cornfield that stretched to daybreak; to the west, a corral that reached to sunset; between the conquests of peace, dearer bought than those of war.

The passage is a masterstroke of evocation. Willa Cather has given us Venusberg through Clark's musical consciousness. How could the delicate pilgrim-artist, Georgiana, defeat the powerful, ancient forces of such mysterious blackness and waste and aridity?

Aunt Georgiana is transfixed by the music. In answer to Clark's self-query, "Had this music any message for her?", there are only the fingers working upon her black dress in sympathy with the melodies of *The Flying Dutchman*; she had owned the piano score when a student. Like the prelude to *Tristan and Isolde* which preceded it, *The Flying Dutchman* overture works through opposing motifs (here, the tranquil Senta motif and the crashing Curse motif) and celebrates the eventual triumph of the higher, the Senta, over the lower, the Curse. The last piece before the intermission is the "Prize Song," and here the voice sings with the orchestra of the victory of the ideal. The *"Preislied"* is the musical summation of the contending themes presented earlier in the concert. Walther's musical triumph, in Wagnerian terms, amounts to a victory for the noblest ideals of art, which were the ideals of the Mastersingers' Guild. And as Walther wins Eva's hand along with the mastersingers' emblem, Wagner celebrates the perfect union and the double triumph of art and life. That *Die Meistersinger* is a comic variation of the contest theme in *Tannhäuser* gives the first half of Willa Cather's Wagner matinee a thematic, as well as musical, balance.

Even Cather's choice of a *Wagner* matinee has particular psychological relevance and historical suitability to the kind of awareness Georgiana Carpenter achieves. Clark explains that his aunt left the Boston Conservatory "somewhere back in the latter sixties." At that time Wagner's music was just coming into ascendency among the most knowledgeable musicians, and any performance of his operas would have been a rarity in the United States. Though there were scattered experimental presentations in the 1850's, it was not until the late 1880's that the Metropolitan Opera performed his works. Yet, Aunt Georgiana, whose musical education abruptly ended in the late 1860's, was "perfectly familiar with their respective situations." Moreover, she owned a piano score for *The Flying Dutchman*. So when Clark, who by his own admission had judged his aunt "superficially," says that her musical training "had been broader than that of most music teachers of a quarter of a century ago," he is actually understating the range and depth of her musical sensitivity. She was, judging by her knowledge of Wagner, distinctly *avant-garde*.

Georgiana Carpenter's question to Clark during the intermission—"'And you have been hearing this ever since you left me, Clark?'"—is more than a sad and gentle reproach to the boy's taunt that "'we have come to better things than the old *Trovatore'*"; it is a self-measurement of her spiritual losses. Though the cultural world was once behind her in its admiration for Wagner, it is now she who has been left behind—and alone. Willa Cather has, then, in making Aunt Georgiana's concert a *Wagner* matinee, defined Georgiana's tragedy historically.

Cather's use of music goes deeper than historical perspective. Thematically the Wagnerian numbers serve as ironic comments on Aunt Georgiana's defeat; psychologically they serve to heighten her tragedy of the soul by aligning her struggle with the legendary enactments of it.

> Soon after the tenor began the "Prize Song," I heard a quick drawn breath and turned to my aunt. Her eyes were closed, but the tears were glistening on her cheeks, and I think, in a moment more, they were in my eyes as well. It never really died, then—the soul that can suffer so excruciatingly and so interminably; it withers to the outward eye only . . . . She wept so throughout the development and elaboration of the melody.

After the intermission come four numbers from the *Ring* cycle. The first three are unspecified; the concluding selection is Siegfried's funeral march. In a general way this simple but touching melody of heroic defeat anticipates Aunt Georgiana's taking leave of the concert hall and her return to Red Willow County. It signals the solemn procession to darkness and sadness. And with Siegfried's funeral music are mingled the Venusberg associations in Clark's mind. He sees the desert: "just outside the door of the concert hall, lay the black pond with the cattle-tracked bluffs; the tall, unpainted house, with weather-curled boards; naked as a tower, the crook-backed ash seedlings where the dish-cloths hung to dry; the gaunt, moulting turkeys picking up refuse about the kitchen door."

Though she uses Wagnerian analogues, Cather offers no Wagnerian conclusion to Georgiana Carpenter's pilgrimage in "A Wagner Matinee." There is no victory for the higher yearnings, no triumph of art, no redemption through love or even through renunciation. There is only defeat, the trek back to privation and hardship—to Venusberg and "the inconceivable silence of the plains."

The bustle of the city can also be inconceivably hostile to a feeling for art, especially if, as in "Paul's Case" (1905),[9] it is a teasing reminder that romance is near at hand and yet out of reach. Cordelia Street in a

9. *CSF*, pp. 243–261.

working-class section of Pittsburgh has all the "ugliness and commonness" which a sensitive boy like Paul resents coming back to after concerts at Carnegie Hall and glimpses of elegant life at the Schenley Hotel. He requires a constant romance. Having located his dreads in the ordinary life of his neighborhood, Paul builds of his extraordinary downtown associations a world congenial to his imagination. Paul is Caroline Noble in reverse. He steals a thousand dollars, runs off to New York, and plays the game of the imagination down to each preconceived detail, like the bouquet of flowers in the hotel room. He comes up with the world as fiction. Central Park is transformed into a "wonderful stage winterpiece." Like Wallace Stevens' Crispin, who also voyages for experience, Paul cannot "find/In any commonplace the sought-for aid." The fancy goes the way of "luminous traversing." For Paul, of course, the supreme fiction is that he can keep the brilliant gesture going.

The story is subtitled "A Study in Temperament," and it is important to distinguish that temperament from an artistic one. Cather's point again is made through negation. Paul's attachment to art is false, subjective, and, in an appealing way, insane. His eyes have "abnormally large" pupils and shine with a "glassy glitter" and "hysterical brilliancy," implying a sensuous hunger for gratification. About his hauteur and contentiousness one agrees with his teacher that "'there is something wrong'" with the boy. His mind is a "medley of irrelevant things." At the theater and concert hall he "really lived," but living is a "debauch" punctuated by fitful shifts between rapture and depression. Escapade and artifice are vital things. Art is only accidental to the emotional transport Paul seeks. Music, it so happens, provides the quickest propulsion for his spirit to curvet "blue league after blue league, away from everything," including life itself. His mind makes no qualitative distinctions; "any sort of music, from an orchestra to a barrel organ" ignites him. If not music, then a mere *auf wiedersehen* uttered by a passing performer will do the trick. Paul's temperament lives under the annihilating tyranny of a chaotic imagination. Imagination always alienates a person from the world and then by the pull of discipline drives him back into it. An artist, at any rate, returns to the world. The fallacious promise of an unchecked fancy destroys Paul, and it is not until death that he "dropped back into the immense design of things." His suicide constitutes the last of many warnings about the perils of the imagination and the shortcomings of artistic life which Willa Cather proposes in *The Troll Garden*.

II

> There were ninety and nine that safely lay
> In the shelter of the fold,
> But one was out on the hills away,
> Far off from the gates of gold—
> Away on the mountains wild and bare,
> Away from the tender Shepherd's care.
>
> "The Ninety and Nine"

Of the nine stories appearing between 1907 and 1912, two are inter-
mediate drafts of Willa Cather's celebrated portraits of pioneer heroines;
and both exemplify the growing use of music in her fiction. "The Joy of
Nelly Deane" (1911)[10] relates the pain of Nelly Deane. She is so attractive
that even a town like Riverbend, Nebraska, which is on guard against the
"worldly and wicked" and which prizes its "plain girls," takes pride in her
presence. Affection in a place which suspects feeling is not easily won.
Riverbend is a chilly region as the names of its matriarchs remind us—
Mrs. Dow, Mrs. Freeze, and Mrs. Spinny. Still, Nell's "unquenchable
joy" "always warmed their hearts." Music conveys Nell's warmth:
"When she was not singing, she was laughing." The history of Nell's life
in Riverbend is a tragic one. Music also reveals her fate.

Margaret, a contralto in the choir for which Nell is the leading soprano, tells the story. It is a remembrance in three parts, each colored by
the narrator's idea of Nell's singing. The story begins with a reference to
Queen Esther, a cantata the choir is giving for Christmas. The short
oratorio comes up several times in the first section. *Esther*[11] ("Queen" is
Cather's addition), an enormously popular work for church groups, by
William B. Bradbury, an equally popular nineteenth-century American
composer, relates the story of the Jewish heroine's salvation of her people
from Haman's plans to extirpate them. The oratorio follows the Old
Testament faithfully and provides an ironic frame for the story. Nell and
Esther are unquestionably the best and most beautiful of their respective
people, and each braves danger for her ideals. Both are potential victims of
brutality. They share also in the suffering of their breed, Esther as a Jew
and Nelly Deane as a sensitive among insensitives. But the outcome of
their lives differs: Esther's plea to Ahaseurus results in his sparing the Jews

10. *CSF*, pp. 55–68.

11. *Esther, The Beautiful Queen* (New York: Mason Brothers, 1856). All references are
to this text.

and succeeds in destroying the evil Haman; Nelly Deane is destroyed by the town. The Riverbend variety of Christianity proves more formidable than the ire of Haman. The oratorio is all the more effective because it allows Nell to demonstrate in her singing the very virtuoisty and rareness of spirit which the music honors and which the town condemns.

> The *Queen Esther* performance had cost us three months of hard practice . . . . The country folk for miles about had come in through a deep snow . . . . It was certainly Nelly's night, for however much the tenor . . . might try to eclipse her in his dolorous solos about the rivers of Babylon, there could be no doubt as to whom the people had come to hear—and to see.

The religious hymns which Nell sings so well complete the ironic implications established in *Esther*. The one Margaret loved to hear her sing was "The Ninety and Nine" because it brought out the strength and sweetness of her voice. The third verse, "But one was out on the hills away," is the only part mentioned; but Margaret's choice of this hymn echoes through the story. Nell's life is the story of the "one"—not the ninety-nine secure sheep but the stray with stronger impulses than the herd's. The hymn is a dialogue among the Shepherd, the ninety-nine, and a narrator. For the Shepherd the odd hundredth justifies his suffering. "'And although the road be rough and steep/I go to the desert to find my sheep.'" The hymn functions in two ways. It presents the attitude of the more generous Baptist ladies of the sewing circle who hope that Nell will join their congregation; "they were always looking for 'influences' to change her." But we are given the smug view so that we do not adopt it. It is not Cather's. We are to see Nelly Deane as the hundredth and admire her individuality. She is set apart from others because of virtues—beauty, extravagance, artistic ability—which are at best grudgingly tolerated by the colorless people around her. Being the hundredth implies courage and suffering. The integrity of her nature requires that she avoid "the shelter of the fold" because to follow its ways is to let go of life's joy. The hymn honors what the stray endures.

> Out in the desert He heard its cry—
> Sick and helpless, and ready to die.

Though the stray is lost through sin, the lyric delicately avoids condescension. As Cather uses the hymn, compassion grows into commendation. The music reference shifts the moral advantage in the story. The Baptists patronize Nell as a "stray." Cather turns that attitude around. The hundredth holds the advantage; her exuberance challenges the cautionary rule.

Nell's release from Riverbend depends on marriage to Guy Franklin, a Chicago dry-goods salesman with "very smooth and flattering ways." With him she can live in excitement, which for Nell is mainly the possibility of taking music lessons. "'I'm going to live in Chicago,'" she says, "'and take singing lessons, and go to operas, and do all those nice things—oh, everything!'" Circumstances, however, commit her to Riverbend. Franklin did not return; her father goes broke; and, worst of all, she is to marry Scott Spinny the "grim and saturnine" son of one of the Baptist ladies. This is four years after the first part, and Nell is about eighteen.

The brief second part relates Nell's baptism preliminary to marriage with Spinny. The ritual, as Margaret reports it, is macabre. It not only runs contrary to Nell's nature but also ceremonializes a negative vision of life. Nell's baptism is her funeral. The minister presides "in his long, black gown." Nell descends into cold water in a "cemented pit," the baptistry. Then, "while the minister said the words about being buried with Christ in baptism," she "disappeared under the dark water." Margaret senses doom in the humbling, indeed humiliating and chastening, immersion: "'It will be like that when she dies ...,'" as in fact it is. Margaret's remembrance of Nell's descent into the icy waters of common Riverbend life is touched with music. She recalls the choir singing "Washed in the Blood of the Lamb." The hymn as background and commentary is replete with meaning. It is intended to be sung "joyfully," but neither the occasion nor the theme is particularly joyful. For "those three dear guardians," the mesdames Dow, Freeze, and Spinny, it is a happy event; for those who have not taken the stark messages of religion literally and do not literally apply them to life, however, the idea of "being buried" in youth is less than pleasing. "She seemed changed—a little embarrassed and quietly despairing." The hymn sings of redemption for those "who, in their youthful days,/Found Jesus early":

> These, these are they who, in the conflict dire,
> Boldly have stood amid the hottest fire;
> Jesus now says: "Come up higher,"
> "Washed in the blood of the Lamb."

"So little and meek" now, Nell is something of an innocent martyr to society's ways. The hymn of course concerns the afterlife, and Willa

Cather's interest is with the present life. Through music Cather offers a critique of religious ideas which negate a joy like Nell's and offers in its place a doctrine of denial and emotional strictness. The final stanza offers an assurance for the "washed" which does not obtain for the newly washed Nell.

> Safe, safe upon the ever-shining shore,
> Sin, pain, and death, and sorrow, all are o'er;
> Happy now and evermore,
> "Washed in the blood of the Lamb."

Her fate: nearly ten years later Nell dies in childbirth. Moreover, Scott Spinny's hard and penurious ways made those years painful. The final pietism about Nell is uttered by Mrs. Dow to Margaret. "'When it was all over, she did look so like a child of God, young and trusting, like she did on her baptizing night, you remember?'"

Margaret remembers Nell vividly, but not in the static image of baptismal death. Margaret thinks of Nell as a school girl, young and vital:

> ... we two had sat in our sunny seat in the corner of the old bare school-room one September afternoon and learned the names of the seven hills together. In that place, at that moment, after so many years, how it all came back to me—the warm sun on my back, the chattering girl beside me, the curly hair, the laughing yellow eyes .... I felt as if even then, ... that at this moment I should be sitting among the crumbling bricks and drying grass, and she should be lying in the place I knew so well, on that green hill far away.

So intimately does Margaret associate Nell with music that she identifies the two. The sanctuary of "that green hill" comes from one of Nell's hymns. "When she rose and stood behind the organ and sang 'There Is a Green Hill,' one could see Mrs. Dow and Mrs. Freeze settle back in their accustomed seats and look up at her as if she had just come from that hill and had brought them glad tidings." The hymn begins:

> There is a green hill far away
> Without a city wall;
> Where the dear Lord was crucified
> Who died to save us all.

In death Nell escapes the confinement of Riverbend. To borrow from the penultimate portion of Bradbury's *Esther*:

> Our soul is escaped from the snare,
> From the snare of fowlers ....

"The Bohemian Girl" (1912),[12] a long story, depends heavily on music for its final meaning and shape. Characters, as usual, are judged by their involvement with music; occasions are given special musical signatures. Besides what are by now familiar uses, in "The Bohemian Girl" Willa Cather for the first time employs a single composition as frame for a complex of ironies and makes of music a vehicle for wit.

The title provides the musical frame. The story borrows repeatedly from Michael Balfe's opera of the same name. Several of its popular songs are cited and sung in the story; but since those references only confirm what has been going on from the start, it is well briefly to set down the movement of the opera before analyzing Willa Cather's use of it. *The Bohemian Girl* takes place in Austria and portrays a girl who is Bohemian by predilection, not birth. In Act I, Thaddeus, a Polish exile fleeing from the Austrian army, takes refuge with a gypsy band. When he hears that Count Arnheim's young daughter, Arline, has just been attacked by a stag, he ignores danger and saves the child by shooting the animal. During the excitement caused by Thaddeus' refusal to toast the Austrian Emperor at a celebration, the gypsy chief kidnaps Arline. Act II takes place twelve years later. During this time Arline has come to love Thaddeus and the freedom of gypsy life. By an odd turn of events Arline encounters her father, the Count, who restores her to her high rank. In Act III she pines for Thaddeus and the wandering life he leads. Again daring dangers, Thaddeus searches out Arline to bid farewell. When the Count learns of the young man's bravery, he blesses the love between Thaddeus and his daughter, and the lovers go off as gypsies. The opera, so popular that it seemed to start a gypsy revival in music in the nineteenth century, is filled with lilting melodies honoring the migrant and merry life attained by Thaddeus and Arline.

> In the gypsy's life you read
> The life that all would like to lead.

We have only to review the action of Willa Cather's story to recognize her use of Balfe's opera. After an absence of twelve years, during which time he became a wealthy shipper in Norway, Nils Ericson returns to visit his home in Nebraska. The prodigal's homecoming becomes a reunion with an old friend, Clara Vavrika, who is now his brother's wife. The old romance is revived; and defying law and custom, Eric and Clara elope. Like the opera, then, "The Bohemian Girl" is a tale of a daring lover retrieving his trapped beloved. Beyond this basic likeness, however,

12. *CSF*, pp. 3–41.

what is important is their dissimilarity. The Nebraska tale is not a romance of lyric infatuation. Nils Ericson's enterprise has more calculation
than bravery about it and as much self-interest as chivalry. Though the
story roughly parallels the last two acts of the opera and borrows several
of its songs as motif, the works are opposite in tone. The opera takes the
gypsy style seriously. It offers what Balfe thought his audience thought
gypsies were like. The fatuity to which *The Bohemian Girl* appeals allows
Willa Cather to use the opera to show what the story is not, and as
a backdrop for the Nebraska abduction the opera creates some sharp
ironies. The ironies are reversible. The operatic life of carousing and irresponsibility undercuts the drab seriousness and industry of the ambitious
Nebraskans and the ecstatic pretensions of love. At the same time, the
operatic gallantry and heroic abandon put in relief a more mature and
credible idea of love and heroism. *The Bohemian Girl* is a foil. Where the
opera idolizes pleasure through freedom, the story honors freedom
through hard work. The final play on the title is the exchange of a
meretricious Bohemian girl for a real one, a Bohemian by blood. Willa
Cather's readers in 1912 would catch these incongruities and be alive
to her satiric purpose.

Nils's arrival on the transcontinental express is anything but that
of the nervous romantic rescuer. He is poised and haughty, more than
equal to the occasion. Not even the "fierce sunlight" of Sand River
Valley rivals the sun of his vanity in which he basks. He seems prepared to
sport with the prairie world that once checked his frisky ways: "as he
looked out at the ripe summer country a teasing, not unkindly smile
played over his lips." With a smile "of rather kindly mockery" he meets
ripe Nebraska, testing its defensive arrogance ("'It's big enough for us'")
and its inevitable negativism about a style other than its own ("'I don't
suppose you've ever got used to steady work'"). Taciturnity best serves
his purpose. He gives his family the advantage of letting them think he is
shiftless so he can have the greater advantage of knowing they they do not
know how wealthy he is. Disguise furthers his purpose. Nils is something
of a Pan in motley. Panama hat, turned-up trousers, valise swung over
shoulder, and a flute case tucked under his arm, he starts across the field
toward home.

If Nils is not Thaddeus, Clara Vavrika is less Arline. Thirty years old,
she requires no providential thoughtfulness to protect her innocence. She
rises late, dresses with special care, and is fiercely strong-willed. Pressured
by her well-intentioned aunt, Johanna, into marrying Olaf Ericson, she

now compensates for her discontent by exercising tyrannies of her own. Olaf's position in politics, as Clara makes spitefully clear, depends on Bohemian votes; and that block is delivered by Clara. If she leaves him, the vote is lost. Vindictiveness, however, cannot fill the emotional void left by misalliance. The "strain of Tartar or gypsy blood" requires excitement, movement, change. She is not at all, then, the wistful Bohemian girl of Balfe's opera. But the title implies paradox as well as irony. Clara, a Bohemian by blood, longs for the freedom which Arline, a Bohemian by choice, enjoys. Not until the end does Clara find the bright life her name tells us she is designed to lead.

Those in "The Bohemian Girl" who have a capacity for pleasure—that is, share a Bohemian spirit—are all musical. Cather does not use music ironically as a feature of personality here or elsewhere, except when musical ability is abused or pretentious. Clara has been trained in Chicago; her first interest and only release is her piano, one of the two furnishings (the other being a bathtub) she has shown any interest in having in her husband's house. At the piano she can vent her feelings. After being agitated by Nils's return "she practised as if the house were burning over her head." Also, every Sunday she plays for her father at his saloon where she feels free and is encouraged to be herself. Joe Vavrika, her father, was a fiddler and in his youth had been known for his dancing. He is also famous for his generosity and benevolence. As his tedious and ungenerous neighbors have not altered these virtues, so age does not attenuate his desire to enjoy life. Settled back in a rocker he wags his big carpet slipper in anticipation of "'Bohemie songs'" and hums in a "husky baritone." At the barn supper his dance with Clara draws wide applause. He seems to live in the opulent sun which, while sinking, catches the aging man swallowing the last drops of Tokai, and which "glistened on the bright glass, on his flushed face and curly yellow hair." To Clara Vavrika and her father, two blood Bohemians, we can add a third, Nils, who, like Arline in the opera, is Bohemian by disposition. The symbol of his spiritual nationality is his flute.

The flute symbolizes Nils's devotion to pleasure and announces his mission in Nebraska. He returns to the place of "'that old delight'" not simply to renew the sense of youthful joy but to regain Clara who remains essential to his remembered happiness. At Joe's saloon Nils's flute carries the imagination back to the good times of the past and gradually sweetens Clara's bitterness about life to the point where she is susceptible to the "wild thing" within her heart. Music characterizes Nils's own idea of his undertaking. "'The more I thought about you, the more I re-membered how it used to be—like hearing a wild tune you can't resist, calling you out at night.'" The flute allows Nils to test the source of the irresistible melody which he must search out. He finds that people have not lost their eagerness for life. Joe's place and the barn supper are filled with laughter and music. In some the strain is lost, in others, de-stroyed; but in the hundredth the measure of joy lingers, even if dor-mantly. The flute can liberate this tune from quiescence, as Nils's restores Clara's "'love of life.'"

The flute symbolism is not taken from Balfe. It is Cather's, and the use of the instrument so well accords with its mythology that the corre-spondence bears noting. The history of the flute, however scientific or interpretive, invariably connects the instrument with regeneration. Flutes are phallic, according to one authority;[13] and there are numerous legends linking flute-playing with phallic ceremonies to prove his point.[14] In some legends the flute's primitive identification with masculine powers is more abstractly taken as the life-giving principle itself.[15] The association quite naturally extends to love; and Mozart's opera, *The Magic Flute*, which gathers together the traditional symbolic values of the flute, adds several metaphysical implications of its own. Willa Cather does not recount a specific myth involving the flute; but in working out the strangely magnetic force of Nils, which can break the root-tight grip the earth has on Clara, Cather shows how Nils's flute-playing sensitizes Clara to his dominating vigor. We can also see "The Bohemian Girl" as a story of rebirth, the renascence of Clara's love of life; and Nils's influence on the process is emphatically sexual. The flute is the strongest charm at Nils's command. Without reference to an established fable, the life-bearing quality of the flute arises easily out of the drama. Cather's seeing funda-mental meaning in music as well as aesthetic pleasure affirms, I think, the trustworthiness of her feeling for music.

The musical nature of the characters and the dignity of their pursuing the "'wild tune'" tempt the reader to sympathize with their hedonism. My point about Cather's artistry here is that she carefully qualifies the protagonists' values through Balfe's opera. It seems to me that Cather felt

13. Curt Sachs, *The History of Musical Instruments* (New York: W. W. Norton & Company, 1940), p. 44.

14. Curt Sachs, *Geist und Werden der Musikinstrumente* (Berlin: Dietrich Reimer, 1929), pp. 20–27.

15. Christopher Welch, *Six Lectures on the Recorder* (London: Oxford University Press, 1911), pp. 381–382.

the excesses of feeling in her material and sought to moderate them by employing a work simultaneously appropriate for the characters and representative of the very romantic limits her story should not reach. I have already noted the deliberate dissimilarity between the operatic lovers and the lovers in the story. Again, where the opera is soaked in naïveté and kindness, the story involves incest and legal intimidation. Nils and Clara meet each other coyly with music as a greeting.

> The east windows opened directly into the front yard. At one of the latter, Clara, while she was dusting, heard a low whistle. She did not turn at once, but listened intently as she drew her cloth slowly along the round of a chair. Yes, there it was:
>
> > I dreamt that I dwelt in ma-a-arble halls.
>
> She turned and saw Nils Ericson laughing in the sunlight, his hat in his hand, just outside the window.

The song, "The Gypsy Girl's Dream," is Arline's second-act piece in which she tells of her ideal life in splendor and about being won in love. The song has just enough description of wealth to hint that Clara's circumstances bear resemblance to Arline's dream of a life "With vassals and serfs at my side," and the air conveys enough chivalric feeling of love to let us see Nils's self-mockery. He does come to win a "maiden heart" but it belongs to a woman and it will not be won "upon bended knee," as the operatic code requires. Nils claims Clara's hand the way he whistles the song, commandingly. We are, I think, to take the song as a gentle dig. Nils reminds Clara that she is not dwelling in marble halls and that he is really the answer to such a dream. Clara chooses to ignore the implications of the song. She knows that Nils remembers her youthful sensitivity about being called the Bohemian Girl, and she wants to make light of his twelve-year absence and suggest that she has survived the years rather well. The advantage of Nils's song is that it is casual enough to be dis-regarded at the same time that Cather can make her point about the touch of the devil in Nils and the touch of pride in Clara.

Nils is very fond of teasing Clara. When Joe asks for Bohemian songs, Nils plays "When Other Lips and Other Hearts" to reawaken Clara's resentment of the taunting name "Bohemian Girl." Music is a perfect ploy because of its second meaning. Joe regards the song as "'fine music.'" Clara understands it as another reminder that she has surrendered her desire to live by marrying Olaf and meeting the Ericsons on their bickering terms. Specifically, "When Other Lips and Other Hearts" is

Thaddeus' farewell pledge of loyalty to Arline who is expected to marry another. It is also a plea for remembrance "Of days that have as happy been." Nils does not sing the words; he plays the melody on the flute. Words are not needed for Nils's more artful strategy. Through music he appeals directly to Clara's imagination. He avoids the humble entreating of Balfe's hero and instead subtly, but unmistakably, reminds Clara of her need to keep faith with the past. She must do so for herself. He implies no false self-sacrifice. Clara, in turn, proves to be a good sport. She "smiled and leaned back in her chair" and, heeding her father's request, she sings "'I dreamt....'" Momentarily a musical mood takes hold. Nils's flute-song is beginning to be heard by the heart. On her own, Clara offers another song from *The Bohemian Girl*, "The Heart Bowed Down," which is Arline's father's lament over his lost daughter. As Clara warms to the music and as the three come closer to the "old" feeling, there is no need to be ironic in order to awaken the woman to the possibility of joy. Accordingly, Cather uses the song as a direct expression of Clara's loss of "delights that were/Too beautiful to last." In quoting only the song's refrain, she emphasizes the principal way the past can be understood, and the relevance of the melody to Cather's entire canon is obvious:

> For memory is the only friend
> That grief can call its own.

Agreeing with Joe that so frank an expression of loss is insupportably sad, Nils jovially sings "Oh, Evelina, Sweet Evelina!", the merciless jeer he and Clara as children directed at a "very homely girl in thick spectacles." The song lightens the mood and is intended as an indirect assurance to Clara that Nils still knows "'how to play'" as he did in youth. This musical exchange is a pointed, adult version of the games they used to play, especially the game Nils enjoyed most—making Clara "'get so mad.'"

Cather uses the interplay between an atmosphere of music designating fellowship and the same music taken in a different, more private way at a barn supper. E. K. Brown compares Cather's "happy accumulation of detail" in this scene to Flaubert's style in the wedding chapter of *Madame Bovary*.[16] This discerning remark illumines Cather's intention, and I should like to pursue it by suggesting an equally memorable passage, the ball at Vaubyessard, where Emma is first exposed to luxurious living. Flaubert differentiates personalities through music throughout the novel,

16. Brown, *Willa Cather*, p. 164.

but here he catches the feel of aristocratic taste while finely observing the responses of various members of the gathering. Nothing signals the Bovarys' future more vividly than the contrast between Charles, inertly watching a whist game for five hours, and Emma awkwardly and wildly waltzing around. Willa Cather uses music to provide the same focus on the heroine. The whole party responds to the gaiety and music, even the frumpy and shy members. The most radiant is Clara. "Animated and . . . gay" and "eyes . . . full of life," she plays the piano and dances with guests.

Besides celebrating the hospitable manners of the prairie, Cather wants to set the behavior of Nils and Clara against the prevailing decorum. Music occupies the guests' attention differently than it engages the lovers' interest. The effect is felicitous. When Olaf, "in a frock coat and a solemn made-up necktie," leads his mother in the grand march, Clara allows herself the private sarcasm of accompanying them on the piano with "a pompous solemnity." Only Nils appreciates Clara's reproach.

> "Oh, aren't you rubbing it into them, Clara Vavrika? And aren't you lucky to have me here, or all your wit would be thrown away."
> "I'm used to being witty for myself. It saves my life."

Musical awareness allows a privacy (and in this situation a censure) otherwise unavailable in a generally ignorant world. At Joe Vavrika's we saw how music communicated Nils's purpose over Joe's head; now he sings for the world to hear words that Clara alone can appreciate. His brother's wife is his, he feels. "'I don't care. They can't gossip. It's all in the family . . . . Where's my waltz, boys?' he called as they whirled past the fiddlers." With the joy of a conspiracy achieved, Nils sings with the fiddlers. The song is the one he played for Clara before. His insolence now, however, removes the former suggestion of wanting Clara to remember him.

> "When other lips and other hearts
> Their tale of love shall tell,
> In language whose excess imparts
> The power they feel so well."

The old women applauded vigorously. "What a gay one he is, that Nils!" And old Mrs. Svendsen's cap lurched dreamily from side to side to the flowing measure of the dance.

> Of days that have as ha-a-p-py been,
> And you'll remember me.

[57]

Music prepares Clara for Nils's final, less subtle appeal: "'What good is the power to enjoy, if you never enjoy?'" Her resistance weakens. Nils carries her off. Both succumb, it seems, to the splendor of the moonlight and sky which made one feel "as if one were sitting deaf under the waves of a great river of melody"—the "'wild tune you can't resist.'" At the party Nils told Clara that she is "'the real Bohemian Girl,'" implying that freedom will settle her bitterness. Balfe's girl passively accepts the fate assigned to her by others; the real Bohemian Girl fights for freedom and has some misgivings about her departure.

Unhappily "The Bohemian Girl" does not sustain the ironic implications set in motion by the title. The action does not cohere. In the final scene the fate of Nils's younger brother Eric, who runs away from the farm and then returns, becomes prominent though it is irrelevant to the action; and Mrs. Ericson acquires new virtues overnight, at nearly seventy years old. But the unfocused conclusion does not obviate the story's importance. It reveals, especially through music, a tone in Willa Cather's voice usually too soft to be detected. The writer herself defines the quality, wittiness, in *A Lost Lady*. "She had a fascinating gift of mimicry," Willa Cather says of Marian Forrester. "Nothing pleased one more than to provoke her laughter . . . . It was her form of commenting, of agreeing with you and appreciating you when you said something interesting,— and it often told you a great deal that was both too direct and too elusive for words."[17] Music in "The Bohemian Girl" is analogous to Mrs. Forrester's "musical laugh."

17. *A Lost Lady* (New York: Alfred A. Knopf, 1958), pp. 70–71.

CHAPTER THREE

Alexander's Bridge

And when she sang, the sea,
Whatever self it had, became the self
That was her song, for she was the maker.
Then we,
As we beheld her striding there alone,
Knew that there never was a world for her
Except the one she sang and, singing, made.

Wallace Stevens

Willa Cather apologized twice for her first novel, *Alexander's Bridge* (1912);[1] and she did so with such persuasive candor that readers have taken the book at her estimate. In 1922, when Houghton Mifflin brought out a new edition, she looked back on *Alexander's Bridge* with chagrin because it "does not deal with the kind of subject-matter in which I now find myself most at home."[2] Later, in 1931, she was even harsher, putting the novel aside as "unnecessary."[3] Edith Lewis, for one, was not finally taken in by the novelist's categorical dismissal of the first novel. "For many years," Miss Lewis says, "I accepted her estimate of *Alexander's Bridge*. But in reading it over again ... I felt that she had never altogether done it justice. It is true that it is a contrived novel .... But when it at last moves into its true theme, the mortal division in a man's nature, it gathers an intensity and power which come from some deeper level of feeling, and which overflood whatever is 'shallow' or artificial in the story. It is as if her true voice, submerged before in conventional speech, had broken

---

1. *Alexander's Bridge* (new edition with preface; Boston: Houghton Mifflin, 1912 and 1922). All references are to this text.
2. *Ibid.*, p. v.
3. *Willa Cather on Writing* (New York: Alfred A. Knopf, 1962), p. 92.

through, and were speaking in irrepressible accents of passion and authority."[4]

Miss Lewis is right, and one need not look far to find the distinctive Cather passion. *Alexander's Bridge* dramatizes a pursuit of intense life, and no preoccupation is more uniquely Catherian. Like all the characters with whom the writer is sympathetically involved, Bartley Alexander, the novel's hero, is built for exceptional experience but is cut off from it. Life takes him one way, his soul yearns for another. By profession he constructs great bridges and yet he cannot raise a passage into the world elsewhere that satisfies his heart. The psychological *donnée* of the novel is the partition of self; the action a romantic search. Both features are expansions of a dualistic view of man which underlies the preceding short fiction and which deepens into a determinant of Willa Cather's mature art. She is after the real thing in *Alexander's Bridge*, and we can see what that is by looking at the music materials.

Music in *Alexander's Bridge* is used in a seemingly unstudied way to enforce psychological observation and theme. Many of the music references appear to be only casual detail or passing simile. Few allusions are elaborated upon, and those that are seem more decorative than functional. But the inconspicuous naturalness with which music recurs in *Alexander's Bridge* makes its cumulative service more effective as a running metaphorical comment on dramatic event. It is not Cather's principal interest in the book, but it does expand meaning and connect disparate parts. For example, the several worlds which Alexander inhabits have a musical atmosphere about them which measures his response to their peculiar geniality. It is important, also, that the two women in the hero's life are musicians of sorts, because their tastes in music are subtle confirmation of their difference and desirability. What justifies Cather's use of music as figurative gloss is the personality of the central character, Bartley Alexander, whose associations supply the meaning for the music references. As his wife, Winifred, and his mistress, Hilda Burgoyne, are psychologically defined by what they mean to Alexander, so the quality of their particular music takes on the personal meaning which he gives it.

Everything about Alexander's personality goes back to a psychic division between what he is and what he ought to be. At forty-three and

4. Edith Lewis, *Willa Cather Living: A Personal Record* (New York: Alfred A. Knopf, 1953), p. 78.

at the peak of his eminence as bridge builder, he feels sharply the loss of his desire for life. Success brings neither freedom nor power. Recoiling from the idea of surrendering personal liberty to "a professional movement," "he found himself living exactly the kind of life he had determined to escape" (49). The dilemma now confronting him is represented by his Boston home. Though this is the world which Alexander associates with his "dead calm" of middle age, it is not a world without benefit and attraction. The rub, rather, seems to be that it has too many privileges, advantages which are not wholly in keeping with the essential Bartley. The manner is moneyed—elegant, gracious, orderly, and very snug. The style of this world derives largely from Winifred's nature, and her personality is inseparable from her deep musical interest. She is, in fact, first presented not with Bartley or in her home but returning from a concert. The association with music is not fortuitous. A room in the house is set aside for music and becomes something of a sanctuary for her. There is even a second piano in the upstairs study. She reveals to Professor Wilson, a house guest, that she studied in Vienna; and from her playing after dinner we realize that, though she says she does not practice "'a great many hours'" (18), she does spend many hours at the piano. The appreciatory report of her performance is Wilson's, and his judgment is altogether reliable.

> She played brilliantly and with great musical feeling. Wilson could not imagine her permitting herself to do anything badly, but he was surprised at the cleanness of her execution. He wondered how a woman with so many duties had managed to keep herself up to a standard really professional. It must take a great deal of time, certainly, and Bartley must take a great deal of time. Wilson reflected that he had never before known a woman who had been able, for any considerable while, to support both a personal and an intellectual passion. (18)

I do not think it matters that Winifred plays Schumann's "Carnival." It does matter, however, that she plays Schumann, because the choice of composer is another of Willa Cather's private comments on her characters. The complimentary associations of Schumann's music to which Wilson responds are specified in a *Journal* notice on the death of the composer's wife, Clara Wieck Schumann. Clara Schumann is the opposite of George Sand. A brilliant pianist herself, Clara Schumann subordinated her talent for the sake of her husband's higher genius. She inspired her husband to write his most impressive pieces and is the one to whom nearly all his greatest music is dedicated. She provided support and incentive for Robert Schumann's "exquisite temperament."[5] Through the music of Schumann, then, Willa Cather suggests an atmosphere of domesticity touched with inspiration. Music suggests also the limitation of so fine an influence. Willa Cather portrays a woman remarkable enough to be Alexander's wife but not remarkable enough to provide him complete marital happiness. Given her education and careful manners (she is never haughty though always gently reserved), Winifred is almost exemplary. Her absorption in music is not preclusive. She balances interest in music with her husband's emotional demands. The point Cather makes is that Alexander is emotionally larger than Winifred. There remains something more elemental in him than her classical music accommodates, though he finds deep satisfaction in that too. At the end of the book Wilson tells Hilda: "'No relation is so complete that it can hold absolutely all of a person'" (173). No one image of Alexander accounts for the total personality. And so Winifrid's music, brilliant, passionate, and finished, has only partial appeal to Bartley. After she finishes playing, Wilson notices Alexander in a chair, shoulders sunk, hand passively hanging over the arm, "with the glow of an immediate interest gone out" of his face. He wears the "purple velvet smoking-coat" (20) Winifred has chosen for him, but remains disinterested in her Schumann. It was not always this way, however. When they first met he asked her to play for him (25). Music was part of her initial appeal, as it has been a reassuring part of her maturing graciousness.

The hardly discernible separation between husband and wife, which music suggests without violating the surface harmony of their relationship, is best explained in Alexander's letter to Hilda.

> Now I know that no one can build his security upon the nobleness of another person. Two people, when they love each other, grow alike in their tastes and habits and pride, but their moral natures (whatever we may mean by that canting expression) are never welded. The base one goes on being base, and the noble one noble, to the end. (128)

Music voices Winifred's moral nature. It is a cultivated nature and affiliated to a complex order, while Bartley's is really at home in the simple pastoral order of a sandbar. The two are incompatible.

5. *Journal*, June 14, 1896, p. 13; *KA*, p. 170.

Winifred's formal music is one strain within Alexander's double nature. The other, more elemental side is echoed by Hilda Burgoyne's. The sharp contrast between their talents shows the acuteness of Bartley's conflict. In Boston music is deliberate, reserved, and refined; but in London music is impulsive, simple, and direct. Significantly, Winifred's expression takes the form of a piano piece which is less personal than Hilda's songs. The added measure of warmth which is provided by voice corresponds to the general openness of Hilda's nature and the force of her femininity. Alexander, after many years, by chance hears Hilda in an Irish folk musical, "Bog Lights," at the Duke of York theatre while he is in London on business. She enchants him with her fanciful, light touches which make "'the whole thing a fairy tale'" (31). Later, in a scene that parallels in reverse the novel's opening scene with Winifred's piano entertainment, Hilda sings to Alexander after dinner. His face which passively beheld Winifred acquires expression and brightness as the actress goes through "'some good Irish songs'" (73), recently composed for her. Her training, as she admits, is limited. "'Of course I can't really sing, except the way my mother and grandmother did before me'" (74); and this is exactly how Alexander would have her sing. Her voice has power, just as Winifred's Schumann was masterly though she too denied any special claims her music might have, such as power to awaken the youthful feelings Boston and professional routine have dulled. The simple rhythm of her music accords with the rhythm of his "base" nature.

Hilda sings for Alexander on a Sunday evening when he dines at her apartment. The circumstances surrounding her singing reveal how deeply the artless rhythm of her music runs in Alexander. Alone together they recall former days in Paris when they first met and loved. As they reminisce, two moral natures fuse momentarily, but only momentarily. Willa Cather, again using music as metaphorical comment, carefully undercuts the tentative reconciliation. To check the strong emotional appeal in Alexander's remembrance of Paris, Hilda moves over to the piano and abruptly shifts the topic to her newest play. She sings some of the score, but music proves an ineffective denial of the passion each feels. He asks Hilda to sing "The Harp that Once." She nervously hesitates, suggesting first that she cannot sing and then, when Bartley ignores this, that the room is too warm. She never does sing Moore's lovely air. They are in each other's arms too soon. Hilda's real reason for not singing it is not made explicit, but Cather's mentioning the song seems to me apt. The lyric interprets Hilda's silence for us (she fears even a musical reminder of a love lost); and Moore's song obliquely suggests the brevity and fatality of their love renewed.

> The harp that once thro' Tara's halls
>   The soul of music shed,
> Now hangs as mute on Tara's walls,
>   As if that soul were fled.—
> So sleeps the pride of former days,
>   So glory's thrill is o'er,
> And hearts, that once beat high for praise,
>   Now feel that pulse no more.
>
> No more to chiefs and ladies bright
>   The harp of Tara swells;
> The chord alone, that breaks at night,
>   Its tale of ruin tells.
> Thus Freedom now so seldom wakes,
>   The only throb she gives,
> Is when some heart indignant breaks,
>   To show that still she lives.[6]

The youthful spirit from which Alexander's fondness for Hilda grew has fled because the terms of his life which encouraged the desire are drastically altered. But in fleeing, the spirit of early life has left residual energy. Once again Cather represents the soul's deepest strength through music. Success cannot totally destroy Alexander's desire for a higher, indestructable enchantment. His *élan* is imperishable. "'Bartley caught the wind early,'" Professor Wilson tells Winifred, "'and it has sung in his sails ever since'" (9). The song within sensitizes Alexander to the larger rhythm of life. When the external world is bustling, its vitality comes to him as a rich, long chord. London, which "'always makes me [Alexander] want to live more than any other city in the world'" (119), in particular echoes his heart's strain through the surface vivacity of metropolitan sounds.

> There was a blurred rhythm in all the dull city noises—in the clatter of the cab horses and the rumbling of the busses, in the street calls, and in the undulating tramp, tramp of the crowd. It was like the deep vibration of some vast underground machinery, and like the muffled pulsations of millions of human hearts. (119)

6. *The Complete Poetical Works of Thomas Moore* (New York: Thomas Y. Crowell, 1895), p. 171.

The street pianos, even though they monotonously repeat *Il Trovatore*, make him "'feel jaunty'" (120). In a mood of such exhilaration dinner would be preferable at the Piccadilly Restaurant because "'the music's good there'" (120). Music reassures Alexander that his joy in life is honest, and activates his youthful self. The intimate connection between the hero's spirit, his second self, and music is solidly confirmed by Willa Cather's making him an amateur pianist. Alexander's playing the piano serves no formal purpose; his destiny is linked to building bridges. But when he spontaneously plays accompaniment for several young people on the ship —"until the last sleepy girl had followed her mother below" (97)—we know the keen pressure which the "expectancy of youth" (99) creates. Music releases pressure and allows the soul's desire some satisfaction. In one way or another, all of Alexander's happy, unrestrained moments are musical. In London with Hilda when things go well and he feels the delight of the moment, there is music; by contrast, their two tense altercations are without music.

The characterization of Hilda Burgoyne emerges from Willa Cather's constant fascination with backstage life and with the personal history of artists. Without falsifying the novel's emphasis by making the story Hilda's, I think it proper to see the whole London setting of *Alexander's Bridge* as another look into the private life of an artist, something which is very much Willa Cather's subject matter. Like Madame Tradutorri, Frau Selma Schumann, and Cressida Garnet, one of the later artists, Hilda Burgoyne succeeds in art and fails in love.

II

The passage from "Eric Hermannson's Soul" describing the inarticulate hero's violin as "his only bridge into the kingdom of the soul," while it pertains to Willa Cather's general use of music, has special relevance to her technique in *Alexander's Bridge*. The subject in both the story and the novel is integration. Eric and Bartley suffer from a spiritual division. The "vital thing within" (43) longs to be born with its delicacy and fineness alive. In analyzing Bartley's inability to work out a career in keeping with his vital need—and here the novel gathers authority—Willa Cather places an emotional strain on the hero no less severe than the catastrophic stress on Moorlock Bridge, his scientific masterwork. The metal structure reminds Bartley of his spiritual loss. He tortures himself "for the ugliness he had brought into the world" (149) and suffers for losing touch with the past when he brought something beautiful into life. As a symbol of spiritual union, music functions as a bridge to Bartley's soul and the intense life which his youth held before him. As a dramatic pattern, music is the psychological counterpart of the bridge which crashes at the end and kills Bartley. Both bridges are unfinished and disabled.

In the later novels music serves as a bridge into the past by prompting a complex mnemonic excursion. In *Alexander's Bridge* and the short fiction coming before it, Willa Cather's treatment is simpler. Her manner is commensurate with the degree of complication in her characters, and by comparison to the later figures the early ones are uncomplicated. Bartley Alexander "'was never introspective,'" Wilson tells Winifred. "'He was simply the most tremendous response to stimuli I have ever known'" (9). Music indicates how tremendous his response is, and does not initiate a reflection but concludes it. One passage is worth quoting in full since it characterizes Cather's treatment of music as a link to the past up to this time.

> Since then [his first visit] Bartley had always thought of the British Museum as the ultimate repository of mortality, where all the dead things in the world were assembled to make one's hour of youth the more precious. One trembled lest before he got out it might somehow escape him, lest he might drop the glass from over-eagerness and see it shivered on the stone floor at his feet. How one hid his youth under his coat and hugged it! And how good it was to turn one's back upon all that vaulted cold, to take Hilda's arm and hurry out of the great door and down the steps into the sunlight among the pigeons—to know that the warm and vital thing within him was still there and had not been snatched away to flush Caesar's lean cheek or to feed the veins of some bearded Assyrian king. They in their day had carried the flaming liquor, but to-day was his! So the song used to run in his head those summer mornings a dozen years ago. Alexander walked by the place very quietly, as if he were afraid of waking some one. (42–43)

In following Bartley's reminiscence we see how naturally Willa Cather moves toward music as a symbol of intensity. His resurgence of youthful vigor gains power with each association; but beyond music there is no higher persuasion of the old fire and its lingering warmth. Against signs of change and death surrounding him in the form of beautiful but bloodless artifacts is the enduring song of "a dozen years ago," the feeling which once stirred Caesar and the Assyrian king and now pulsates in Alexander.

Alexander associates his condition with music a second time. Whereas the song of a dozen years ago epitomizes rejuvenation, the second reference, also an unspecified song, recapitulates awareness of defeat by success, money, and time. Caught by emotional fatigue, he demurs at the idea of traveling back to England. "'I wish things would let me rest. I'm tired of work, tired of people, tired of trailing about'" (90). Finally, he describes to Winifred the effect of life's indefinite, inexplicable threats: "'All the same, life runs smoothly enough with some people, and with me it's always a messy sort of patchwork. It's like the song; peace is where I am not'" (90–91). The trip across proves therapeutic, but seeing Hilda does not. His note to her admits that he is "never at peace" (129). The fire extinguished, the drive dissipated, Alexander devotes himself to building bridges; and from Chapter VIII, where he leaves Hilda, to the end there is no music. The musical bridge to the past and youth, momentarily reconstructed, breaks.

Before Bartley dies, when he is back in London for a second time, Cather catches him pensively looking out the Savoy Hotel window at the flashing Thames; and it is the same attitude of dreamy thoughtfulness in which all the characters are frozen at the novel's conclusion. After the catastrophe Winifred sits in the carriage "Hour after hour . . . watching the water, the lonely, useless stone towers, and the convulsed mass of iron wreckage over which the angry river continually spat up its yellow foam" (162). The Epilogue dealing with Wilson's visit with Hilda ends with a comparable tableau: "They both sat looking into the fire" (175). Wife, teacher, mistress are "'only onlookers at the best'" (174). Alexander made the play, and the play has ended. But as Wilson tells Hilda, "'He left an echo.'" Our final impression of those who heard and felt the vitality of his original song is of their waiting intently for its return, poised so that with the echo they can create for themselves a musical bridge across to Alexander's life.

CHAPTER FOUR

O Pioneers!

The night-bird's song,
The evening breeze,
All nature's sounds together say,
"He loves thee!"

Faust

O Pioneers! (1913)[1] honors the new beginnings of civilization. In Willa Cather's writing before this novel there is strong sympathy for the adventurer, there is deep appreciation for a world untouched by man, and there is serious questioning of the place of art both in a world too rude to promote it and in the very enterprise of living; but for some reason Willa Cather did not bring her principal interests together. She does so in *O Pioneers!* The exploration in the stories of artistic egotism and the narrow views of art's service provides a base from which Willa Cather develops a kinship she discerned between the man who gives form to the thing within and the man who gives form to the soil. Like the heroine of *O Pioneers!*, the novelist had to know the meaning behind man's work because it is more from the idea of the thing than from the thing itself that one derives satisfaction. The idea Willa Cather sees behind prairie life is that the pioneer venture in a corner of Nebraska bears the great responsibility of civilization, and this idea unifies her themes. A meager start continues the cycle of humanity's remaking the land according to desire. The task draws upon the heart, the arm, the imagination. Carl Linstrum,

1. *O Pioneers!* (Sentry Edition; Boston: Houghton Mifflin, 1962). All references are to this text.

having returned to the Divide after sixteen years, says to Alexandra about the conspicuous changes in life on the land: "'Isn't it queer: there are only two or three human stories, and they go on repeating themselves as fiercely as if they had never happened before; like the larks in this country, that have been singing the same five notes over for thousands of years'" (119). The great human story, of course, is the founding of a culture.

There are two human stories in O *Pioneers!* Both are stories of youth and imagination. Where the force of youth is disciplined and used to work the land, as in the case of Alexandra Bergson, the story is one of success; where the passion is unchecked and misdirected, as with Emil Bergson and Marie Shabata, the story is tragic. An important function of music is to emphasize the contrapuntal pattern of these stories. This is done in a familiar way. Music measures the characters' promise of love, their accomplishment, and potential heroism. A capacity for musical expression or an encouragement of music are synonymous with creative human powers.

The two human stories are set within the larger history of breaking the Nebraska land. After countless years of following its own beautiful but not bountiful way and after a brief span of human toil, the red earth suddenly sprouts new life and yields rich, yellow wheat. Willa Cather complements the song of youth with a medley of natural sounds, earth's natural music, to express both its complex temper and its gradual enrichment under human care. This twinned beginning of life constitutes the start of civilization, and Willa Cather subtly underscores the cultural blending of European style and American material through musical talent in representatives of four generations. In doing so, she introduces in O *Pioneers!* what will come to be one of her major uses of music—as referent for her grand theme, culture.

II

The significance of the prairie in the novel resides in the power it has over those who strive to cultivate it: the land is the great enigmatic fact of life. It undergoes natural change and submits to man's desire, all the while retaining its essential temper which does not alter and which cannot be fully known by man, though occasionally it is deeply felt. On the surface the Divide seems at times friendly and at other times hostile, but it is really unfeeling and neutral to the interests of man. What accounts for the philosophical importance of the prairie in O *Pioneers!* is the attitude the settlers adopt toward it. These attitudes range from mystical to profane, depending on the person's awareness of the mysterious, immutable spirit beneath the physical properties or his exclusive concern for the fruit it may bear.

The ambivalent temper of the Nebraska land is caught in the first half of the poem-prologue, "Prairie Spring"; and to express the theme in poetry is already to elevate it to a form of music.

> Evening and the flat land,
> Rich and sombre and always silent;
> The miles of fresh-plowed soil,
> Heavy and black, full of strength and harshness;
> The growing wheat, the growing weeds,
> The toiling horses, the tired men;
> The long empty roads,
> Sullen fires of sunset, fading,
> The eternal, unresponsive sky.

As the poem's title implies, the tableau catches the prairie at a high point in its birth; but in its natural state nature is much more resistant. The novel opens when the land is largely untamed and the conditions of human life hardest, one January day when "the little town of Hanover, anchored on a windy Nebraska tableland, was trying not to be blown away" (3). A howling wind envelops the precarious community, ready to erase the slight human alteration of nature; and always the tough red grass seems ready to come back and carpet man's work. Nature is harsh, yet its harshness is its strength and beauty. The silence mentioned in the poem is a respite in what is really commotion, mystery, chance. Human claims for dignity against the mighty elements must be equal to the strength of nature. They must be heroic.

When this majestic force does reveal something of its secret identity, it does so through the wind, which is, as the human voice is for man in Willa Cather's work, the most impressive medium of its inner self. The wind is nature's breath, releasing its climatic mood. Mood of course refers to the meaning man ascribes to natural phenomena. Early in the novel when Carl takes Alexandra and young Emil back to the country from Hanover, the sound in the wind is an echo of Carl's call. Man puts meaning in natural events just as he gives meaning to the soil's potentiality by bringing it to fertility. The first setback Alexandra experiences coupled with the prospect of Carl's departure, for example, deeply colors her sensitivity to the noise of a tornado and frightened cattle. The sounds of nature are heard as antagonistic, chaotic. The lowing and bellowing animals seem to catch the plangent quality of frontier life. With the qualification that emotional disposition generates meaning, one can say that nature appears to stay silent when neutral to man's aspirations and appears strident when inimical.

In its uncultivated state, nature has a delicacy which balances its primitive roughness. Significantly, nature first shows this side of its personality at Ivar's isolated pond where, out of the old Norwegian's religious regard for nature's perfection, all is kept in a sacral splendor. If the wind is nature's breath, then the birds are its voice, a voice with a unique beauty in its melody. The sound of birds is all the more beautiful and impressive because it arises amid the uninterrupted silence of the prairie. When they are young, Alexandra and Carl visit the hermit's sanctuary and hear this natural blend of sound. We are not told about Carl's response, but we do know Alexandra's. Her strong sense of place and her respect for Ivar prompt in her a reaction sympathetic to the old Norwegian's. She catches something of the earth's sacredness in the hymnal unison of lark, quail, and locust. "If one stood in the doorway of his cave, and looked off at the rough land, the smiling sky, the curly grass white in the hot sunlight; if one listened to the rapturous song of the lark, the drumming of the quail, the burr of the locust against that vast silence, one understood what Ivar meant" (38). Ivar's "meaning" follows from his sacramental view of nature. Through his eyes nature appears as a richly varied expression of the Lord's work and His love; in his ears the earth's sonority is an antiphon praising the Creator.

The religious quality of the earth's sounds from this one point of view is underscored in several ways. The integrity of the setting remains unviolated and tenderly fostered. The visit occurs on a Sunday afternoon, and immediately after the narrator's observation on the song of the earth, Ivar closes the Bible and recites several sections of Psalm 104, which he conveniently runs together for his purposes:

> He sendeth the springs into the valleys, which run among the hills;
> They give drink to every beast of the field; the wild asses quench
> their thirst.
> The trees of the Lord are full of sap; the cedars of Lebanon which he
> hath planted;
> Where the birds make their nests: as for the stork, the fir trees are
> her house.
> The high hills are a refuge for the wild goats; and the rocks for the
> conies. (38)

The juxtaposition of the earth's auditory effects and the psalm is apt. Like the psalmist who contemplates the natural world and admires its magnificence, Ivar sees God's wisdom and love manifested in creation. Later, when trying to discourage the Bergson boys from killing birds, he pleads, "'But these wild things are God's birds'" (41). And so their high song, attuned to the bass burrings of the locust, is to Him.

The three years after Mr. Bergson's death are prosperous ones. The crops are good. But the second three years "brought every one on the Divide to the brink of despair" (47). The land, taking back what it gave, does not yield to the plowshare. Everywhere there is discouragement: drought, failure, foreclosures. The land cruelly and finally distinguishes among its challengers. The weak "follow in paths already marked out for them" and leave for the cities. The strong who are meant "to break trails in a new country" (48) not only meet the challenge but raise the stakes by accumulating more land. Against the advice of her timid mother and unimaginative brothers, Alexandra puts the homestead back into mortgage and makes arrangements to acquire land from those who give up the fight. Speaking of the more prosperous farms along the river which she has just visited, she says to Emil, her younger brother: "'Down there they have a little certainty, but up with us there is a big chance. We must have faith in the high land, Emil'" (64).

Alexandra's decision to remain on the Divide and work seems to be the kind of strong loving commitment the land succumbs to. It responds and bears fruit when it receives love and is firmly worked. The rather long section (Chapter V of Part I) which treats Alexandra's insight into the value of land and her positive pledge to it begins and ends with music. Her five-day trip to the prosperous river farms has shown her the value of her own land up higher. She says to her younger brother: "'I want to hold on harder than ever, and when you're a man you'll thank me'" (64). Her return to the high land is almost rapturous. She urges the horse up the first long swells of the Divide; and in her happiness she "hummed an old Swedish hymn" (65). It is the only occasion in the novel when Alexandra expresses herself musically, and for a woman who is "armored in calm" (135) and "about her own feelings . . . could never write very freely" (286), this humming amounts to an outpouring of sentiment. Even Emil "wondered why his sister looked so happy. Her face was so radiant that he felt shy about asking her." The reason is clear enough. She has achieved a vigorous awareness of the land's spirit and its relationship to the meaning of her life.

Her attitude toward the land is very much like Ivar's, but with an important distinction. Alexandra's view is emotional, where the hermit's is mystical. Her relationship to it requires action and work to bring forth its riches; her attitude is productive. His relationship requires continuous worship and custody; his attitude is protective. Above all, Ivar sees the land in specifically Christian terms; Alexandra regards it in broader, naturalistic, almost atavistic, terms. Yet both treat it with love and respect. The difference between the sacral and naturalistic dispositions toward the land is strongly suggested in the way both Ivar and Alexandra respond to its sounds. Both hear the same beautiful effects. For Ivar, as we have seen, the sound of the birds is something of a devotional chant to the Creator. For Alexandra the earth's sound is a song of herself, a song of self-discovery, love, and illumination. Her new consciousness is represented through a unison of the aural movement in nature and the pulse of the heart. Insects chirping come to Alexandra as "the sweetest music," and there "with the quail and the plover and all the little wild things that crooned or buzzed" (71) was the rhythm of her spirit.

Later in the novel Carl Linstrum, having returned from St. Louis for a visit before going west, hears the same pastoral music while walking to his old farm. As the sun comes up, the small creatures "began to tune their tiny instruments" (126) and a profusion of chirping, twittering, and whistling arises. But just as Carl's life belongs away from the Divide, so its sound holds no personal message for him. For Alexandra the rustle of natural life signifies her heart's work, while for Ivar the prairie's noise has a sacramental ring; for Carl, however, it is something sensuously lovely and nothing more. He left the Divide earlier because he saw no relationship between himself and the land, and now he perceives nothing of the earth's spirit in its song. The morning sound is a haunting reminder of his weakness and defeat in leaving the land some twenty years before. The day before he hears the insects and the birds he expressed his surprise to Alexandra about the changes two decades have brought to Hanover, and he remarked his preference for the untamed land. Never having understood it then, yet eager to know it now, he finds it wholly unrecognizable.

> "This is all very splendid in its way, but there was something about this country when it was a wild old beast that has haunted me all these years. Now, when I come back to all this milk and honey, I feel like the old German song, 'Wo bist du, wo bist du, mein geliebtest Land?'" (118)

His dear land is of course where it always was; he hears it once again as he did then (with Alexandra at Ivar's), and it still tells him nothing about himself.

Carl Linstrum at least responds to the earth's voice. There are those in the novel who are altogether insensitive to it. The Bergson boys, Oscar and Lou, who certainly "would have been happier with their uncle Otto, in the bakery shop in Chicago" (47), comprehend very little of the land which they work and which gives them so much. They work methodically as horses would, unconsciously and by instinct. They have no life apart from the soil, and such a life is incomplete unless one can savor the meaning of pioneering. Oscar and Lou cannot. Their lack of perceptivity renders them victims to the soil they work. Its hard ways become their style and they are enslaved by the physical comforts the land brings. Alexandra is alive to the loss of mental elasticity on the prairie. "'We grow hard and heavy here,'" she says to Carl, who is given to romanticizing about the frontier which he has not really understood. "'We don't move lightly and easily as you do, and our minds get stiff. If the world were no wider than my cornfields, if there were not something beside this, I wouldn't feel that it was much worth while to work'" (124). Ways of living for Willa Cather are ways of perceiving, and Oscar and Lou are just about deaf to the delicate sounds of the prairie. In Lou, there is a trace of musical sensitivity; he plays the dragharmonika. But Oscar, who "worked like an insect, always doing the same thing over in the same way" (55), lives in the oppressive silence of his spirit.

III

It is to the young that the world appears bright and resonant, and that quick responsiveness is represented through musical sensitivity and dancing. The function of music in relation to the theme of youth is suggested in the introductory poem:

> Against all this, Youth,
> Flaming like the wild roses,
> Singing like the larks over the plowed fields,
> Flashing like a star out of the twilight;
> Youth with its insupportable sweetness,
> Its fierce necessity,
> Its sharp desire,

Singing and singing,
Out of the lips of silence,
Out of the earthy dusk.

Wild roses, larks, and a shooting star commemorate the beauty in the charged brevity of youthful life. The music metaphor heightens that beauty into an expression of dynamic release from silence, harshness, toil, gloom—"all this" potentiality.

The young for Willa Cather are innately musical. The adventure of youth invariably has musical associations, as it does in the opening poem and when Emil Bergson writes to Alexandra of his Mexican holiday which was filled with music and dancing during the fiestas. Emil preserves some of that southern excitement through song. He returns from Mexico with a guitar and a Latin swagger (a "shoulder-motion he had acquired among the Mexicans"). When he starts to play on one occasion, his strummings prompt sympathetic responses in all the young people present: "[They] drifted to the other end of the hall where the guitar was sounding" (226). Wherever the young gather in the novel— at university dances, church suppers, weddings, in the fields—there is music which manifests the quickened pace and "'acceleration of life'" (305) that Carl experiences when he is near Emil Bergson and Marie Shabata.

Emil, Alexandra's youngest brother, and Marie, the wife of a neighbor, are the most important young people in the novel; and it is to the quality of their youth that the music motif is most applicable. In their case the generic "singing" of the poem-prologue becomes a song of love: the "sharp desire" is for each other; the "fierce necessity," for a life-in-love. Music seems a natural metaphor to convey the significance of their lives, because everything about Emil and Marie is characterized by rhythm, vivacity, and grace.

The story of Emil and Marie is recounted in the middle three parts of *O Pioneers!* By this time Alexandra already has achieved success on the Divide, and the land now "yields itself eagerly to the plow" (76). "Yes," Alexandra thinks, "it had been worth while; both Emil and the country had become what she had hoped . . . . She felt well satisfied with her life" (213). Against this background of fulfillment and hope, Emil and Marie enact their fatal drama. Our first impression of Emil as a young man (he is twenty-one in Part II) is one of rhythmic movement. Standing at the gate to the Norwegian cemetery, he sharpens a scythe to the melody he is whistling; and this image is deepened by a bearing of strong masculine grace. "He was a splendid figure of a boy, tall and straight as a young pine tree, with a handsome head, and stormy gray eyes, deeply set under a serious brow" (77). The details of his life also suggest vitality and speed. He is known at college for his whistling, plays the cornet in the band, and holds the interstate record for high jumping. The appeal of Emil's tragic counterpart, Marie Shabata, is principally visual. On the day Emil is whistling away as he sharpens his scythe, Marie appears wearing a wide hat circled with red poppies. "Her face, too, was rather like a poppy, . . . with rich color in her cheeks and lips, and her dancing yellow-brown eyes bubbl[ing] with gayety" (79). The impression is of a spatial fluidity animated by her lovely eyes and set in motion by the wind which fetchingly lifts her chestnut-shaded hair. The public sign of Emil's and Marie's vivacity is dancing. They dance whenever they can, so often, in fact, that Marie warns Emil about offending the other girls by his attention to her.

The stronger power music exercises over Emil is private, not public. It permits him to express his love for Marie—Frank Shabata's wife—by transforming her into a *donna angelicata* and therefore securely above the mundane implications of sensuality and adultery. It is another of those total surrenders to musical enchantment which puts Emil in the company of Peter Sadelack and Paul in the kingdom of the unattainable; and like those bizarre mental excursions, Emil's, too, is fatal. The occasion is a confirmation service for the French children at the church of Sainte-Agnes, and the atmosphere could not be more conducive to rhapsodic indulgence. While half the community joyfully celebrates the confirmation on this Sunday, the other half prepares for the funeral on Monday of Amédée Chevalier, Emil's close friend who died suddenly from acute appendicitis. Already laden with sharp feeling, the air is further burdened by religious music; and for Emil there is the special anxiety about the reasons for Marie's absence. In the middle of the well-rehearsed Rossini Mass comes the exuberant melody of Gounod's devotional "Ave Maria." "The Choir had never sung so well and Raoul Marcel, in the 'Gloria,' drew even the bishop's eyes to the organ loft. For the offertory he sang Gounod's 'Ave Maria,'—always spoken of in Sainte-Agnes as 'the Ave Maria'" (254). Like Aunt Georgiana in "A Wagner Matinee," Emil is caught up in conflicting whirls of emotion as he hears Raoul's rich voice worshipfully sing the name of the absent Marie. Suddenly music illumines an uncertainty and Emil believes that he can love Marie Shabata above any sinful implication. The word "rapture" is repeated four times, and it is not too strong a description of Emil's emotional flight in music. "He coveted nothing that was Frank Shabata's. The spirit he had met in music was his own" (255). Music endows Marie with spiritual identity and thereby provides access to a forbidden relationship. Once again Willa Cather has soul speak to soul through music. Raoul's wailing of the magic words, "San—cta Mari-i-i-a, . . . O—ra pro no-o-bis!" rounds off Emil's rationalization of his illicit love for Marie. He assumes "this equivocal revelation" (256) of music to be uniquely his.

That Willa Cather specifies Gounod's "Ave Maria" appears particularly apt in the light of another allusion to his work. The composer's romantic lyricism has, it seems, a special attraction for Emil. Earlier, when we first see Emil cutting the grass, he is heard whistling an aria from *Faust*: "When the grass required his close attention, or when he had to stoop to cut about a headstone, he paused in his lively air,—the 'Jewel' song,—taking it up where he had left it when his scythe swung free again" (78). The passing allusion to Marguerite's aria foretells the quality and destiny of Emil's love and life when it is considered in the context of the opera and then compared to the situation in *O Pioneers!*

The third act of *Faust* opens as Siebel, a youth in love with Marguerite, enters her garden to pick flowers which are to convey his affection. "*Faites-lui mes aveux,*" he sings; but the flowers cannot bear his avowal. They shrivel as he plucks them because his hands have been cursed by Méphistophélès. If he dips his fingers in a font of holy water by the wall of Marguerite's house, however, the flowers will not wilt. Like Emil who purifies his desire for Marie through the agency of sacred music before offering his love, Siebel must cleanse his gesture of the impiety. The bouquet Siebel arranges and leaves for Marguerite, then, symbolizes the claim of ideal love. Méphistophélès replaces the bouquet with one of his own along with a casket of jewels. The gems are to arouse the girl's vanity and thereby dispose her to Faust's flattery. They are emblems of profane love, and the "Jewel Song" voices the naive delight in sensuous beauty and the awakening of physical passion. As Marguerite adorns herself with the jewels, she sees beauty smiling back in her reflection and imagines herself transformed into a nobler woman:

> Oh! could he see me now,
> Here, deck'd like this, I vow,
> He surely would mistake me,
> And for noble lady take me![2]

2. *The Authentic Librettos of the French and German Operas* (New York: Crown Publishers, 1939), p. 74.

This romantic power makes the girl susceptible to Faust's flattering advances, and both lovers are destined to be destroyed by the blinding force of their lust. For Marguerite as for Emil, the revelation of love comes through music. She sings: "*J'écoute!... Et je comprends cette voix solitaire/ Qui chante dans mon coeur!*" Their passion casts a spell from which they cannot escape, and the consequence of their lust is gloatingly predicted in Méphistophélès' invocation to darkness:

> 'Twas high time!
> By night, protected,
> In earnest talk of love,
> They will return! 'Tis well!
> I'll not disturb
> Their amorous confabulation!
> Night, conceal them in thy darkest shade.
> Love, from their fond hearts
> Shut out all troublesome remorse.
> And ye, O flowers of fragrance subtle,
> This hand accurs'd
> Doth cause ye all to open!
> Bewilder the heart of Marguerite![3]

In its dramatic setting, then, the "Jewel Song" not only expresses the birth of physical love but also discloses its destructiveness. The justness of Willa Cather's alluding to the aria in O *Pioneers!* might be explained by examining it as a comment on the love theme. Like the operatic lovers, Emil and Marie are victims of a reckless, physical passion; thus, Emil's whistling the "Jewel Song" ironically prefigures his death. Willa Cather seems also to be contrasting this profane love with the sacred love of the "Ave Maria." The contrast, a favorite of Willa Cather, adds a further irony. In music Emil thinks he discovers that "he could love forever without faltering and without sin"; he takes his love to be an idealized one. It is not. Precisely this misrepresentation of his feelings allows Emil to justify his embracing Marie. Just as Marguerite sees what she wishes to see in the mirror and hears what she wants to hear in "*cette voix solitaire*," Emil projects his own profane longing for Marie into the devotion to the Virgin.

Later that afternoon, Emil, unable to be away from Marie, dashes to the Shabata farm, sees the girl lying under the white mulberry tree, embraces her. Marie surrenders to Emil's desire just as he gave himself up to music. But the "new life of perfect love" (259) is brief. Her husband,

3. *Ibid.*, p. 78.

Frank, discovers them and shoots them both. Emil dies in the ecstacy of passion, Marie, wearing "a look of ineffable content" (269). Their death marks the end of the old story of human desire and failure writing itself over, this time on the Nebraska Divide. It was written with "'the best you had here'" (305) to be sure, but it was not a successful story, only a beautiful one. The beauty of Emil's and Marie's life is seen by contrast in the effect their murder has on Alexandra. She becomes cold, heavy, numb, and gripped by a death wish. "What was left of life seemed unimportant" (286) to her. And as the fire of youth is represented through music, so the extinguishing of that flame brings an end to the music references in O Pioneers! In Part V, the concluding section, the dominant image is of incarceration. The penitentiary in Lincoln where Frank Shabata is imprisoned becomes for Alexandra the form that defines the grief in which she is locked. As in early stories like "The Clemency of the Court" and "On the Divide," enclosure is the counter-image of music. It indicates the absence of all the humanizing and liberating things music stands for. The positive implication of music is emphasized in Willa Cather's shifting to a poetic allusion to define Alexandra's heavy heart and "disgust" (298) after leaving the penitentiary. The allusion to Byron's "The Prisoner of Chillon" works as do the music references in expanding meaning but it does not invite the reader to hear a melody as well. The withdrawal of musical appeal subtly indicates a deep loss of joy. Her memory slightly alters the words. The two verses in proper order run: "And the whole earth would henceforth be/A wider prison unto me."

But the novel's final statement is not negative. Like "The Prisoner of Chillon," O Pioneers! ends with freedom regained. For Alexandra there will be a new life with Carl Linstrum who, after hearing about the disaster, returns to Hanover to rescue her. In taking leave of the Divide, Alexandra bears knowledge of the freedom in the land. For the human heart, the prairie offers repose as Alexandra herself felt it and believes that others shall; and within its geological growth resides the endless design of regeneration which endows the land with freedom from the surface change effected by time and human affairs. "'We come and go,'" Alexandra pensively says to Carl, "'but the land is always here'" (308). The tableau in the introductory poem suggested this permanence in picturing the prairie in spring on the verge of new things, and Willa Cather underscores the cycle of exchange between man and the earth in several characters whose personality determines the new versions of the old story that was and will be written on the Divide.

We know from earlier pages in the book what will happen. The magnificent bequest of the Bergson story will go to Milly Bergson, Alexandra's favorite niece, the daughter of Lou Bergson. An "'especial favorite'" of Ivar's as well, Milly is, as her mother proudly puts it, "'the musician of the family'" (110). The young girl is close to her Aunt Alexandra from whom she has learned both the old and new ways. Together they have gone over Swedish songs and read stories of the American frontier. To the customs of Europe and America are added the refinement which a new prosperity allows. Milly's family will move "'into town as soon as the girls are old enough to go out into company'" (111), and her aunt has promised Milly a piano so that she can improve her playing. In fine, Milly is something of a cultural custodian, and her musical ability forecasts a rich spiritual increase from the little beginnings of civilization as the cycle of prairie life moves into an upward course.

CHAPTER FIVE

The

Lyric Artist

> ... he wept
> By Strymon's lonely wave under soaring
> cliffs,
> Unfolding his tragic song to the frozen
> stars,
> Enchanting tigers, moving oaks with his
> theme ....
>
> *Georgics*

Of the three American singers about whom Willa Cather wrote appreciatively while they reigned during the Metropolitan Opera's golden age, one commands her total favor. Louise Homer, a contralto born in Pittsburgh, famous for her Orpheus, had power and persuasion, "but she had set for herself no goal that it would break her heart to lose."[1] Geraldine Farrar, a soprano from Massachusetts, was known for the lyric sensuousness of her interpretation and had that personal quality of voice which her great teacher, Lilli Lehmann, taught the world to prize. Farrar gave fresh feeling to her roles, but even in her full vocal measure the emotion she gained was at the expense of "the intellectual side" of music. Neither the "'frozen heights'" of talent (as Madame Farrar called the region where one risks being stupid in order to be sublime) nor the idea behind the music intimidated Olive Fremstad, the Swedish-born Wagnerian soprano who was reared in Minnesota. She overreached for the one and dug for the other, and her voice could accommodate both intentions. She was Willa Cather's artist *par excellence*—powerful, passionate, daring, intellectual.

Madame Fremstad's expansive vocal range, intelligent singing, and sheer melodic beauty were reasons enough for esteem, but as always it was

1. "Three American Singers," *McClure's*, XLII (December, 1913), 33–48.

the force behind the instrument that fascinated Willa Cather. The history of artists whom she greatly admired offered her a possible way into the mystery of artistic creativity; also, she learned from analyzing her own experience. She did not hesitate to put her own ideas in the mouths of others, and frequently the pronouncement that issues from a personality she is interviewing echoes what she herself has written earlier.[2] In "Three American Singers," the profile of Olive Fremstad has elements of projection, but it also has something more. The homage derives from a meeting of two minds which think and feel alike. The diva had large, strong ideas and she was enjoying the highest success. For once, there is not the slightest hint of superiority in Cather's attitude, not a trace of disapproval. Several of Fremstad's quoted observations would fit neatly in such early stories as "A Singer's Romance" and "Nanette: An Aside," and do certainly seem to color the conception and conversation of the prima donna figure in *Youth and the Bright Medusa* (1920). The artistic principles tentatively urged in Willa Cather's early nonfiction, too, are echoed by remarks attributed to Fremstad and borne out by her practice. On responsibility: "'What voice is necessary for the part I undertake, I will produce.'" On integrity: "'My work is only for serious people.'" On interpretation: "'It ought to mean something.'" On life: "'We are born alone, we make our way alone, we die alone.'" The sympathies here are so fundamental that, as Willa Cather goes on to analyze Olive Fremstad's genius, the essay seems less an extension of the writer's personal standards than the unfolding of a mutual fealty to the nature and needs of art. First, Fremstad's reading is from a shaping idea, thought "so intensely experienced that it becomes emotion." The conception, however, only broadly and austerely defines the portrayal. Much of the character is kept in mental reserve. The excitement is not on stage; "the fateful drama actually went on behind her brow." Willa Cather locates the origin of Madame Fremstad's musical ideas in those "cardinal needs of humanity" that she specified in an 1899 piece on Lillian Nordica.[3] The expression Fremstad finally employs "has it roots deep in human nature, it follows the old paths of human yearning . . . ." Those old paths lead to what Bernice Slote explains as the primitive vitality behind creation, the life force of the earth.[4] Because Fremstad grew up "in a new, crude country" she had to

2. As a case in point, Farrar's reference to the "'frozen heights,'" cited above, is strangely reminiscent of "She [Duse] is utterly alone upon the icy heights where other human beings cannot live" (*Journal*, November 4, 1894, p. 12; *KA*, pp. 152–153).

3. "An Open Letter to Lillian Nordica," *Courier*, December 16, 1899, p. 3.

4. *KA*, p. 47.

fight "her own way toward the intellectual centers of the world." The untamed land anchors many ideas behind her impersonations. She says of her Kundry at the end of *Parsifal*: "'There is much of my childhood in that last act. You have been to revivals? Well, so have I.'"

There is much of Willa Cather's artistic childhood in Olive Fremstad's, just as there is much of the writer's view of art in the singer's statements. The complex meshing of Willa Cather's personal experience and attitudes with the great accomplishment and career of Olive Fremstad constitutes the substance of *The Song of the Lark* (1915).[5] Other influences enter into the book, like the discovery of the Southwest, which takes on the force of a permanent preoccupation, or the attempt "to reproduce the emotional effect of the Wagner operas upon the printed page," which Cather admits to trying.[6] But *The Song of the Lark* finds its essential inspiration in the use of a singer's creative growth as an ideal analogy for the discovery and expression of all art. The portrait of an artist as diva serves too as an ingathering of Cather's association with grand opera's golden hour. In New York, as on the Nebraska frontier, she witnessed history. Edith Lewis recalls:

> We went constantly to the opera at this time. It was one of the great periods of opera in New York. Nordica and the de Reszkes, Melba and Calvé were still singing during our first years in New York. From 1905 on our old programmes continually list such names as Sembrich, Farrar, Chaliapin, Plançon, Destinn, Renaud, Mary Garden, Caruso, Amato, Homer, and Tetrazzini. Toscanini, not then half so famous, but at the height of his powers, was conducting two or three times a week at the Metropolitan. But the most thrilling, to us, of all the new stars that came up over the horizon was Olive Fremstad. We heard her nearly every time she sang.[7]

The atmosphere of music in *The Song of the Lark* is more inclusive and democratic than the posh confines of the Met, though its high pressure does gauge the other musical conditions in the novel. The Met is the summit of musical expression. Nevertheless, the origin of music is in the earth, in the sound of things and the rhythm of life. Between the physical beginning in man and the spiritual culmination are different levels of talent. There are untrained musicians who transmit the lore in

5. *The Song of the Lark* (Sentry Edition; Boston: Houghton Mifflin, 1963). All references are to the revised edition of 1937 of which the Sentry Edition is a reprint.

6. Willa Cather, Preface to Gertrude Hall's *The Wagnerian Romances* (New York: Alfred A. Knopf, 1925), p. vii.

7. *Willa Cather Living* (New York: Alfred A. Knopf, 1953), pp. 89–90.

their blood and many skilled lyric artists who perform the masterworks of musical heritage. The combined passion of the folk artist and the educated intelligence of the professional make up the cultural patrimony to which Thea Kronborg, the heroine, is heir. Her gradual laying claim to the double legacy is the drama of the novel. Her generous distribution of the treasure reveals to us the value of the struggle. As Thea Kronborg comes into her own as a magnificent singer, music figures the spiritual bridge between men.

II

"Friends of Childhood," the first of six sections, covers Thea's eleventh through seventeenth years, that period of her life when she was pure artist. "'I am more or less of an artist now,'" she says to Doctor Archie when she approaches the peak of her career, "'but then I was nothing else'" (551). She has as a girl an aesthetic freshness which allows her to experience things wholly. Her receptivity is grounded in nature. The sand hills around Moonstone, Colorado, and the Turquoise Hills ten miles off tantalize Thea with a message of freedom, courage, and aspiration. The eagle living up on a windy ridge teaches her more of the spirit and desire of man than does the most ambitious man in the town below. From people she learns a great deal, but it is small in comparison with the tidings in the naked vigor of the earth. Frequently the lesson learned from man is negative. She must preserve a certain solitude, protect her feelings from the sentimental intrusions of her sister or from the elaborate familial doings which can blot out her identity. She must hold her own against the cheap taste and rivalry of a Lily Fisher, who connives to get a show-stopper at the church Christmas concert and would sing anything which pleases the crowd. More frequently, the experience of childhood positively contributes to the development of her aesthetic sense. Among Moonstone friends Thea realizes that human relationships are matters of the heart and not applications of social or religious tenets. The final communion that Thea Kronborg creates on the Metropolitan stage at the novel's end comes back to the first trust in the social choices young Thea makes in Moonstone. A confidence shared is permanently honored. The continual and enlarging spiritual return, in fact, is one of the personal gratifications of her singing.

The accumulated wealth of childhood, apart from the unaccountable inborn power to receive the creative passion in the first place, is exemplified in four friends. Each has a different personality, but all share in a common friendliness toward one another, a love for Thea, a personal integrity; and each lives in the paradox of being a failure in the public view and a valued person to Thea. The mark of this kinship is music. Each friend is talented or appreciative of music, and in all four musical response implies the higher self which society does not discern and which the friends themselves cannot reach or release on their own.

With Spanish Johnny, the unreliable alcoholic, Thea comes nearest to the elemental impulse of the earth as it is echoed in man. The music Johnny makes on a mandolin is frenzied and exceptionally skillful, but its strength and beauty reside in the racial consciousness which is at the heart of his songs. In the second part of the novel, after Thea returns from a year of formal study in Chicago, she identifies the emotional freedom she enjoys with the Mexicans through the ethnic current in their music. Among Mexicans, and especially with Johnny, music is a felt reality and a common expression. Even their movements have "a kind of natural harmony" (289). When she sings before a "really musical people" like the Mexican neighbors, Thea receives "the response that such a people can give" (292)—pleasure and affection. Transcending social or racial fact, music unites Thea with emotional allies for whom society provides no regular means of exchange. Among the Mexicans she unearths a collective human feeling through songs of joy, love, riches, and delicate swallows: "Ultimo Amor," "Noches de Algeria," "Fluvia de Oro," "La Golandrina." The spiritual transfer with simple people is important. During her operatic career, Thea constantly draws from the deep reservoir of basic human yearning. At the close of *The Song of the Lark* the final measurement of her brilliant Sieglinde is the "'Brava! Brava!'" of "a grey-haired little Mexican" (572) perched in the top gallery. His excitement assures us that Thea Kronborg's voice reaches the sympathetic center of those from whom she first learned music's primitive energy.

Ray Kennedy, a railroader-romancer, brings the young artist to other beginnings, those of history. From his tales of Old Mexico and the Southwest Thea learns how man pulled himself up from a primitive to a civilized creature. About the Cliff-Dwellers and their cities, Ray says, "'You begin to feel what the human race has been up against from the beginning. There's something mighty elevating about those old habitations'" (149). Ray's own life has little of the heroism of his dreams, but he is able to communicate heroic ideals. The meaning of the human story is his gift to Thea. As a child she instinctively comprehends the timelessness of man's fight for the civilized things which make him man, because she has within herself a yearning to create and because she requires direct contact with the vital source of life Ray speaks of. Later of course she does live fully by the natural pull of things in the Southwest—actually immersed in the life-water of the earth—and the conception of art which Thea achieves during this baptism is an enlargement of Ray's idealism.

Thea's closest Moonstone friend is Howard Archie, a physician, who is too timid to call a halt to an unsuccessful marriage and to leave a town he finds limiting. He cares for her from cradle to artistic coronation. The intellectual of the town, Archie is able to explain questions of religion, personal responsibility, and human destiny which puzzle Thea. He makes no concessions to her young mind; he speaks maturely. The nasty death of a tramp, who spites the town's meanness by drowning himself in the standpipe and contaminating the water supply, for example, shocks Thea; and Archie does not sentimentalize experience to lessen the shock. The indifference of everyone to the tramp's needs strikes the girl as a mockery of the Christian principles society asserts. She is also disturbed by a man's falling desperately far out of good fortune. Perplexities of these kinds will, Archie assures her, always arise, and her bookish notions of religion will not solve them. He offers in place of conventionalized restriction a doctrine of pleasure: the important duty is "'to live . . . ; to do all we can and enjoy all we can'" (175). That she does overcome the inevitable, momentary reverses of desire and circumstance demonstrates an ability to brush ugliness and misfortune aside in favor of searching out "'the best things of this world'" (175).

A piano teacher, psychically lame like the other three Moonstone friends, has the most to do with Thea's artistic preparation. Professor Wunsch gives Thea all he can; that would be quite a bit for a normal child, but not enough for one intending to study the piano seriously. As desire outweighs discipline in his personality, so his teaching emphasizes emotion and ignores, except in a wayward fashion, the literature of the piano. Music is Wunsch's life and love; because it was not submitted to discipline of any kind, it has become an inadequate source of livelihood and an emotional frustration. The imbalance of his musicianship is not without a compensatory benefit, however. His name states what Thea receives from him—desire.

Willa Cather uses the famous lament in Gluck's *Orpheus and Eurydice* to represent Wunsch's tragedy. The music and myth shaping the opera reference contain as well the symbolic locus of the novel. The opera is first mentioned as one of Wunsch's favorite works of music, "'the most beautiful opera ever made'" (89) he tells Thea, and when she shows interest, he cannot resist going over the lament. The deep feeling he brings to the melody shows the identification of his personal loss of music with the operatic hero's loss of Eurydice. As usual, Willa Cather provides a few verses of a piece to suggest background and draws upon the implied context in developing the action. The aria runs:

> I have lost my Eurydice.
> Nothing can equal my despair.
> Cruel fate, no hope is left me.
> Nothing can equal my despair.
> This is more than life can bear.
> Eurydice, Eurydice, reply!
> What torture! Answer me!
> It is thy faithful Orpheus;
> Hark to my voice that calls to thee.
> I have lost my Eurydice.
> Deathly silence,
> Hope is vain,
> What suffering,
> What torments tear my heart![8]

When Wunsch plays and Thea sings of a life without the thing one needs most, the reader is invited to participate aurally in the moment when two talents, following separate paths on the Orphic landscape, intersect. The high thoroughfare that the young girl, not fully aware of her genius, will take to success crosses the worn trail of an old man resigned to wanderings. Again, the larger service of music is to introduce the classical legend that Willa Cather is reworking in *The Song of the Lark*. Two complementary ways of deepening meaning come together. Myth holds the old human stories; music the old feelings. In this novel it is the legend behind Gluck's opera that Willa Cather uses, but her thematic sense frequently calls for a particular tonal emphasis which music supplies.

The story of Orpheus, the eponym of art, recounts the lasting drama of man's search for expression. Specifically for Willa Cather, the story glosses the relationship between art and life and the relationship between instrument and material. For Orpheus, the supreme lyric artist, the emergency of life determines the emergency of art. Only through art can

8. *Orpheus and Eurydice*, Act III, scene i. I have taken the English translation from the *Metropolitan Opera House Libretto* (New York: n. d.), p. 9.

he retrieve his beloved. Art can redeem life for the singer. If he can articulate his grief, hell can be won over to his need. Not only must the feeling be intense, then, but the intensity must be released in communicable form and adapted to those it must sway. This Orpheus can do. But the course is parabolic. Even if art can rise to triumph over the will of hell, there remains the descent back into personal passion for which discipline of self is required. The law of hell is cunning; it makes no concession to human weakness though that weakness is the substance of the song it respects. When Orpheus must check his feelings, he fails: he looks back at Eurydice. Success in the greater task aids not at all in the lower. Art gives meaning, emotion in communicable shape, to life but does not necessarily provide a way of meeting its demands.

Willa Cather's canonical treatment of Orpheus, the artist-quester, varies. The artists in *The Troll Garden* and *Youth and the Bright Medusa* fail to enchant themselves. They duplicate the failure of the historical Orpheus. In *The Song of the Lark*, however, Willa Cather proposes a triumphant solution. It is not quite so mechanical as Gluck's union, which is arranged by Cupid, but the novel does waive the fatal clause in the pact between the singer and hell and bring together seemingly incompatible things, life and art. The marriage between life and art is brought about through the sublimation of life into art. Art for Thea Kronborg solves the crisis of life by absorbing it. When Archie expresses concern about the singer's lack of personal life, she replies: "'My dear doctor, I don't have any. Your work becomes your personal life. You are not much good until it does. It's like being woven into a big web. You can't pull away, because all your little tendrils are woven into the picture. It takes you up, and uses you, and spins you out; and that is your life'" (546). It is toward this final integration that *The Song of the Lark* moves.

In leaving the fellowship of childhood, in embarking to seek Eurydice, Thea has only the interior "friendly spirit" (100), nourished by four soul-friendships, to guide her.

III

Thea's quest takes her to Chicago where she finds a proper discipline for her desire. Art requires hard work, she learns, especially for those few with great ability. She realizes also that she cannot be a concert pianist. The lack of early training cannot be overcome. Her true medium is the voice, the instrument through which she can unlock the strong, intimate spirit inside her. The conversion from piano to voice, like the larger artistic and intellectual ripening, is from the artificial to the natural.

Andor Harsanyi, Thea's piano teacher, accidentally discovers her real gift. Once exposed, the voice is gently encouraged to follow its natural strengths. The method Harsanyi adopts in training Thea's voice recalls Willa Cather's literary approach—as expressed in "Three American Singers"—from the controlling idea of a piece to the individual passage, from the larger feeling or intuition to interpretation, from intention to specification. The approach also corrects the aimless freedom Wunsch permitted. Thea's reading of "Die Lorelei" instances Harsanyi's technique. Simply singing the song does not satisfy Thea. A beautiful voice alone does not properly convey the meaning of music. The concluding bars of the song as she first sings them displease her because her conception does not mate Heine's lyric with the melody. Unless each part belongs to an inclusive conception a reading has no cogency. When she grasps the idea of a river enduring beneath the havoc above it, Thea gives the end of "Die Lorelei" an "'open, flowing'" (240) tone to suggest continuity. That quality pleases her and Harsanyi. Before she perceived the idea behind a melody "she wandered like a blind man surrounded by torments" (241); after the "'revelation'" she sails with steady sureness. The beauty of the voice is always there; it is the idea which must be sought out.

Harsanyi has his own reasons for giving Thea "Die Lorelei"; he is suggesting a method congenial to her nature and testing the girl's ability to reach the idea behind a melody. And Willa Cather has her own novelistic reasons for giving us the song. Liszt's setting is beautiful and popular enough to evoke for the reader an atmosphere "'reeking of a song'" (243), as Harsanyi describes the studio to his wife; but Heine's poem is Willa Cather's way of connecting an artistic discovery in a character with theme. Like the persona in the poem, Thea's mind is haunted by an indefinite "tale of past times." Though the facts of the tale are in the future, "Die Lorelei" foreshadows a journey beset with danger. It will be Thea's journey on the Rhine of artistic ambition, the old tale of man's need for expression. The strange splendors and exquisite allurements which in the end destroy the voyager are the countless obstacles hindering expression. "Die Lorelei" is the Orphic journey, the voyage perilous again.

The same intuitive grasp of a musical idea seen in Thea's singing of "Die Lorelei" is shown again at a symphony concert a short time later. On this occasion Thea is listening, not interpreting, and the process is reversed. By the transposition Cather suggests that instinctive sensitivity works in two directions, in appreciation as well as in execution. The exchange is doubly beneficial for the artist, as we shall come to see more clearly from Thea's appreciation of the earth's life-giving music in the Southwest. The aesthetic feeling in the concert-hall scene is more limited in effect than her response to the cañons. She is brought to a union with her aesthetic desire, but it is an impressionistic and momentary experience compared to the intellectual (as well as emotional) and permanent recognition of a creative force that comes later in Arizona. Thea has been to very few concerts and in the beginning is distracted by the novelty of her surroundings. Not until the second number is she ready to listen. Her imagination seizes on the first theme of Dvořák's Symphony in E minor, "called on the programme, 'From the New World'" (251). She visualizes her own West with wagon trails, wind, and eagles—the old sights of childhood recovered through melody. Blending into the nostalgic evocation of the past is the Walhalla motif from *The Rhinegold*, the next number the orchestra plays. Her knowledge of the opera is vague, we are informed. In Willa Cather's treatment of Thea's response, however, the Walhalla music bodes her destiny as a distinguished Wagnerian soprano. Wagner mingles with Dvořák to create Thea's New World of Music. Suggestively, Willa Cather announces a thematic image that recurs throughout her fiction in various forms and at the end of *The Song of the Lark* with complex associations: "The cold, stately measures of the Walhalla music rang out, far away; the rainbow bridge throbbed out into the air, under it the wailing of the Rhine daughters and the singing of the Rhine" (252). Thea is "sunk in twilight" now, but soon she will cross the rainbow bridge to success. In the Walhalla of her power she, as singer, will construct the rainbow bridge back to the musical spirit of her audience. The future is revealed to the reader; it is not in Thea's awareness. Her response stops at a firm decision to fight for the joy she felt in the concert hall. "As long as she lived that ecstacy was going to be hers. She would live for it, work for it, die for it; but she was going to have it, time after time, height after height" (254).

It is one thing for Thea to know that the voice and not the piano will transport her across the rainbow bridge and quite another for her to act on the knowledge. It requires a second birth, and the artistic bringing forth of the deeper self is more difficult to undergo than the first, human birth. With friends Thea's feeling and love provide the standard for singing; with the impersonal public the mind as well as soul are demanded. Approval would open the way to unusual fulfillment and self-knowledge;

failure would be killing because the judgment of the voice involves a judgment of the soul. Defeat at the piano, for example, does not break her because the voice is there to absorb disappointment. Thea's fear of action is understandable from another viewpoint. Defeat is more usual than victory on the concert or operatic stage, and she has yet to meet anyone who has succeeded in the way total dedication deserves. The models have been negative. Two things do work in favor of her taking the risk, however. She cannot forget how their responsiveness to her singing gave an entrée into the "second selves" (273) of people like Ray and Spanish Johnny. And she realizes during her brief return visit to Moonstone that she cannot live in a choking moral atmosphere. The struggle would be worth while just to escape pettiness and emotional restraint. She needs glorious air to breathe. "'I only want impossible things,'" she says brusquely to Archie. "'The others don't interest me'" (305).

Thea's growth up to now is largely psychological. She finds out what she is not and comes generally to sense what she must be. Ironically, when she begins formal study of voice, her progress seems slow. The bitter part of every Orpheus' "bitter struggle" (221) shows itself in the acquisition of control. Discipline checks at the same time that it cleanses. Also, proximity to the profession dims the shine a tyro tends to see. The idealistic Thea encounters the hard-nosed careerist, who has finish but no fire, the coarse audience, which savors only the banality it knows, and the compromised singer, who fattens her reputation by feeding the Cerberus-audience its sop.

Encouragement of the sort she received from Archie or Harsanyi is hard to come by. The old inspiration is replaced by empty routine. Her voice master, Madison Bowers, personifies the uncongenial situation. He is good as a master but personally "cold" and "academic" (315), contemptuous of the public (and of some of his students). One might think of him as an Orpheus with the power to resist turning around to see Eurydice if only he could move hell in the first place. Thea's chief personal contact is not much brighter. Philip Frederick Ottenburg, a "florid brewery magnate," entertains her in a style to which she is unaccustomed and introduces her to the Nathanmeyers, whose knowledgeable approval of her singing and personality momentarily cheers her; but Ottenburg's interest is only ostensibly musical. The Bowers period when she tries to emerge as herself is filled with irritations intense enough to embitter Thea and to make her cynical of everyone's motive or aspiration. Everywhere about her she sees compromise, contempt, and vanity. The warmth and idealism of Moonstone and her first Chicago teacher have vanished, leaving the life of art merely another way of meeting daily hardness with comparable artistic obduracy. Icy expertise is the best attribute of this world. In Part III, "Stupid Faces," the young artist is offered two alternatives. Thea can fashion a career according to the crassitude that works so well and be assured of popular success, or she can abandon the art Bowers and his students stand for—and all art—and retain her personal integrity. A third possibility, rising above careerism, is not suggested through characterization, but it is there by inference. Again Thea moves in the dark without guidance from others. As her decision to sing was implied in music, so the future course she must take is charted in the song which she sings for Fred Ottenburg the first time they meet. Grieg's "Tak for dit Råd" ("Thanks for Your Advice") stands as Thea's implicit rejoinder to Bowers and all the "Stupid Faces" whose help she acknowledges and whom she will surpass. That Cather intends to emphasize this song is evident from her providing the translation of Grieg's lyric. Thea is doing the explaining:

> "Well, it goes something like this: 'Thanks for your advice! But I prefer to steer my boat into the din of roaring breakers. Even if the journey is my last, I may find what I have never found before. Onward must I go, for I yearn for the wild sea. I long to fight my way through the angry waves, and to see how far, and how long I can make them carry me.'" (338)

"Tak for dit Råd" is the singer's adieu to Chicago, and its significance derives from the perilous voyage motif of "Die Lorelei" and Orpheus and Eurydice, which it echoes. The song speaks for Thea's spiritual courage which must combat storms of hostility. With the dauntless sailor in Greig's air, she must carry on the struggle for guidance which comes only from the friendly spirit inside. Thea takes a high ideal to be a hard command.

IV

The fourth, fifth, and sixth parts of The Song of the Lark treat the liberation of Thea's "treasure of creative power" (333). Willa Cather does not delineate a rapid ascent to achievement from the desire of childhood and the direction of youth. Between consecration and action there falls a quiet pause for reflection. In Willa Cather's view of artistic growth the reposeful lull is a crucial moment. It is particularly restorative for Thea Kronborg. The pause is the retreat before the great advance, a return to the origin of all creativity—the earth. Thea's experience in the spacious, powerful cañons of the Southwest incorporates the early excitement of childhood among the open sand hills; and intellectually it goes back further, to the nature of history. Contact with the earth removes data from history to leave only the basic thing: man's continuous fight to achieve something beyond himself. That fight holds value, and it repeats itself in everyone at every stage of human development. The contest is the basis and embodiment of art. Thea achieves this understanding among rocks, air, birds, and sky, the first things which tested man's power to control and shape.

Transformation is brought about in Panther Cañon in Arizona where she lives alongside relics of the Cliff-Dweller civilization. She is able to divine the daily tone of the Cliff-Dwellers' life, and this empathy helps her to shed the Chicago bitterness and to enjoy immersion in "the earliest sources of gladness" (369). Even in extinction, ancient Indian life testifies to taste and aspiration. Its art suggests a unity between utensil and spiritual need. Especially beautiful to Thea are the jars which hold "the precious water" (377). The vessels are functional but also expressive and consecrated to the water they house. "Their pottery was their most direct appeal to water, the envelope and sheath of the precious element itself" (377). The Cliff-Dwellers transformed nature but still lived according to it. Elevation was a way of life, the vistas a way of seeing and regarding life—widely, freely. They civilized themselves. That is the ultimate heroism for Willa Cather. The severe and mighty geography dignifies, it does not falsify, the hardness of human labor.

It is while Thea is physically immersed in the "precious element" that she gains the deepest knowledge of art. Not when she practices or performs, but when she bathes in a stream comes the understanding that art is the giving of human shape to physical nature.

One morning, as she was standing upright in the pool, splashing water between her shoulder-blades with a big sponge, something flashed through her mind that made her draw herself up and stand still until the water had quite dried upon her flushed skin. The stream and the broken pottery: what was any art but an effort to make a sheath, a mould in which to imprison for a moment the shining, elusive element which is life itself—life hurrying past us and running away, too strong to stop, too sweet to lose? The Indian women had held it in their jars. In the sculpture she had seen in the Art Institute, it had been caught in a flash of arrested motion. In singing, one made a vessel of one's throat and nostrils and held it on one's breath, caught the stream in a scale of natural intervals. (378)

The experience in Panther Cañon restates one of Willa Cather's long-standing beliefs about art. In a *Journal* piece of March 1, 1896, she wrote: "Art is not thought or emotion, but expression, expression, always expression." The challenge is to preserve the first excitement one feels when receiving the idea until the idea is put into words, sound, or color; ". . . that is the greatest of all the gifts of the gods. And that is the voyage perilous . . . ."9 In *The Song of the Lark* the voyage is from brain to voice. The voice activates in beautiful tones the "elusive element."

That this period of Thea's life, which bears so deeply on her future art, should be nearly without a music reference is not at all curious. The treatment accords with Cather's idea of art and with the mythic sense in the novel besides. For a time the singer lives on a level of pure sensation, in a world of natural impulses where understanding "came up to her out of the rock-shelf on which she lay" (376). She is in the source of art, the "life in the air" with its "rhythm of feeling and action" (392). The response is "not expressible in words" (376). One might call the experience an extension of the daybreak in Panther Cañon when "the golden light" (389) gradually soaks the gorge until everything swims "in the liquid gold" (390). The near-absence of music implies a return to the sun. And it is from Apollo, after all, that Orpheus receives the gift of a lyre. With the sun one finds the inmost melody among the world's parts.

The sixth and last section of the novel brings the voyage to port. In portraying the artist's great hour in New York Willa Cather uses two devices to emphasize the achievement. She shifts the point of view to Archie and defines Thea through a series of musical personages. The limited vision of Archie preserves the "admiration and estrangement" (500) of the non-artist before creative genius which Willa Cather recurrently shows. Cather is fond of examining the aristocrats of experience through democratic spokesmen. Also, up to now Thea's musical self has been tucked in the recess of desire; the new view in a way protects the soul's privacy. Though exposed, Thea's personality is known through musical guises. The difference between the childhood world of aspiration and the time of fulfillment is suggested in the title of the last part: "Kronborg." The coldness is fitting. The matter-of-fact notation of talent has the impressiveness of a poster listing conductor and famous principal

9. *KA*, p. 417.

singers without individual emphasis, thereby making genius common-place. "Kronborg" also, appropriately enough, suggests detachment and intimidation. Single names for Cather, after Balzac, are noble epithets, "'names that tell all and make the passer dream.'"[10]

The admiration derives from a series of Wagnerian roles which Madame Kronborg interprets. The principal ones are: Elizabeth (*Tann-häuser*), Elsa (*Lohengrin*), Venus (*Tannhäuser*), Fricka (*The Rhinegold*), and Sieglinde (*Die Walküre*). Actually there is a sixth because Willa Cather gives us two Sieglindes; the significance of duplicating the role will be taken up later. The list of appearances suggests a general movement from the more lyrical to more complex and dramatic, which hints of Madame Kronborg's style, but the important thing is that it shows the soprano's range, her rapid ascent at the Metropolitan, and her indefatigable energy.

The first important role was sung in Dresden where, thanks to the "'lucky chance'" (485) every daughter of music needs, Kronborg got to sing Elizabeth. The role and the circumstances of her debut are brought to mind during Archie's visit to the ailing Mrs. Kronborg. The doctor notices a "photograph of the young woman who must have been singing '*Dich, theure Halle, grüss' ich wieder*,' her eyes looking up, her beautiful hands outspread with pleasure" (492). Willa Cather's music allusion is perfectly clear and perfectly apt. The song, which is Elizabeth's entrance and praises music itself, doubles as Madame Kronborg's artistic entrance into her personal Hall of Song. It is a joyous symbolic debut, this saluta-tion of the hall.

> Oh, hall of song I give thee greeting!
> All hail to thee thou hallowed place!
> 'T was here that dream so sweet and fleeting,
> Upon my heart his song did trace.
> But since by him forsaken
> A desert thou dost seem—
> Thy echoes only waken
> Remembrance of a dream.
> But now the flame of hope is lighted,
> Thy vault shall ring with glorious war;
> For he whose strains my soul delighted
> No longer roams afar![11]

10. *Journal*, March 1, 1896, p. 9; *KA*, p. 167.
11. *The Authentic Librettos of the Wagner Operas* (New York: Crown Publishers, 1938), p. 40.

Elizabeth's sacred salute balances Orpheus' sad valediction. "*Dich, theure Halle, grüss' ich wieder*" heralds the triumphant induction into music for Thea Kronborg while "*Ich habe sie verloren*" signals the defeated farewell from music for Professor Wunsch.

Kronborg's move from the opera house in Dresden, which was no ordinary affiliation (first or last) at the beginning of the century, to the Met signifies her arrival at the top. But the top is where the scramble is fiercest and footing most precarious. Too many sopranos are tussling for too few roles. The surplus of talent forces major artists to take on assignments which are neither entirely suitable to their voices nor up to their expectations. Merely to survive in that era a diva needed the comprehensive repertoire of an Olive Fremstad. When Cather remarks that Kronborg sings Elsa in *Lohengrin* the first time that Dr. Archie sees her in New York, she conveys both the competitive state of affairs in opera and her heroine's capacity to cope with its demands. Kronborg's Elsa is brilliant, but, as Fred explains to Archie, "'The fact is, *Elsa* isn't a part that's particularly suited to Thea's voice at all, as I see her voice. It's over-lyrical for her. She makes it, but there's nothing in it that fits her like a glove, except, maybe, that long duet in the third act. But wait until they give her a chance at something that lies properly in her voice . . .'" (511–512).

Her next assignment is Venus in *Tannhäuser*, but the proper role for Kronborg is Elizabeth. In Dresden it was hers; in New York she must take the lesser part. "'Will they never let you have a chance at *Elizabeth*?'" Fred asks, and she answers philosophically, "'Not here. There are so many singers here, and they try us out in such a stingy way'" (522).

Chance helps her out. When Madame Gloeckler breaks down after the first act of *Die Walküre* and the two likely replacements are indisposed, Kronborg is asked to finish Sieglinde, a part she has studied but never sung. Fatigued, anxious, and unable to recall a bar of the score as she rushes to get ready, once on stage Kronborg meets the challenge and turns in a magnificent performance—despite the psychological disadvantage of having to sing at a moment's notice a role she has worked on for years and hoped to do to perfection.

Always there comes the let-down. Her next role is the ungrateful one of Fricka in *The Rhinegold*, but Kronborg brings her special touch even to this secondary task. So long portrayed as a nagging, frumpy German *Hausfrau*, in Kronborg's interpretation Fricka emerges as the personification of wisdom she originally had been, glittering with a gold quality. She becomes a goddess again, her divine status restored by "'a beautiful idea'" (539) in the singer's mind. Thea certainly is one to surprise. Even Fred, who knows Kronborg's gifts well, would not have thought Fricka her style; but after hearing the opera he realizes that she "had a distinct kind of loveliness for this part, a shining beauty like the light of sunset on distant sails" (538).

Soon she is scheduled for a Sieglinde of her own. It is a command performance. "On Friday afternoon there was an inspiring audience; not an empty chair in the house" (565). Music unifies variety. Fred Ottenburg is there, of course, along with the soprano's benefactor, Howard Archie. Andor Harsanyi, back from a successful engagement in Vienna, and his wife also are in the house. From Moonstone, from Chicago, from Europe have come Kronborg's friends; and joining them from some rare, indefinite locale is Spanish Johnny. Old friendships are present to lay spiritual claim on the voice whose growth they shared in. The older nonhuman companionships which enriched this voice are also present, for music blends the Southwest with the Metropolitan stage. "'You're as much at home on the stage as you were down in Panther Cañon. Didn't you get some of your ideas down there?'" Madame Kronborg answers Fred: "'Oh, yes! Out of the rocks, out of the dead people'" (554). A voice such as Kronborg's, which Wunsch recognized during its incipience as a "nature-voice" (97), is corporate, reaching down to the procreative force of the earth and up to human yearning. This is the sign and wonder of the artist's divine adoption: "Like the spring indeed, it blossomed into memories and prophecies, it recounted and it foretold . . ." (568). Of all the grace gifts the artist possesses, the most magical is the power to vault the barriers between time and place and person and construct a rainbow bridge to them all. Willa Cather does not count the curtain calls, but the fierce "clamour" (569) of the audience makes it unmistakably clear that Thea Kronborg is the kind of singer who leaves beautiful memories behind her. A soul has touched a soul.

V

Willa Cather continued to write about the lyric artist after *The Song of the Lark*, but not as the principal figure of a novel. Singers are, though, the subject of several sketches published within five years after the study of Thea Kronborg, which serves as something of a model for the short studies. Of the eight stories published between 1915 and 1920, four portray artists who live by their voice, whose singing is their work. Along with four stories from *The Troll Garden* ("Paul's Case," "A Wagner Matinee," "The Sculptor's Funeral," and "'A Death in the Desert'"), they appeared in the 1920 collection, *Youth and the Bright Medusa*. This pairing of stories from two phases of her career shows the way in which an imaginative encounter with Thea Kronborg's success affected Willa Cather's attitude toward artistic life.

It is less a change in theme or situation than a shift in emphasis that distinguishes the early stories in *Youth and the Bright Medusa*, which are fully representative of the total argument of *The Troll Garden*, from those published after *The Song of the Lark*. In both groups the artist confronts possible misunderstanding by the public, exploitation in personal affairs, professional failure, and the inevitability of death. The stories from *The Troll Garden* stress defeat or death. While death and defeat also enter into the lives of the artists in the newer stories, their sting is lessened by the artists' resignation to pain and impermanence. The earlier stories vent outrage and bitterness; the later ones express courage, assurance, and forgiveness. Katharine Gaylord, the dying singer in "'A Death in the Desert,'" laments to Everett Hilgarde after hearing his brother's new sonata: "'This is my tragedy, as I lie here spent by the race-course, listening to the feet of the runners as they pass me—ah, God! the swift feet of the runners!'" Looking back on her career which, though not abruptly ended like Katharine Gaylord's, is declining, Cressida Garnet, the heroine of "The Diamond Mine," says of her days in Columbus, Ohio: "'Of course, it was a bleak country and a bleak period. But I've sometimes wondered whether the bleakness may not have been in me, too; for it has certainly followed me.'" The consciousness and acceptance behind Cressida's suspicion that the dark forces of life are within herself as well as in the world and the anger and astringency of Katharine's cry which locates misfortune mainly in an antagonistic world (and, in a way, externalizes evil into the surrounding desert) mark the tonal change between the two sets of stories in *Youth and the Bright Medusa*. The later stories, in effect, bring the reader from the Wyoming desert around Katharine Gaylord to the adjacent region of the mind which Cressida Garnet acknowledges, the unsheltered desert places within.

Willa Cather develops this interest in the artist's disposition toward the world by creating a highly successful artist, or one destined to be famous, and placing two terrors before her, the exigency of personal affairs and the mutability of the voice. Because the artist is a singer, the loss of voice is a grave eventuality. This gravity adds a tragic sense to

Cather's treatment of the artist. Finally, the characterization of the singer in these stories presupposes a mental detachment deriving from Thea Kronborg's knowledge that for the master artist the stamp of public approval is incidental. The artist's satisfaction comes from meeting his standards, which are more exacting than the taste of the public whose approval counts for billing but not for art.

"The Diamond Mine" (1916)[12] describes the last transatlantic voyage the narrator, a fellow musician, made with Cressida Garnet who was lost on the *Titanic*. Through flashbacks the story recounts Cressida's career from her early life in Columbus through her four marriages. The narrator, a life-long friend, functions as a sounding board and adviser to "a great voice, a handsome woman, a great prestige" which "all added together made a 'great artist,' the common synonym for success." Cressida went the Catherian route to fame. "For twenty years she had been plunged in struggle; fighting for her life at first, then for a beginning, for growth, and at last for eminence and perfection; fighting in the dark, and afterward in the light,—which, with her bad preparation, and with her uninspired youth already behind her, took even more courage." To the world she is a glamorous figure, a great and honored artist; but to her brother and sisters, her impossible son, and her accompanist, Miletus Poppas—"a vulture of the vulture race," who receives a retainer and a percentage of her fees—she is simply "a natural source of wealth; a copper vein, a diamond mine." Moreover, her married life has been consistently disastrous: her first husband, a romantic young music teacher, died of tuberculosis; the second, an industrialist, could not put up with the ubiquitous Miletus Poppas; the third, a gifted but feckless composer, betrayed her with her own cook; the fourth a scoundrelly promoter, has succeeded in dissipating most of her large fortune. "Her family, her husbands, her son, would have crushed any other woman I have ever known," says the narrator. But because the essential Cressida Garnet, her musical self, remained unassailable, her private story is neither sordid nor pitiful; instead, we agree with the narrator that hers was a "large and rather splendid life."

The heroine of "A Gold Slipper" (1917) and "Scandal" (1919) is another first lady of opera, Kitty Ayrshire. Like Cressida Garnet, she is a paragon of musicianship and generosity, but is more intellectually ready and forensically inclined than Cressida. Kitty is Willa Cather's wittiest

12. *Youth and the Bright Medusa* (New York: Alfred A. Knopf, 1920), pp. 79–139. All quotations are from this text.

spokeswoman for art. "A Gold Slipper"[13] matches her pointedness against the dullness of an intractable Philistine, Marshall McKann, a prominent Pittsburgh coal dealer, who is badgered by his wife into attending Kitty's recital. Music holds no interest for him. He thinks in categories: artists are, in his own clumsy language, "'fluffy-ruffles'" lacking in depth and practicality. The whole lot, performers and audience, are bogus. There are serious matters at stake here, but the story is little more than a playful duel.

The contest is in two parts. The first is impersonal but direct, and it is conducted chiefly through music in Carnegie Hall. Kitty appears for her recital in attire which Pittsburgh feels is a bit too dashing for Mozart and Handel—a gown of "reviling, shrieking green" with the "skirt split back from a transparent gold-lace petticoat, gold stockings, gold slippers." The effect was calculated to put the audience off, for Kitty knows that "to shock the great crowd was the surest way to get its money." More than that, however, "she liked the stimulus of this disapprobation." She proceeds to dissipate the chill in the air with "clean singing" and "finished artistry." After a group of Mozart and Beethoven songs, for which she receives guarded approval, she continues with "romantic German songs which were altogether more her affair," and the audience responds with increasing warmth. Her final number is made up of modern French songs rendered "enchantingly," and "at last her frigid public [is] thoroughly aroused." After an encore which "brought her audience all the way," Kitty abandons them. While they are clamoring for more, she blows them a kiss and is gone.

Throughout this splendid contest McKann sits untouched and bored —indeed, at one point during the concert Kitty has noticed him yawning behind his hand—"he of course wore no gloves." But on the train back to New York City she has a second chance at him, and on this occasion she speaks for her art and her profession. The prima donna's wit and insouciance are all the more sympathetic because they are grounded in her awareness of limitations in herself. Despite her public hauteur, Kitty concedes that certain music lies beyond her voice. Speaking of the revelation given an artist when he is lifted above himself to an ideal, the singer says: "'It is even the subject of the greatest of all operas, which, because I can never hope to sing it, I love more than all the others.'" The admission is reassuring. She values what she has, and that fortifies her. She admires what she cannot have, and that endears her to us. McKann's derision of the

13. *Ibid.*, pp. 140–168.

music he does not understand articulates a Babbittry which acts as foil for Kitty's moral awareness of art and self.

"Scandal"[14] probes the perishability of genius. When we know that the story is about a diva, the first sentence of "Scandal" is ominous. "Kitty Ayrshire had a cold, a persistent inflammation of the vocal cords which defied the throat specialist." The Metropolitan has cancelled her engagements, and a new soprano is literally waiting in the wings to replace her. Money worries her, too. But "what was worse, she was losing life; days of which she wanted to make the utmost were slipping by, and nights which were to have crowned the days, nights of incalculable possibilities, were being stolen from her by women for whom she had no great affection." The throat ailment brings Kitty to reflect on the brevity of human life and the checks on human desire. "'But the world is big, and I am missing it,'" she explains to her doctor in justification of a wish to have a caller. The world, actually, proves to be no bigger than a reminiscence, just as her belief in a glamorous world proves as fragile as the imperfect vocal instrument that brought her desire for enchantment into being.

A visit with Pierce Tevis, an old friend, tells us more about Kitty. She is warm and generous, virtues which are vulnerabilities as well. Her impulse to help others exposes Kitty to exploitation by artistic and social adventurers. A careerist like Peppo Amoretti does not hesitate to invoke her good offices for roles and introductions. A man like Siegmund Stein, the department-store millionaire who wanted to be thought a success with women, uses a model resembling Kitty to suggest an impressive affair with a famous diva to others in the retail trade and to out-of-town buyers. Eventually both opportunists unite to further their own ends. Stein asks Peppo to sing at his home, with the proviso that Kitty join him, which she reluctantly does to help Peppo along. After she sings, cameras flash and guests crowd her with their presumptuous attention; but the diva manages to get away from "'such unscrupulous cordiality.'" In retrospect, as she and Tevis talk the Stein party over, Kitty views the matter philosophically. She shrugs off a newspaper picture of her with the Steins at their house-warming and Peppo's using her for publicity. She remains above rancor because the important problem, the one which she cannot control, is the throat ailment and the rumors that her voice is gone. And that is the real scandal, that a beautiful voice is not forever.

Willa Cather examines two artistic dispositions in "Coming,

14. *Ibid.*, pp. 169–198.

Aphrodite!" (1920),[15] that of a painter, Don Hedger, and a singer, Eden Bower. Both are destined for a great success, but what interests Cather here is the way Hedger proceeds by instinct and Eden by calculation. About his genius Hedger is confident. "'I'm painting for painters,—who haven't been born.'" His sense of method is equally strong. "'You see I'm trying to learn to paint what people think and feel; to get away from all that photographic stuff.'" His sense of discipline and direction do not, however, touch his personal life. Before Eden's physical beauty he is weak, and the business side of art does not much interest him. Art is something separate from personal life for Hedger. In spite of his belief in a great future, "Don Hedger knew that nothing much would ever happen to him." Eden Bower sees things very differently. She "understood that to her a great deal would happen." Art for the singer offers an entrée into greater living and a fuller understanding of herself. "She was like some one standing before a great show window full of beautiful and costly things, deciding which she will order. She understands that they will not all be delivered immediately, but one by one they will arrive at her door."

The lyric artist in "Coming, Aphrodite!" represents an early stage of the mature intelligence and ambition found in Cressida Garnet and Kitty Ayrshire. At the end of the story we see Eden at thirty-eight back in New York "after years of spectacular success in Paris" and in an elegant style comparable to Cressida's and Kitty's, but the action centers on Eden at twenty, recently arrived in New York from Chicago where she began her singing career. She is poised for her years. Though she grew up in a small Illinois town, she knew that the capitals of the world held the things she wanted. Like Thea who felt something special inside, Eden "from her earliest childhood . . . had not one conviction or opinion in common with the people about her." Beauty, discretion, and self-awareness make getting what she wanted easier. Eden stayed with wealthy people in Chicago and accepted assistance from a rich admirer; nevertheless, "she thought her own thoughts, and laughed." The singer advises Hedger, whose lack of business sense annoys her, to paint what the public understands "'and then, after you're successful, do whatever you like.'" For all her self-interest, she is not cynical. It's just that "she believed in Fate" and lives in accordance with her wonderful sense of self. "People like Eden Bower are inexplicable," finally. Where fate does not go her way, as with her desire for Hedger, she goes fate's way. Eden is not one to kick boulders.

15. *Ibid.*, pp. 11–78.

Financial acumen is only a sign of a sharper insight into life. She knows that "a 'big' career takes its toll, even with the best of luck."

The four later stories in *Youth and the Bright Medusa* are, then, brief supplements to *The Song of the Lark*. If the strength of character and steadiness of commitment in these singers are reworkings of Thea Kronborg's personality, the idea of loss of genius in these stories is, I believe, something new in Cather's treatment of the great artist. The voice provides Cather with the right metaphor for the transience of artistic power because it combines fragility and beauty and soul. The vocalist learns to resign herself to the fact of death earlier than must other artists because her singing voice goes before she dies. The prima donna cannot entertain for long the fallacy of the immortalization of self through art. The novel or poem or statue remains, but nothing preserves the singing voice. Its momentary, living presence constitutes the beauty of the voice. In keeping with her particular concern, Cather does not pursue in these pieces the implications of story, situation, or words of the music, as she frequently does. She mentions the music of certain composers but does not allow the works to deflect attention from the voice which interprets the music. In place of allusion Cather provides thematic imagery to enhance her use of the voice as the fleeting, natural agency of art.

One image-complex is of the precious, the ethereal, and the soaring. Around Cressida we find: the name "Garnet," "the goose that laid the golden eggs," a diamond mine, "this golden stream," jewels, sable coat, velvet cloak, Paris dresses. To these signs of luxury Cather adds the image of flight and freedom; "*les colombes*" were her third husband's memories of Cressida. The flight of pigeons, repeated several times in "Coming, Aphrodite!", suggests Eden Bower's rise to fame. Around Kitty Ayrshire are similar touches of richness: she is "the green apparition" in the daring gown, apparelled with gold accessories. Her custom is invariably elegant. Her voice is compared to a bird-song, and she herself reminds McKann that many things are meant to "'go high.'" Art relates to the celestial upper regions over which, in her name, Kitty reigns—Ayrshire.

There are also a number of references to chaos and selfishness which contrast with a steady, industrious drive to succeed in the singer and the generous pleasure that the voice gives. Cressida is circled by the "habitual, bilious, unenterprising envy" of her sisters, the sequence of husbands who pick at her store, and a general "indolence and envy and discord—even dishonesty and turpitude." "Undependable" and "wild" describe her beneficiaries; Madame Garnet is "sane," "conscientious," "reliable," "'a charming exception to rules.'" To be away from her dependents is to be "unincumbered," and the word suggests the spiritual freedom she enjoys above the tempest about her. Kitty Ayrshire also must subdue the forces of dispersion. "She had been unyielding through storms," which is the only way to reach the calm heights. Opera-house politics are shifting and brutal. Only when the "'throng'" at Stein's party is "'scattered'" can the singer feel free. The loss and danger implied in the images figuring the voice and the singer's life are confirmed in the action. Hints of the impermanent become tragic suggestions. Cressida Garnet drowns and Kitty Ayrshire lives in the mortal fear that her voice is gone. Eden Bower, the reader conjectures, must pay the final toll of life itself for a big career.

The complexity and personal relevance of the theme of art challenged Willa Cather to see it many ways. The emphasis on the human voice shows that she is seeing artistic life more tragically than before. These few minor stories tell us that Cather has learned something she either had not known in *The Song of the Lark*, or did not feel secure enough to admit. She confesses one of the "artist's saddest secrets," the sealed thing Madame Garnet would reveal only to her accompanist—and then only because she cannot keep it from him if she is to rely on his assistance. "He knew where she was sound and where she was mended. With him she could share the depressing knowledge of what a wretchedly faulty thing any productive faculty is." Once Cather makes the confession, her fiction acquires a tragic quality. The novels in the offing show how deeply she knew that man's gifts are fugitive.

CHAPTER SIX

My Ántonia

The crier soon came, leading that man of
  song
Whom the Muse cherished; by her gift
  he knew
The good of life, and evil—
For she who lent him sweetness made
  him blind.

Odyssey

Willa Cather's classical work, *My Ántonia* (1918),[1] shows the expansion of
her now recognizable uses of music. There is, as always, music as medium
of the inner spirit. Again, music voices the alternating beauty and brutality of
the untamed Nebraska land and indicates the severe conditions under which
the frontiersmen live. Among characters, both major and minor, musical
ability or musical insensitivity go hand in hand with Cather's favor or dis-
favor. In the case of certain figures, Mr. Shimerda and Leo Cuzak, for example, music is intimately linked with their fortunes. Collectively, musical
spirit connotes a constructive view of life; and this commitment to living
is configured in two musical patterns: the dance, which vivifies an inner
rhythm, and the violin, which represents the cultural progress born of man's
positive, creative energy. Finally, music becomes the metaphorical equiv-
alent for Ántonia's greatness, her capacity for love and her inner spirit. If
there is no "clear reason"—as Thea Kronborg would say—to account for
the Bohemian girl's immediate and lasting response to life, it is because her
joie de vivre cannot be conveyed in words. It is more a rhythm than a reason
that the narrator gives. Ántonia's vitality is felt and thus rightly represented
through a sensuous form. Music in *My Ántonia* captures what is ineffable

1. *My Ántonia* (Sentry Edition; Boston: Houghton Mifflin, 1961). All references
are to this text.

in the heroine: her warmth, naturalness, spontaneity, freedom, strength, and her haunting presence in the memory of those who knew her.

The spokesman for those who remember Ántonia Shimerda is Jim Burden, the narrator, whose aesthetic responsibility is to recast for himself and then for the reader "the precious, the incommunicable past." As a memoirist, Jim relies heavily on music to catch an exultant moment in his personal history. Music helps Jim arrive at one of his most important insights into human experience: the shared intensity of childhood is only lived and once lived, lost. Insofar as the past can be regained it is through imaginative shaping, through art which endows remembrance with a new emotional form. Like his boyhood in Nebraska, music exists in time, and the inevitable end of its beauty, its insupportable pleasure, gives music a nostalgic quality which is congenial to Jim's mind and which is in keeping with the heightened sense of loss he gives to his memoir. Music helps by recalling specific occasions to him, but it performs a higher service by providing a form flexible enough to hold his rather intuitive observations and the impressionistic episodes which make up the book. In fine, music acts on Jim as a mnemonic evocation of Ántonia and life on the Divide.

Willa Cather did use music to connect two temporal or spatial orders in works before *My Ántonia*. *Alexander's Bridge* has something of this technique in the retrospective sections, but it was not developed into a principle of composition. *My Ántonia*, then, in addition to incorporating previous uses of music, adds a new one and brings music from the center of moral interest which it held in *The Song of the Lark* to a position of structural determination. Music amounts to the "sheath" or "mould" for recollection—the form by which art could "imprison for a moment the shining, elusive element which is life itself," as Cather put it in *The Song of the Lark*. The relation of music to form in *My Ántonia* is first suggested by Jim Burden's description of the way he wrote his memoir of Ántonia and Nebraska: "'*I didn't take time to arrange it; I simply wrote down pretty much all that her name recalls to me. I suppose it hasn't any form.*'" There are several controlled patterns in the novel, like the seasonal cycle, which imply more exactitude than Jim realizes; but one pattern, music, while ordered with diligence, reveals a pliant, associational coherence which Jim would allow as proper to his subject.

II

The novel spans thirty-one years. It opens in the fall of 1885 when Jim Burden, ten years old, coming from Virginia to Nebraska, meets

Ántonia Shimerda, who is fourteen and has emigrated with her family from Bohemia; and the book closes with their reunion in the fall of 1916, when Ántonia is established in Nebraska as the mother of a large family. As Jim Burden recalls his first arrival on the Nebraska prairie, the land's "empty darkness" (7), mystery, and monotony return to his memory. Nature hostilely greets the apprehensive immigrants, American and European alike, with a vast sameness whose fearfulness is intensified by the absence of human touch. "There was nothing but land," as Jim remembers Nebraska, "not a country at all, but the material out of which countries are made." The frontier gives one the feeling of being "outside man's jurisdiction"; and though at first overwhelmingly expansive, this new world does offer the boy an immensity into which he can be assimilated. "Between that earth and that sky I felt erased, blotted out" (8). The ambivalent rapport he feels with the frontier comes to Jim more comprehensively a short time later through the land's music, its voice, the wind. Sitting in the middle of his grandmother's garden, he "could hear it [the wind] singing its humming tune up on the level" (18) and "could see the tall grasses wave" under its gentle pressure. This music is especially audible in spring, as when the lark's song heralds the earth's floral bounty:

> It was a beautiful blue morning. The buffalo-peas were blooming in pink and purple masses along the roadside, and the larks, perched on last year's dried sunflower stalks, were singing straight at the sun, their heads thrown back and their yellow breasts a-quiver. (127-128)

As the land's roughness is gradually smoothed by human hands, the yield from tilled soil seems audible.

> July came on with that breathless, brilliant heat which makes the plains of Kansas and Nebraska the best corn country in the world. It seemed as if we could hear the corn growing in the night; under the stars one caught a faint crackling in the dewy, heavy-odoured cornfields where the feathered stalks stood so juicy and green. (137)

Nature's other mood is also interpreted in music. The singing wind has a "bitter song" as well as a soothing hum. This is its winter mood, a mood with a stark message in its melody:

> When the smoky clouds hung low in the west and the red sun went down behind them, leaving a pink flush on the snowy roofs and the blue drifts, then the wind sprang up afresh, with a kind of bitter song, as if it said: "This is reality, whether you like it or not. All those frivolities of summer,

the light and shadow, the living mask of green that trembled over every-thing, they were lies, and this is what was underneath. This is the truth." (173)

The bitter wind-song rises to the surface of Jim's association when he is musing about Mr. Shimerda's suicide. As he thinks of the lonely man, he "could hear the wind singing over hundreds of miles of snow" (101). Against this harsh, melodic accompaniment, Jim's thoughts form vivid pictures of "all that Ántonia had ever told me about his life before he came to this country; how he used to play the fiddle at weddings and dances" (101–102). But for Mr. Shimerda that music was silenced some time ago. Surely his sensitive ear heard in the wind-song the harsh truth that happiness is a lie. His life is proof of the message. That is why he shot himself.

It is the dark background of hardship and hostility that defines the special place of music in prairie life. In a world which is largely a com-posite of deprivations, music becomes an important consolation, providing an occasion for camaraderie, for a reassuring moment of community amid isolation and solitude. When Jim thinks of the savage descent of winter on Black Hawk, the little town into which he and his grandparents moved after three years in the country, he recalls how "a hunger for colour came over people" (174), how they used to linger outside the Methodist Church "when the lamps were lighted early for choir practice or prayer-meeting," held there by "the crude reds and greens and blues" of its "painted glass window," and his memory associates music with the effort to parry the bleakness of the outside world, to bring that world within man's jurisdiction—in short, to humanize it. Thrown back on their own devices by nature, the pioneers sang and played in their infrequent hours of leisure. These sounds are the memorable man-made sounds on the desolate plains; they are the soft, human rejoinders to nature's strident howls and the "hungry, wintry cry" (68) of coyotes.

A number of musical occasions highlight Jim's memoir. Russian Peter's "gaudily painted harmonica" (37) and the tunes that "were either very lively or very doleful" revive the thought of Russian Peter's tragic life. Those days in Jim's youth when "lives centred around warmth and food and the return of the men at nightfall" (66) were enlivened every Saturday night by musical entertainment. Otto Fuchs, the Burdens' amiable handyman, lingers in Jim's memory as one of the "good fellows" (67) who had kept the faith with many things, and the feature of Fuchs's personality which Jim remembers most is his "good baritone voice" which he lent to folk songs and which "always led the singing when he went to church services at the sod school-house."

The events in Jim's memory which are most clearly linked to the lost happiness of boyhood are mostly musical. There are, in particular, those Saturday nights at the Harlings' when, as he puts it, "one always felt at ease." In that cheerful home, which was "'like Heaven'" to Ántonia and Jim, the natural impulse for musical expression was nourished.

> Frances taught us to dance that winter, and she said, from the first lesson, that Ántonia would make the best dancer among us. On Saturday nights, Mrs. Harling used to play the old operas for us—"Martha," "Norma," "Rigoletto"—telling us the story while she played. Every Saturday night was like a party. (175)

In retrospect the "jolly evenings at the Harlings'" (156) are a significant part of the unregainable happiness of childhood. Jim's recollections of those evenings are filled with music and with amateur musicians. "There was usually somebody at the piano" (158): Julia Harling practicing seriously; Frances playing after Julia until dinner; Sally drumming "the plantation melodies that Negro minstrel troupes brought to town"; and even the smallest child, Nina, playing the Swedish Wedding March. As Jim's mature memory turns to the vivacious household, the musical associations are so strong that its mistress is caught in a musical attitude: "I can see her at this moment: her short, square person planted firmly on the stool, her little fat hands moving quickly and neatly over the keys, her eyes fixed on the music with intelligent concentration" (158).

Music is also a tie between the prairie and the outside world. Through this universal medium the settlers learn something of the metropolitan life from which they are separated. At the Saturday night gatherings of traveling salesmen in the parlor of the Boys' Home—"all the commercial travellers in that territory tried to get into Black Hawk for Sunday" (170) in order to stay at the Boys' Home, "the best hotel on our branch of the Burlington"—the man who traveled for Marshall Field's "played the piano and sang all the latest sentimental songs." And one could count on talk about "actors and actresses and musical prodigies" (183).

When an Italian family, the Vannis, come to Black Hawk and begin giving dancing lessons and holding dances in their tent pavilion, the young people eagerly welcome this escape from the humdrum routine of life. "At last there was something to do in those long, empty summer evenings, when the married people sat like images on their front porches, and the boys and girls tramped and tramped the board sidewalks . . ." (196). Now music breaks the dark silence which settles on a small Nebraska town. Music improves the conditions of life.

> That silence seemed to ooze out of the ground, to hang under the foliage of the black maple trees with the bats and shadows. Now it was broken by lighthearted sounds. First the deep purring of Mr. Vanni's harp came in silvery ripples through the blackness of the dusty-smelling night; then the violins fell in—one of them was almost like a flute. They called so archly, so seductively, that our feet hurried toward the tent of themselves. Why hadn't we had a tent before? (196)

Music whets youth's appetite for life and brings out the dormant impulse for gaiety; when it has music, youth also has its happy hour.

In the scenes at the Vannis' pavilion, Willa Cather does more than dramatize how music transforms frontier life; she uses it to make certain observations about the social structure in a prairie town. In these instances, music redefines the social system of a prairie town. In Book II, "The Hired Girls," Jim goes out of his way to indict the haughty and narrow small-town mind and tells of a "curious social situation in Black Hawk" (197), the class distinction small-town mores created when Bohemian and Scandinavian country girls went into service with town families. "The daughters of Black Hawk merchants had a confident, unenquiring belief that they were 'refined,' and that the country girls, who 'worked out,' were not" (199). Moreover, Black Hawk boys were supposed to marry Black Hawk girls, and "the country girls were considered a menace to the social order. Their beauty shone out too boldly against a conventional background" (201). Jim considers the attitude of the townspeople "very stupid" (200), and in proof of the equality—superiority, rather—of the foreign-born girls to the native Americans—cites the "'popular nights'" at Vannis' tent, which "brought the town boys and the country girls together on neutral ground" (203). Since dancing has nothing to do with artificial social superiority and everything to do with natural charm, Black Hawk's young men were willing to "risk a tiff with their sweethearts and general condemnation for a waltz with 'the hired girls'" (197). But no matter how strongly the town blades are attracted, their mothers have no need to be alarmed—"The respect for respectability was stronger than any desire in Black Hawk youth" (202). Music gives the hired girls a status which society denied. Even those who live by this decorum of suppression, the clerks and bookkeepers, even they could not help but feel the happiness from such musical heartiness.

Throughout *My Ántonia* music, musical talent, and musical interest are honorific qualities and designate a constructive commitment to life. Music implies a spirited and sensitive nature. Where that nature expresses itself spontaneously and freely, one finds joy and harmony; and in general, where there is music, there is happiness. Conversely, where there is no music or where music is forced or where the musician is constrained, there is profound unrest. In giving the music motif a negative treatment, Cather wishes to underscore the positive and restorative value of musical expression. There are a number of examples of this technique in the novel. The most conspicuous one is the development of Ántonia's father, Mr. Shimerda, in whose isolation and cultural yearnings Jim sees shadows of himself.

Mr. Shimerda, as his daughter reveals and as his actions confirm, immigrated to America against his will. "'He not want to come, nev-er!'" Ántonia tells Jim. "'My *mamenka* make him come'" (89–90). He was altogether unsuited to the demands of the rugged Nebraska frontier, and he felt his inadequacy deeply, all the more deeply because he was a sensitive man. Unlike his quarrelsome wife, he had come to terms with life in the old country; and for him, acclimation to the new world is degeneration. The horror to Jim of this misplaced gentleman is conspicuous. Jim observes: "I suppose, in the crowded clutter of their cave, the old man had come to believe that peace and order had vanished from the earth, or existed only in the old world he had left so far behind" (86). In that "old world . . . left so far behind," Mr. Shimerda has been a musician. Unlike the other musicians in the novel, he seems to have had some training though we are never sure just how much (Ántonia, for example, recalls her father's lively discussions of music). He shares with the other musicians in *My Ántonia* an inborn talent and inner warmth which make their music humanly compelling even if it is artistically deficient by the highest standards. His refinement and culture, the two features of his nature which Cather emphasizes through his musical talent, isolate him on the great plains and deepen his tragic condition. After crossing the ocean, the Bohemian retains the form of his old life. To compensate for the disorder of his new life he rigorously attends to the orderliness of dress; and to defy the mysterious and uncultured world—or, perhaps, to cling to the old—he refuses to play his violin. Mr. Shimerda's renunciation of music signals desperation; psychologically, his decision denies the possibility of happiness. With music goes his desire for life. At the center of his soul there is deadness where there was once great, vigorous life. In Ántonia's words:

> "My papa sad for the old country. He not look good. He never make music any more. At home he play violin all the time; for weddings and for dance. Here never. When I beg him for play, he shake his head no. Some days he take his violin out of his box and make with his fingers on the strings, like this, but never he make the music." (89)

Mr. Shimerda's abstention from music, which he valued above his other cultural interests, points up the sharpness of his misery and the completeness of his detachment from the human community. The final tribute to the old gentlemen is, suitably, a musical one—a tender interruption of the silence he sought. Otto Fuchs leads the mourners in a hymn, "Jesus, Lover of My Soul," at Mr. Shimerda's grave. The hymn offers a compassion which the prairie withheld from the man, and Charles Wesley's reverent words balance the emotional farewell of the Shimerda family with a tribute to precisely the kind of "helpless soul" Mr. Shimerda was. And the comfort for which the hymn asks is a deeply human one. The final words do not violate our good impression of the Bohemian gentleman as do the family's manners and pietism.

> Thou of life the Fountain art,
> Freely let me take of Thee;
> Spring Thou up within my heart!
> Rise to all eternity![2]

The alienation of the artistically sensitive person in this cultural outpost comes up a second time in the novel. In Book III, which covers Jim's university years at Lincoln, Willa Cather once again observes through music the artist in society. Where she dramatized the tragic consequences of the artist's plight with Mr. Shimerda, in the third book she portrays the comic, almost farcical, dimension of artistic life on the prairie.

Lena's neighbor across the hall is a Polish violin teacher, a Mr. Ordinsky. Fundamentally he feels the way Mr. Shimerda does about the cultural life in Nebraska. But where Mr. Shimerda turns within and becomes shy and retiring, Ordinsky turns on society without and be-

---

2. *Franklin Square Song Collection*, selected by J. P. McCaskey (New York: Harper and Brothers, 1881), p. 133.

comes bold and rather hilariously pompous. Formal even in his shabbiness, Ordinsky becomes arrogant to the extent that society is hostile to music. With his waistcoat held together by safety pins he stalks about remarking how "'the noblest qualities are ridiculed'" in "'a place like this'" and asserting the primacy of "'delicacy'" and "'*noblesse oblige*'" (286–287). There is something pathetically hopeless about this man. His seriousness about music is admirable of course, and his affectations are not without charm; but his "furious article, attacking the musical taste of the town" (287) and his calls for "'chivalry'" and "'*amour-propre*'" are futile gestures. His vain show before the "'coarse barbarians'" (288) is embarrassing and only confirms the incongruity of art in this society; but still, beneath Ordinsky's mad histrionics is the lamentable circumstance of a society which is unprepared either to receive or aid the few artistic members who seek to improve it. Such a state of affairs either prohibits a violinist from playing or, if he performs in spite of the hostility, turns him into a doubtful and absurd sort, the man in motley. Ordinsky's own flamboyant hauteur finishes the job society starts.

At the end of the novel the full symbolic value of the violin becomes clear when Willa Cather relates it to Ántonia's heroic career. When Jim returns to Black Hawk many years later, Mr. Shimerda's violin, "which Ántonia had always kept" (347), sings again, this time in the deft little hands of Leo Cuzak, Ántonia's son and the youngest musician in the novel. The previously opposing values of divided worlds, Europe and America, are reconciled in the promise of Leo's success; and the old world's ideals and joys which are embodied in the musical instrument are preserved in Leo himself. Willa Cather stresses the point by insisting upon the Bohemian-ness of the young boy. Like his brothers and sisters, he understands and speaks Bohemian, and yet he seems comfortably placed in the new world, the pleasures of which he fully appreciates. When Leo plays, it is as if cultural progress, held in check while the settlers contended with the tough, daily tasks, moves forward from where it left off.

Little Leo seems equal to the responsibilities of a cultural custodian. He is playful, lively, sensitive but still bold, and he has those "deep-set, gold-green" eyes (348) which characterize such heroic Catherian creations as Thea Kronborg and Professor St. Peter. Moreover, he is instinctively a musician. Old Mr. Shimerda's instrument, as Jim Burden notes, is too big for Leo, "but he played very well for a self-taught boy" (347). What was literally dead, what Mr. Shimerda had cultivated and loved in Prague, has been reborn—and it is the violin, first put aside and then taken up again, which represents the process of transformation and regeneration in *My Ántonia*.

III

The most sustained and revealing development of music in *My Ántonia* occurs toward the end of Book II, "The Hired Girls," in the seventh through twelfth chapters which cover the events from late winter to spring of 1892. The section is pivotal because it brings to a close Jim Burden's high school education and Ántonia Shimerda's education in the ways of town life and leads up to "the summer which was to change everything" (193) for the two friends, when Ántonia's vitality lapses into irresponsibility. Both narrator and heroine are entering adulthood. Jim leaves for the University of Nebraska in the fall; Ántonia begins to assume moral independence. Music, the metaphor for freedom and vitality, elicits signs of their emotional growth.

The principal musical occasion in this section is the Blind d'Arnault interlude. This sequence, which might seem disproportionately long and extraneous, like the grotesque Russian story of Pavel and Peter's involvement with a bridal party who were thrown to the wolves, holds special importance for an understanding of Ántonia's magnificent capacity for life. The mulatto's performance, initially described as a welcome break in a desolately monotonous winter on the prairie, through Jim's appreciation enlarges into a metaphorical description of Ántonia's inner nature, of the burning fire of life that warms her spirit, of the "inner glow" that never fades.

The occasion is one of those Saturday-night gatherings of commercial travelers in the comfortable parlor of the Boys' Home which Mrs. Gardener, the owner, arranged around a grand piano. For Jim and Ántonia the presence at the hotel of Blind d'Arnault, the Negro pianist who is to give a concert in the Opera House on Monday, promises particularly gay music on this cold March night. His arrival in the parlor does brighten the musical atmosphere. In fact, his music generates a festivity which exceeds Jim's expectation. D'Arnault begins by leading the men in "'some good old plantation songs'" (184) and ends with fiery dance music that brings Ántonia and her friends from the adjacent dining room to spin with the gentlemen visitors in the parlor. Jim finds in Blind d'Arnault's piano-playing a talent capable of arousing the animal as well as spiritual impulses in man. The mulatto is, really, the nonpareil of musicians in *My Ántonia*. He has to an extraordinary degree the instinctive musical facility that Mr. Shimerda and Leo Cuzak have in more normal measure. If Leo plays by ear, then d'Arnault plays by body. He literally possesses the instrument. We are told that when, as a child, he first touched a piano, he "coupled himself to it, as if he knew it was to piece him out and make a whole creature of him" (188). He is described as a sheer, sensory mechanism, a mechanism that is not so much designed to receive sensory information from the external world as to transmit the impulse that comes from within. What comes from within is a basic, sensuous rhythm of unusual strength. His body emanates that rhythm.

> When he was sitting, or standing still, he swayed back and forth incessantly, like a rocking toy. At the piano, he swayed in time to the music, and when he was not playing, his body kept up this motion, like an empty mill grinding on. (184)

Mrs. Harling has told Jim about Blind d'Arnault, and he relates the case history of this "nervous infirmity," as he calls it. D'Arnault was born on a plantation in the Far South. He had been blind almost since his birth, and the nervous motion of his body became apparent when he was old enough to walk. When he was six he began running off from home, blind though he was, to stand outside the Big House and listen to Miss Nellie, the plantation's mistress, practicing on the piano. One time when she went out of the room, the blind child made his way into the house and to the source of the sounds that held him spellbound. With the keyboard at his finger tips, the boy began to play passages from pieces Miss Nellie had been practicing but which had already taken so definite a form within the blind child's brain that the "pattern . . . lay all ready-made on the big and little keys" (188). Melody, harmony, modulation are the conditions of the child's responses to the world. The tactile and auditory terms that Jim uses to describe the child's approaching the piano insist upon the irrational hypersensitive nature of Blind d'Arnault's mind.

> Through the dark he found his way to the Thing, to its mouth. He touched it softly, and it answered softly, kindly. He shivered and stood still. Then he began to feel it all over, ran his finger-tips along the slippery sides, embraced the carved legs, tried to get some conception of its shape and size, of the space it occupied in primeval night. (187)

In his dark universe there is but the light of music. Music bridges his world and the outside world. It is expression and identification. With an uncanny musical instinct come his gifts of absolute pitch and accurate memory. Everything about the mulatto prodigy—his being a blend of races, his blindness, his spastic touching and keen hearing—contributes to the total impression that he is elemental musical sensation itself. "It was as if all the agreeable sensations possible to creatures of flesh and blood were heaped up on those black-and-white keys, and he were gloating over them and trickling them through his yellow fingers" (189). When he plays, his body and inner being undergo a transformation. He is divested of consciousness in the way that Thea Kronborg loses hers. In both instances the body becomes an unconscious, effortless medium for art. The word Willa Cather uses in *The Song of the Lark* is "vessel"—"In singing, one made a vessel of one's throat and nostrils and held it on one's breath, caught the stream in a scale of natural intervals." The term describes the still emptiness of the artist's consciousness and body, and it fits Blind d'Arnault. He is a vessel, ten yellow fingers through which trickle musical sensations.

The fascination with the pianist's past and the warm response to his stirring, if crude, music are, first of all, comments on the narrator. We see in Jim Burden a preference for strong emotion. That preference makes his account of Blind d'Arnault a celebration of an emotional genius which triumphs over barriers of mistaken judgment and physical infirmity. Jim, we observe, is growing into a more generous attitude toward human behavior than society or even his charitable grandparents could teach him. Reason and logic, he begins to learn through Blind d'Arnault's music, are less helpful at times than are emotions and intuitions. Jim's record of the impromptu concert presupposes a capacity to respond to something elemental, like the blind pianist's interior fire, and a capacity to realize that spiritual vigor of this kind makes its claims above ordinary standards of judgment, like the quality of musicianship, for example. This sensitivity to the irrational and irreducible in man is requisite for Jim as celebrator of Ántonia, whose distinction, like the pianist's, remains beneath appearance and whose success, again like d'Arnault's music, cannot be measured by conventional rules. The heart or a mind with supersensory impulses is required.

Recognizing that d'Arnault's music with its frenzied and wonderful qualities invites a special kind of spiritual response and therefore defines a way of perceiving human attributes, we can go on to consider Ántonia's connection to that music. On that Saturday night in March her reaction to his playing is no different from that of her friends Tiny, Lena, and Mary Dusak. They all enjoy the lively waltzes and, with Mrs. Gardener away in Omaha, enjoy the generally free atmosphere of the hotel. The strong rhythm from the piano floats into the dining room of the hotel where Ántonia and the other country girls are listening and has a contagious effect on them. "In the middle of a crashing waltz, d'Arnault suddenly began to play softly, and, turning to one of the men who stood behind him, whispered, 'Somebody dancing in there.' He jerked his bullet-head toward the dining-room. 'I hear little feet—girls, I 'spect'" (189). The Marshall Field's man, Kirkpatrick, looks over the transom and sees the country girls waltzing. He insists that they join the "'roomful of lonesome men on the other side of the partition'" (190). Then, "at a word from Kirkpatrick, d'Arnault spread himself out over the piano, and began to draw the dance music out of it, while the perspiration shone on his short wool and on his uplifted face" (191). This "glistening African god of pleasure" generates waves of musical excitement. When the dancers pause to change partners, he urges them not to "'let that floor get cold,'" and he plays until his manager stops him by shutting the piano. The excitement his music has aroused is strong enough to keep Jim and Ántonia stirred up for some time afterward. "I walked home with Ántonia. We were so excited that we dreaded to go to bed. We lingered a long while at the Harlings' gate, whispering in the cold until the restlessness was slowly chilled out of us" (192).

In the fuller context of Ántonia's story, especially the sections treating the arrival of the Vannis' dancing pavilion in June of 1892, the Blind d'Arnault passage relates closely and specifically to the heroine. As music pieces d'Arnault out and makes "a whole creature of him" (188), so it brings Ántonia into a new awareness of herself. D'Arnault's music signals the awakening of something strong and passionate in Ántonia which the subsequent dances at the tent and the Firemen's Hall kindle. The dances mark Ántonia's rapid progress toward an understanding of herself. Dancing broadens the margins of her life and desire beyond the pleasant but narrow confines of the Harling house. Given her natural exuberance, Ántonia has only to find rich soil in order to bloom. And so she does. "The Vannis often said that Ántonia was the best dancer of them all" (205). Jim tells us later that when spinning onto the floor with Tony "you set out every time upon a new adventure" (223).

Dancing also sets Ántonia out on a new adventure, a moral adventure for which she is not prepared. She becomes preoccupied with the pavilion and is absorbed in the idea of following her desire. She hums dance tunes all day and "at the first call of the music, she became irresponsible" (205)

—remiss in her household chores and careless in her personal relations. Sudden freedom and pleasure carry Ántonia away, as first great pleasures can, and rather than surrender her new liberty she quits her job with the Harlings to work for the Cutters. "'I guess I want to have my fling, like the other girls'" (208), she announces to Mrs. Harling, whose concern for the girl's "'reputation'" is genuine. As things turn out, that fling creates a special seclusion, not the freedom Ántonia expected. With the Cutters she is caught in an atmosphere of emotional tension and lives under a threat of physical harm. And her premature independence is expressed in a style which separates her from Jim's and Mrs. Burden's sympathy. Ántonia's clothes become showy, cheap imitations of Mrs. Gardener's flashy mode. The country girl cannot control every situation with the ease she displayed in the Harling kitchen and yard among children and generous adults. Evil assumes subtler forms than Ántonia can cope with and misfortune follows. Wick Cutter's devious attempts to seduce her and Larry Donovan's success in doing so qualify the prize of freedom for which Ántonia fought and are the comeuppance for self-reliance not grounded in experience. But another qualification is in order here so that we do not judge Ántonia more strictly than Willa Cather does. The Cutter and Donovan affairs arise from no serious fault in Ántonia. She suffers because of virtue: she is too innocent, too trusting, too kind to suspect the sly intention of Cutter and the confidence game Donovan specializes in. Her response to both situations reveals deeply sympathetic traits. The Cutter experience does not teach her to be suspicious but, admirably, not to be so vain; and the illegitimate child Donovan fathers becomes for Ántonia a possibility for great love. Besides quickening a desire within Ántonia, Blind d'Arnault's music suggests the heroine's blindness and foreshadows the reckless spree her lack of foresight brings about. Finally, Blind d'Arnault's crashing music reminds us of a passion which vitalizes even Ántonia's erratic behavior and which transforms isolation into independence, sorrow into joy.

The Blind d'Arnault passage is the pulsating center of *My Ántonia*. Occurring as it does in the very middle of the novel, it gives off the emotional—the musical—impulse which reverberates throughout. We are led up to this outpouring of music and spirit by a series of references to Mr. Shimerda's violin, the Saturday musicales at the Harlings', and Ántonia's own enjoyment of music, especially the kind she can dance to. We are led away from this generative center by the dances at the Vannis' tent and the Firemen's Hall and by Leo's tender playing of his grand-

father's violin. The treatment of Blind d'Arnault's performance is ambivalent. His music invokes ignorance, indiscretion, hot-headedness;
but it draws out freedom, fancy, courage.

The spiritual kinship Willa Cather establishes between d'Arnault
and Ántonia brings us directly to the novelist's revelation of those musical
souls whose "yearnings . . . first broke the silence of the world," to return
to one of her first statements about the power of music. Cather penetrates
behind surface difference to show spiritual likeness. The pianist's kind of
music corresponds to Ántonia's kind of life in that both are intense and
passionate, following something primal, almost primordial. "No matter
how many wrong notes he struck, he never lost the intention of a passage,
he brought the substance of it across by irregular and astonishing means"
(189). Ántonia has the same talent. She knows what is morally right instinctively, without the aid of code or commandment; she converts
defeat into triumph. Seen in this way, d'Arnault's gift of absolute pitch
matches Ántonia's absolute love, and his retentive memory suggests her
power to bring together the disparate experiences of Europe and America,
country and city.

To read the d'Arnault passage as a musical commentary on Ántonia
is not to reduce that passage to a delimiting metaphor; such a reading,
rather, reveals the richness and intensity of Ántonia's life and also something of Willa Cather's masterly use of musical figure. The evaluative
summation of d'Arnault's life and musical accomplishment runs a parallel
course to Ántonia's life: from imitation to originality, from confinement
to release, from excitement to expression, from frustration to self-
expression.

> As a very young child he could repeat, after a fashion, any composition
> that was played for him. No matter how many wrong notes he struck, he
> never lost the intention of a passage, he brought the substance of it across by
> irregular and astonishing means. He wore his teachers out. He could never
> learn like other people, never acquired any finish. He was always a Negro
> prodigy who played barbarously and wonderfully. As piano-playing it was
> perhaps abominable, but as music it was something real, vitalized by a
> sense of rhythm that was stronger than his other physical senses—that not
> only filled his dark mind, but worried his body incessantly. To hear him,
> to watch him, was to see a Negro enjoying himself as only a Negro can.
> It was as if all the agreeable sensations possible to creatures of flesh and
> blood were heaped up on those black-and-white keys, and he were gloating
> over them and trickling them through his yellow fingers. (188–189)

Like d'Arnault, Ántonia has a kind of blindness, and it is a deficiency which, like his, produces compensating benefits. Ántonia says: "'The trouble with me was, Jim, I never could believe harm of anybody I loved'" (344). As the pianist's blindness sharpens his auditory and tactile awareness, Ántonia's inability to believe anyone unworthy of love creates an over-balance of love. Surely she is all the more heroic because she cannot comprehend evil and because she cannot hate. Homer's passage on the harpist, Demokodos, which I have used for this chapter's epigraph, tells us how we must judge Ántonia—by her great talent, love, for that is how she judges others. He who lent her sweetness did make her blind.

IV

Finally, music has a broad associational importance for the special kind of heroic life Ántonia represents. While music helps to bring back to Jim's mind the Nebraska past and his relationship with Ántonia, it also serves as a bridge to a still more distant past—the European past. Mr. Shimerda's music, unheard in America but frequently heard in Europe, is altogether of that distant world. But for Ántonia that world is not lost. She transplants its traditional values. The past is a shaping part of her present. In her inner ear the music of Prague lingers in various forms. It comes to her from nature. When she hears the katydid sing, for example, the recollection of a village beggar woman who sang songs for a warm place near the fire evokes her European childhood. "'I ain't never forgot my own country'" (238). Her country, in a way, is still heard.

> "In summer, when they [flowers] were in bloom, he [Mr. Shimerda] used to sit there with his friend that played the trombone. When I was little I used to go down there to hear them talk—beautiful talk, like what I never hear in this country." (236)

In her own household at the end of the novel there is music as there was at the Harlings' place and in her Prague home. Impressively, music is deeply rooted in the Cuzaks' everyday life.

The impromptu concert after the festive dinner Ántonia prepares to honor Jim's homecoming is a beautiful tribute to her special musical nature. As the flourishing orchards represent the interior quality of Ántonia's genius, her profound repose, the musicale marks the familial quality of her greatness, her large love. Yulka, one of the Cuzak girls, accompanies Leo's playing of the violin; and though her effort is less

successful than Leo's, Yulka succeeds in the way that counts. Music fills
the parlor with expression and love. During the duet, little Nina gets
up from her corner and begins to dance in the middle of the floor, and
no one would think of being so ungenerous as to check the child's spontaneous demonstration of emotion. The assumptions in the air of
Ántonia's world are deeply human, and they go back to all the good things
she herself discovered in music when she was young and which she lives by
when old—feeling, freedom, rhythm, openness, and love. No wonder Jim
"was conscious of a kind of physical harmony" (349) among the people
around Ántonia. It is in the music of the air. Again a soul has touched
a soul; again a rainbow bridge is raised into the kingdom of the soul.

Ántonia is not a musical artist as is the great Thea Kronborg. But
then Willa Cather's ultimate interest in Thea's artistic eminence is more
than a fascination with a fight to become a great lyric singer. Cather sees
the artistic life as one aspect of the universal striving for selfhood and
meaning. So, too, does she see in Ántonia's struggle and domesticity an
aspect of the artistic. These lives represent two expressions of the inex-
tinguishable human spirit.

Still, so much about Ántonia *is* musical. Her life is musical in the final
harmony she achieves with the world around. In its spontaneity and its
direction, the music of Ántonia's life is attuned to the whole music of
nature, a music which ranges from the frailest katydid's thin, rusty chirp
up to the earth's symphonic florescence. Ántonia's power and perfection
come from the unison achieved between her life and all of life—a concord
between the cadence of the universe and of her spirit. The measure of her
artistry is the harmonic activity around the farm. The place abounds with
life. Numerous children and animals run about; the land flourishes; and
the orchards are laden with autumn fruitfulness. All this physical growth
goes back to a spiritual growth in Ántonia. Beauty and youth are gone.
Only an "inner glow" remains. But "whatever else was gone, Ántonia
had not lost the fire of life" (336). That fire within warmed her in the
winter of adversity and precipitated her growth as a person. She made of
her foreign ancestry a cultural asset and heritage of family life; she made
of her stay in town an opportunity to refine the farm life of her family;
she made of her illegitimate child a fine, loved daughter; she made of
foreign American soil a home. Her gift is a perennial transformation of
want and weakness into pleasure and strength.

CHAPTER SEVEN

One of Ours

> Send the word, send the word over there
> That the Yanks are coming the Yanks are
>   coming
> The drums rum-tumming ev'rywhere—
> So prepare, say a pray'r . . . .
>
> George M. Cohan

One of Ours (1922)[1] occupies as separate a place in Willa Cather's canon as the hero holds in the novel. While the book offers another act in the artist's drama of civilization and is played within the familiar *mise en scène* of her imagination, Europe and the Middle West, unlike the earlier *O Pioneers!* and *My Ántonia*, which are mainly pastorals and novels of feeling, *One of Ours* is a war novel and a novel of cultural protest. Never before and never again are topical issues like war, the status of ideals, or cultural crisis quite so compatible with Cather's temperament or intention. On this occasion she could not retreat from forces which called into question the very tradition of youth, idealism, individuality, and culture which her art commemorates. The events of the early twentieth century darken her triumphant view of human destiny into pessimism; and as her confidence in the outcome of man's struggle for destiny wanes, she relegates heroic action to the irrecoverable past.

   One of Ours is the first novelistic expression of Willa Cather's response to the moral and cultural dissolution she perceived. The lament,

   1. *One of Ours* (New York: Alfred A. Knopf, 1922). All references are to this text.

once voiced, becomes the ruling tone of the novels that follow—*A Lost Lady* (1923), *The Professor's House* (1925), and *My Mortal Enemy* (1926)—all of which treat failure and go so far as to honor it. Willa Cather's sense of defeat makes the hero a spiritual stranger in a transitional world; and while the *isolato* is certainly not new in her work, he is now a principal figure and a model of integrity where he was once minor and pathetic. In the frontier novels Cather conceived of the hero's separation as the means to individuality, to freedom, and to community of men. Now the hero converts isolation into a personal knowledge which bears no relation to the new, corrupt manner around him.

The first of Willa Cather's dark middle novels, *One of Ours*, is set in a torn and tired nature and deals with destruction, illusion, violence, defeat. It reads like a chronicle of despair in which human affairs run down like a clock. But the power of this novel does not come from the clichéd horrors of war. A soldier's death is sorrowful to the extent that his future held the possibility of self-discovery. Without a chance to find himself, he is not yet a man. His catastrophe is caught by Biff Loman's apology for Willy in *Death of a Salesman*: "He never knew who he was."

The intensity of Willa Cather's response to this tragic condition is rendered by the large sense of loss which permeates the novel. She continually measures her grief against the common sadness of the age. There is no occasion for heroism save the dubious invitation to war. Strife controls; and no department of human activity remains untouched, no region of life a sanctuary from evil. The characters endure the resultant attenuation of traditional values, and the setting bears the scars.

A special responsibility of music in *One of Ours* is to impart the authorial vision. In a 1922 interview Willa Cather tells of several non-commissioned officers who recognized that one of the characters, Lieutenant David Gerhardt, was based on an officer they had known, Lieutenant David Hochstein.[2] Like the character in the novel, Hochstein was a violinist—"an artist of high aims," according to the New York *Times* obituary of January 28, 1919. His army friends knew nothing of his musical career, but apparently a genius of character did shine through—something to which the men had responded and which confirmation of an attribute like musical fame would clarify. They took "a good deal of trouble" to look up Willa Cather, as she puts it, "merely to ask me whether Hochstein 'amounted to much' as a violinist." They "knew

2. New York *Herald*, December 24, 1922; reprinted in the Red Cloud (Nebraska) *Advertiser*, September 2, 1923.

nothing and cared nothing about music . . . . But they seemed to need this fact to complete their memory of him, to pull their mental picture of him together, though it was merely as a soldier that they had admired him." Cather comprehended their need. The soldiers, like Willa Cather the artist, somehow required a dimension outside their experience to shape their feeling. She, too, needed a reference beyond the life of her hero and the temper of an age to pull her aesthetic picture together. Coincidentally, but not by accident, the reference is music. Music motifs indicate the protagonist's exposure to culture and symbolize the disjointed state of the world. Not wishing to intrude in her own person and yet feeling obliged to take a stand on the events, Cather seems to express through music what she does not overtly state, thereby making music the bridge between dramatic action and private vision. Her use of music goes even deeper: ultimately, it relates the novel to the cultural heritage which has been disrupted by the modern world. *One of Ours* is a threnody for the noble ambition to make the world free for democracy and to save ideals.

II

Roughly divided, *One of Ours* falls into three parts. The first three books portray the central character, Claude Wheeler, in various aspects of midwestern life and during his first months in the army. The fourth book takes place aboard a troopship on the Atlantic, and the fifth, which is set in France, juxtaposes Claude to established European civilization in wartime. Symbolically, the eastward journey traces a course of misfortune. It is a flight, not a heroic rise above thwarting circumstances but an unheroic escape from them—and a final destruction by them.

The midwestern section shows Claude thrice defeated: first, in education, then in marriage, and finally, in farming. Though he is a young man of intelligence and aspiration, Claude is unsuccessful in all of these categories because the forces set against him overwhelm his individual strength. He does not have heroic stature, does not stand alone and above life as most Catherian heroes do. A psychic cripple—the name Claude means lame—he remains among the anonymous multitude, "one of ours." His temperament and defeats are conveyed both through music and, more importantly, through music's absence, as we recognize once we understand the significance of its presence.

More specifically, one of music's functions in *One of Ours* is to represent what Willa Cather in *The Song of the Lark* calls "the best things of this world." In *One of Ours* culture and fraternity are positive and good. Claude's fate is to be cut off from both sources of gratification. First, his parents prevent his transferring from inadequate Temple College to the State University, where there is a genuine intellectual community. Eventually, he must leave even Temple and his few friends in Lincoln. Education exposes Claude to a mode of living which he finds agreeable, and fate takes that satisfaction away. He stands equally apart from a human community and from cultural tradition. Idealistic values separate him from those who do not hold these values, and circumstances keep him away from the few who do. Cultural and social enrichment are inaccessible to Claude, and there in that distant region of the inaccessible resides music faintly heard.

It is precisely the near-absence of music which marks Claude's double alienation from history and society. His spiritual isolation is first seen in his family. Mr. Wheeler is a Philistine, a practical joker, and mercenary. Mrs. Wheeler is pietistic and timid. "She thought dancing and card-playing dangerous pastimes . . ." (25), and she is ignorant of life as Claude thinks it should be led. If she does have faith in "'whatever is noble in this world'" (87), she does not feel any personal responsibility to preserve these nobilities. His brothers are of the final coarseness. Bayliss, the older, feeling himself misunderstood and underrated, envies the achievement and vitality of others. He pursues material gain—for itself. Appropriately, he peddles farm machinery. The younger brother, Ralph, is acquisitive and unproductive. The family's prosperity provides means for his limitless interest in new-fangled devices. In sum, the Wheelers' attitudes and ambitions bespeak the plight of the new agrarian prosperity—"stingy and grasping, or extravagant and lazy" (102). Significantly, their narrow mentality is without musical sensitivity. If not downright opposed to musical expression, the Wheeler men are indifferent to it. We can judge the significance of this insensitivity by examining the worth which music has for others in the prairie village of Frankfort, Nebraska.

Besides Claude's mother, who is "'fond of good music'" (371) even though her fundamentalist views make her condemn dancing, there are three people in Claude's Frankfort world who are musical. Each is an outcast in some way; each is a friend of Claude's; and collectively they occupy the sympathetic center of the hometown world. The least sophisticated of the three is Mahailey, the Wheeler housekeeper. She is illiterate, but her values are of the highest order. She stands for rural tradition and personal loyalty. At a time when everyone around her hastens to keep up with new gadgets and new modes, Mahailey resists the temptation to change and clings to what she knows to be true. Household machinery bewilders her. With apparatus she becomes lost, but with people she finds her place; and her judgment is respected just as her domestic talents are sources of comfort. Her world is anachronistic, yet her values are timeless. Contentment and warmth are her musical signature:

> Claude could remember warm spring days when the plum bushes were all in blossom and Mahailey used to lie down under them and sing to herself, as if the honey-heavy sweetness made her drowsy; songs without words, for the most part . . . . (23)

Another friend, Ernest Havel, is no better a musician than Mahailey, but he is more articulate about a philosophy of life. He is Claude's foil. Where Claude is timid and hesitant, Ernest is temerarious; where Claude is idealistic, Ernest is practical and literal-minded. He has no use for "ideas," since natural desires are his absolutes. Even in disagreement there is friendship, an easy relationship in an "atmosphere of mental liberty" (11). In essence, Ernest Havel is a young man with hearty, earthbound values and with a lusty commitment to life. His music evokes just these qualities through certain pictorial associations.

> Ernest Havel was cultivating his bright, glistening young cornfield one summer morning, whistling to himself an old German song which was somehow connected with a picture that rose in his memory. It was a picture of the earliest ploughing he could remember.
>
> He saw a half-circle of green hills, with snow still lingering in the clefts of the higher ridges; behind the hills rose a wall of sharp mountains, covered with dark pine forests. (137)

Claude's third friend in Frankfort is Gladys Farmer. She is his closest spiritual ally, and she is the most accomplished musician in town. These two young people are of the same fated disposition. They expect more of life than they ever will receive. Where they differ is in their capacity to accept frustration. Gladys makes her separate peace through resignation. She desires art and love but can live without them because she believes them ultimately unattainable.

> She had worked out a misty philosophy for herself, full of strong convictions and confused figures. She believed that all things which might make the world beautiful—love and kindness, leisure and art—were shut up in prison, and that successful men like Bayliss Wheeler held the keys. The generous ones, who would let these things out to make people happy,

were somehow weak, and could not break the bars. Even her own little
life was squeezed into an unnatural shape by the domination of people like
Bayliss. She had not dared, for instance, to go to Omaha that spring for the
three performances of the Chicago Opera Company. Such an extravagance
would have aroused a corrective spirit in all her friends, and in the school-
board as well . . . . (155)

Claude, of course, cannot adjust through passivity. Though his will is
inoperative, he is a man of action. Besides, idealism always begs for a
solution of controversy.

Claude's separation from Gladys is a failure of love. These young
people with imagination and generous impulses cannot love each other.
The affection between them is disabling, not redeeming. Willa Cather
distributes the responsibility universally, blaming especially society,
which renders sensitive youth timid by silly convention and sentimentality.
Gladys offers Claude such spiritual and womanly companionship as he
calls for, but he lacks the confidence to claim them.

Willa Cather represents spiritual aridity in one hard symbol—the
machine. Mechanization in *One of Ours* amounts to dehumanization. The
more man involves himself with mechanical devices, the further he is
removed from essential realities—from love and kindness, leisure and art.
The whole Frankfort landscape is strewn with mechanical litter. Broken
devices clutter the Wheeler basement and mar the rural prospect. The
"belching black engine" (157) constitutes the dead center for its human
worshipers, the little machines "with the springs broken inside" (156).
Machinery, then, is the counter-symbol of music, and this tension
thematically contrasts dehumanization with civilization, decay with art,
sorrow with happiness—and the world with Claude.

Claude's musical sensitivity assures us that he yearns for something
beyond gears and cash. He is touched by Mahailey's song without words,
sensitive to Ernest Havel's whistling, and pleased by Gladys's piano-
playing. His inner ear is especially attuned to the physical music of the
earth. Nature's rhythm calms him and offers an identification with something outside himself which human relations deny.

> To lie in the hot sun and look up at the stainless blue of the autumn sky,
> to hear the dry rustle of the leaves as they fell, and the sound of the bold
> squirrels leaping from branch to branch; to lie thus and let his imagination
> play with life—that was the best he could do. (212)

Characteristically, Willa Cather associates musical receptiveness with
noble impulses emanating from the heart—with longing and peace.

The world in which "love and kindness, leisure and art" thrive is that of Lincoln, the prairie's cultural center. Claude is introduced to a life of amenity through his visits to the Erlich home. These cordial and civilized people represent everything his hometowners lack. As musical insensitivity reveals Frankfort's limitations, musical activity suggests Lincoln's possibilities. In fact, one can think of the Erlich home as a musical storehouse much in the same way that the Wheeler place is a dumping ground for machinery.

In Frankfort, people are closed and suspicious. At the Erlichs', they are warm and open, qualities which training stamped out of Claude. "He had never heard a family talk so much, or with anything like so much zest" (41). They live the life which Gladys Farmer thinks open only to rich people. But the Erlichs are poor: "The father was dead, and all the boys had to work, even those who were still in school. They merely knew how to live, [Claude] discovered, and spent their money on themselves, instead of on machines to do the work and machines to entertain people" (43). Diversions range from informal discussion (so scarce in Frankfort) to formal musicales and concerts (nonexistent in Frankfort). Each member of the Erlich circle positively contributes to a civilized life, and it is noteworthy that many of the contributions are musical. The boys play the guitar and the piano; Mrs. Erlich sings old German songs. Indeed, the family's musical connections extend into the professional artistic world, for Mrs. Erlich's cousin, Madame Schroeder-Schatz, is a member of the Chicago Opera Company, and comes to Lincoln as soloist for the May Festival.

Regrettably, Claude cannot free himself from restraint and become part of the Erlichs' world. When he lived at home, he "had come to believe that the things and people he most disliked were the ones that were to shape his destiny" (31), and life in a world of things and people he prizes does not alter that fatal shape. Exposure is not assimilation. Having the taste for fineness does not necessarily imply the ability to savor it. Actually, he meets the Erlichs too late and for too short a time for the encounter to correct his deficiencies. When Madame Schroeder-Schatz asks Claude to turn the pages for her while she sings, the youth apologizes, "'I'm sorry I'm so stupid, but I don't know one note from another'" (60). The admission is not damaging (the Erlichs are fond of him for more important virtues), but it is indicative of Claude's detachment from the cultural world for which he has an affinity but for which he lacks training. Once again he stands apart from human community. This particular separation is all the more painful because Lincoln offers affection and the opportunity for identification.

But fate takes him from college; he is needed to run the family farm. As a result of an injury—his team is frightened by a noisy "gasoline motor-truck" (138)—Claude gets erysipelas; and his one visitor—fate's personal choice—Enid Royce, becomes his wife. The marriage had been in the offing, but Enid's daily visits precipitate it. His decision to marry her could not have been more foolish. The marriage inevitably fails. Claude is to blame for idealizing her qualities—the major one seems to be condescension—but the larger blame rests with Enid herself. There is little to be said in her defense and almost too much that could be said against her. Some of her attitudes are silly and fussy; most of them are irritating; and her religious mania heightens the constriction we feel when confronted with her bloodless world. Enid is a parody, really, of the unfeminine feminist, the pre-World War I woman in motley who works for Prohibition and bumps about the countryside in her electric car with posters and proscriptions. She takes her Prohibition work so seriously that she prohibits her spouse from being her husband. Physical contact is abhorrent to her—as are cigars, dancing, meat. Her one kindness to Claude—leaving him—comes from her self-indulgent resolve to go to China to take care of her sick missionary sister. To have a cause and a calling to be of service—this makes her happy. So pleased is Enid about the China jaunt that she is heard singing (the only time) while she works about the house: "Enid was singing in the kitchen in a subdued, rather lonely voice" (219). It is the only music Claude has heard since he married. Gladys and Ernest, the regular sources of music and verve, rarely see Claude now because they dislike his wife. Music stopped for him in church after Gladys Farmer played the wedding march for his marriage. As for Enid's "voice," it seems to intensify Claude's dark silence rather than relieve it.

In the prefatory note to a 1936 book of essays Willa Cather bitterly complains that "the world broke in two in 1922 or thereabouts."[3] In the fictive anticipation of the historic division, *One of Ours*, the two parts are symbolized, as we have seen, in the machine-music opposition. It is Claude's tragedy to be suspended between the two parts. Mahailey's and the Erlichs' world is remote, Bayliss', revolting. In musical terms the old melody is sad and distant, and the new sound is strident. Claude himself expresses the individual's plight in a divided world: "'I have a way . . . of

3. *Not Under Forty* (New York: Alfred A. Knopf, 1936), p. v.

beginning things and not getting very far with them'" (235). His final acceptance of defeat in Nebraska is more anguished:

> His life was choking him, and he hadn't the courage to break with it . . . .
> What a hideous world to be born into! Or was it hideous only for him?
> Everything he touched went wrong under his hand—always had. (220)

Grim the world, indeed; and unlike the lost world of gladness, it has no healing and elevating music in it. Depressing silence it has—and repellent sounds: "belching" engines, the cranking of cars, drills "tearing" the air.

III

The conditions worsen as the novel progresses. Mechanization and materialism are shown to be related to an even harsher force at large in the world—the Great War. "On the twenty-third came the news of the fall of the forts at Namur; again giving warning that an unprecedented power of destruction had broken loose in the world" (167). Thematically, small-town hostility gives way to nationalistic contention; confinement becomes devastation; personal greed waxes into general avarice. Willa Cather underscores the thematic change in the music references by making certain distinctions about the kinds of musical expression possible under such conditions and, finally, by silencing what little real music there is.

For Claude war is doubly significant. It releases him from Nebraska and provides a test for his idealism. He enlists to put order back into a disordered world. For the first time he has a sense of purpose. "He believed that he was going abroad with an expeditionary force that would make war without rage, with uncompromising generosity and chivalry" (248). Romantic that he is, Claude squarely pits his personal strength against the grand impersonal force of evil. One admires him for doing so at the same time that one realizes the futility of such a gesture. In any event, thus equipped with lofty hope one of our doughboys voyages to France and the front line.

"The Voyage of the *Anchises*," as the fourth book is entitled, recounts his crossing. In the main Willa Cather does two things in this book. She romantically celebrates Claude's military journey, and she shows him exposed to the unexpected minor crises which attend warfare. For both purposes Cather uses music.

The *Anchises*' sailing for Europe acquires a special importance through an implicit epic comparison. Two thousand young men from the hinterlands fearlessly sail with an "indomitable resolution" (273) to set things straight. The "scene was ageless; youths were sailing away to die for an idea, a sentiment, for the mere sound of a phrase . . . and on their departure they were making vows to a bronze image in the sea" (274). To this archetypal picture of bravery, music adds a patriotic touch and sends the valiant word abroad. There is a rousing flourish of "Over There" from the Kansas band with two thousand voices taking it up and "booming" (273) the Cohan song "over the water" as the *Anchises* departs from the Hoboken docks. We sense in the bravura that the Yanks are indeed coming, and they are coming to redeem the oppressed.

If Cather is somewhat sentimental about the departure, she is not about the voyage. It is a rugged, almost endlessly trying journey for the men. Military service may seem noble in the abstract, but the doughboys themselves can be cynical, bitter, and timid. Claude discovers that not every one is going to fight Germany for his or any exalted motive. Some are fleeing responsibility. Some are just going. Also, there is a severe epidemic of influenza on the ship, during which Claude learns the paradox of military life, that robustness does not insure well-being and that a soldier's routine demands tenderness as well as valor.

At the beginning of the trip, there are band music on deck and concerts below. But with the spreading of influenza, those sources of pleasure are cut off. The musicians must be nurses before they can be entertainers, and attention turns to a basic issue—survival. The fanfare of "Over There" at the pier was momentary. In its place comes a disturbing stillness. "The band concerts, the Lindsborg Quartette, the first excitement and novelty of being at sea: all that had gone by like a dream" (298). Once again Willa Cather dramatizes the fateful turn of human affairs by diminishing the music in the background. Twice stillness is interrupted in this section, and the effect here is comparable to Enid's breaking Claude's quietude with her lonely voice. First, there is the funeral accompaniment to the sea burial of a young doughboy: "a gentle boy [is] thrown into that freezing water and forgotten" (293). "The Chaplain read the burial service while they stood with uncovered heads. The Kansas band played a solemn march, the Swedish quartette sang a hymn" (292). Everything about the burial except the music seems destitute of benevolence and remembrance. The ocean's energy is a "mocking cruelty" to the boy's lifeless body. His fellows forget him because they have their "own miseries to think about" (293). Music, however, does offer its brief tenderness to the "already forgotten" lad.

The second musical moment is less somber but by no means cheerful. Toward the end of the crossing after a long period of silence and sickness, Claude hears "one of the Swedish boys . . . playing softly on the old piano" (305). Life during the epidemic is too hard and too filled with tiring duties to permit one the full luxury of music. In keeping us from music and then calling it momentarily to our attention, Cather suggests that war does not just take us from our normal occupations and recreations. It deprives man of the natural joy so essential for his soul. One can snatch a moment now and again, as the Swedish boy does, but the pleasure, like his music, is brief and vague. It is no wonder that upon arrival Claude muses with such exhausted concern about those who died at sea:

> They were merely waste in a great enterprise, thrown overboard like rotten ropes. For them this kind release,—trees and a still shore and quiet water,—was never, never to be. How long would their bodies toss, he wondered, in that inhuman kingdom of darkness and unrest? (319)

IV

In the third major part of the novel, Book V, "'Bidding the Eagles of the West Fly On,'" the two thematic strains are resolved. As the cleavage between the older and younger halves of the world deepens into a historical Divide, the tenuous bond between the present and the past, between Claude's idealism and the possibility of its realization, between war and music is irreparably severed. Willa Cather marks this development through thematic counterpoint. There is a descending line from engagement to death as the war progresses. Simultaneously there is an ascending development in the growth of the protagonist as Claude Wheeler gradually comes to know something of himself and the world. His psychological ascent is not, as one might expect, a movement from aspiration to achievement or from unawareness to illumination. Such a progress is heroic. Claude, rather, goes from ambiguous faith to false belief, from disappointment to illusion.

Like the thematic design, music's part is twofold: it heightens the tragic sense of waste and loss in war while it hopefully suggests that somehow a warm human spirit will reassert itself when this fearful contest ends. The wreckage of a rare violin symbolizes the great, irreplaceable loss of values in modern life; faint stirrings of music in the earth, victory dances, and national songs utter a promise of cultural renewal.

Willa Cather makes her plea for the human spirit by means of finely discriminated music references which double as a scale of moral values. The musical scale starts with deafness, which is an extreme form of the silence that descends on the prairie in the earlier section. Deafness is the chief deprivation of war: "The German occupation was like a deafness which nothing pierced but their own arrogant martial airs" (434). In the main, surdity indicates the absence of joyful human activity and the severity of human suffering. War paralyzes and desensitizes the human spirit by its alternating assaults of hurtful noise and numbing silence. A bombardment—"Then the shrapnel broke loose; not the long, whizzing scream of solitary shells, but drum-fire, continuous and deafening" (449)—is followed by a reprieve: "The silence was like a heavy anaesthetic" (451). Cather adds to the war scene mechanical junk, "bodies of wrecked motor-trucks and automobiles lying along the road, and everywhere endless straggling lines of rusty barbed-wire . . ." (358).

Breaking through the new deafness are murmurings of nature. While glancing over the parapet between mounds of sandbags, Claude sees entangled wire fences with birds hopping on them. Indifferent and superior as they are to the wire and the war that erects it into imprisoning barriers, the birds sing: "Clear and flute-like they sounded in the heavy air,—and they were the only sounds" (363). In nature if not in the human world there is a vestige of harmony and verve, an audible sign of life's persistence through the havoc of war. Somehow life continues, even when it appears to be suffering attenuation. "The birds, that always came to life at dusk and dawn, began to sing, flying home from somewhere" (393). At dusk and dawn, despite setback and death, the thrust of life's energy breaks through containment, just as the birds always begin to sing when taking flight.

There is an interesting extension of this musical impulse in the soldiers' songs. Their music, the human echo of the vital force in the bird-song, comes with a stark loudness. Indeed, their martial airs are so loud as to seem vindications of an energy too long quelled. From café door-ways "music-machines poured out jazz tunes and strident Sousa marches. The noise was stupefying" (332). As the doughboys trudge through France, one hears clamorous patriotic band music meant "'to show that the morale was high'" (358). The soldiers' shouting, their public display of high morale, is more a proof to themselves of high spirit than it is a spontaneous demonstration of courage. Paradoxically, too, it is as though music is enlisted by war, and made to serve the purpose of death and destruction, the "big show" (358) ahead.

Where music is spontaneous and tender, it is remote and muted:

> In the far distance the big guns were booming at intervals. Down in the garden Louis was singing. Again he wished he knew the words of Louis' songs. The airs were rather melancholy, but they were sung very cheerfully. There was something open and warm about the boy's voice, as there was about his face . . . . (391)

Gun blasts render the song melancholic and remind Claude of the abiding ruin in the world, but that a French veteran should be happy enough to sing augurs of something beautiful "on the horizon," the blond voice suggesting golden wheat fields. "Claude sat alone for half an hour or more, tasting a new kind of happiness, a new kind of sadness" (391). "That was life": the ebb and flow of things, birth, death, regeneration. Music conveys to Claude the principle of life which subsists beneath superficial change and through time. Such is the "undreamed-of quality of sound" (342); such is the revelation of the great bell at the Church of St. Ouen which Claude heard on an earlier occasion.

With the arrival of the American troops in a French town comes a moment of freedom, and with freedom comes musical expression. The doughboys are bearers of a musical gift besides the special gift of liberation. "The Americans were the first to bring 'Madelon' to Beaufort" (434). When the children roundly beg, "'*Chantez-vous la Madelon!*'" the soldiers realize "how far and how long out of the world these villagers had been" (434). These Frenchmen had not known one of the most popular French tunes of the time. After the Americans are in the village a while, the musical atmosphere intensifies. They teach the French girls "to dance the 'Pas Seul' and the 'Fausse Trot'" (435). They discover an old, unused violin (obviously, a symbol of suppression) and provide instrumental accompaniment for the dancing which becomes a popular nightly affair. Music brings the liberated and the liberators together, into a kinship so close that Beaufort is "'our town'" for the soldiers. Here as everywhere in Cather's fiction, music creates a universal bond of feeling.

This is music at its highest pitch in *One of Ours*, but popular songs do not mark the highest music reference in the novel. As expressive as dancing and singing are, they do not touch the sublimity which man occasionally experiences. Such delicacy and transcendence are the features of great art, the expression of artistic genius; the rest remains but a simple echo. Artistic music remains silent. However easily man is restored to a certain peace and freedom, higher peace and independence require long periods of time and an established tradition. Man himself can rebound from a crisis like war, but the restoration of civilization, especially after this war, comes only with unusual effort and gradual preparation.

Willa Cather, then, handles the musical pattern in such a way as to provide tonal and metaphorical emphasis for her fictive argument. The musical gradation starts in deafness, moves through suggestive stirrings in nature and then in humanity, and ends ironically in silence. And there, Cather implies, is where the great war has left civilization. From the brilliant cultural heritage of the past, humanity is heir only to a "suppressed, bitter melody" (417).

Willa Cather underscores this silence in the characterization of Lieutenant David Gerhardt, a violinist of international acclaim who gave up a promising musical career when he was called to the colors. As has been noted, the character derived from Cather's casual acquaintance with David Hochstein, whose increasing success on the concert stage was cut short by war; and, as happens in fiction, the real personality is transformed by the needs of the story. Musical sensibility lends itself most agreeably to Cather's power. She wanted Claude, her "red-headed soldier from the prairie" to have a "fine friendship" in the course of daily life.[4] That he has. Gerhardt blends sophistication and achievement with humility, a quality Claude is sensitive enough to admire. Special talent does not exempt one from war; as Gerhardt says, war is "'too big for exceptions; it's universal'" (354). "'You are a musician?'" Claude asks him; and he answers, "'I was.'" Rather like Mr. Shimerda in *My Ántonia*, he rebukes the age by voluntarily silencing his violin. There is a cruel finality about such a decision. Perhaps it is a gesture of disaffection which finally is suicidal, like Mr. Shimerda's decision. "'I haven't any profession at present,'" Gerhardt says. "'I'll never go back to the violin'" (407). The time lost in the army possibly can be made up; but the desire to go on creating cannot be recaptured. "'I've lost much more than time.'"

His violin, a Stradivarius, was "'smashed into a thousand pieces'" (409) in a car accident, and his career seemed to go along with it. In this collision the submerged tension between music and the machine is violently concretized, and in such a direct confrontation music has no defense against its adversary. Once killed, music and beauty can only be

4. New York *Herald*, December 24, 1922.

painstakingly revived. This makes manifest how "'much more'" Gerhardt lost. Speaking of the broken violin, he says: "'I didn't know what it meant then; but since, I've seen so many beautiful old things smashed . . . I've become a fatalist'" (409). His fatalism seems warranted. First the machine destroys the violin and then its uglier counterpart, war, destroys the violinist.

David breaks his self-imposed musical silence just once, and that is when he is visiting the family of a fellow student he knew at the Conservatoire in Paris, René Fleury, who was killed at Verdun. The Fleury family is a more elegant version of the Erlich household. While there, Gerhardt is asked to play René's Amati, the sixteenth-century counterpart of the instrument unearthed in Beaufort, which the family reveres as a sacred legacy of exquisite skill designed to create beauty. The young boy, Lucien, who is "*très sérieux* with his music" (416), brings the rare violin forward, opens the case carefully, and "took off the velvet cloth, as if this was his peculiar office, then handed the instrument to Gerhardt." Lucien's sister, Mlle. Claire, goes to the piano and begins the orchestral introduction to the Saint-Saëns concerto. Reluctantly at first, and then by disciplined reflex, David breaks into "that suppressed, bitter melody" which begins with the entrance of the violin. He stops at the taxing third movement, then resumes playing when Mlle. Claire tells him that it was the last thing her brother played on the Amati during his final leave. It is also the last thing David plays. The Saint-Saëns piece serves as a final genuflection in this house where "music has always been like a religion" (418). The music becomes "part of [Claude's] own confused emotions." Torn between admiration and envy, he wonders what it would be like to be able to do anything so well, "to have a hand capable of delicacy and precision and power" (418). War, he thinks further, is the first and true test of his ideals. David has his dream, and Claude, his. If Claude dies for something larger than himself, he too shall achieve something. So runs his rationalization after hearing the concerto:

> Ideals were not archaic things, beautiful and impotent; they were the real sources of power among men. As long as that was true, and now he knew it was true—he had come all this way to find out—he had no quarrel with Destiny. Nor did he envy David. He would give his own adventure for no man's. (420)

Ways of hearing are of course ways of knowing for Cather, and the way in which Claude responds to the sound of war supports his homage to ideals. "The sound of the guns had from the first been pleasant to him, had given him a feeling of confidence and safety . . ." (419). War elicits high purpose by bringing great issues into the life of the common man. "Well, History had condescended to such as he; this whole brilliant adventure had become the day's work" (312). Living by desire gains for Claude in France the youth denied him in America. He sees his life as fulfilled. Without violating the sympathy created for Claude, Cather does qualify the hero's view of his pact with destiny. The sound of guns is not pleasant and the novel does not represent that din as anything but dreadful. More importantly, the sense of what might have been, which exerts a strong pressure on the novel, suggests that Claude's private campaign is no more successful than was the political enterprise of putting an end to war. Claude, feeling deeply the disparity between his artistic ineptitude and the creativity of Gerhardt and the Fleury family, confesses "that a man might have been made of him, but nobody had taken the trouble to do it; tongue-tied, foot-tied, hand-tied" (418). Claude Wheeler's final salute to idealism, like all gestures of a visionary, converts dream into achievement. Also, the events of the novel undermine his trust in the power of ideals. Music, the emblem of the ideal, has stopped. Claude must be satisfied with the idea of beautiful things because the living forms are gone. David plays brilliantly, but his music is brief. We are left in silence with only a recollection of his bitter melody. Claude turns recollection into hope. Fortunately this hope is not submitted to a test. Claude Wheeler is shot in the heart. Just before Claude is shot, David Gerhardt, like his rare Stradivarius, is blown to pieces.

CHAPTER EIGHT

A Lost Lady

We've wander'd mony a weary foot,
Sin' auld lang syne.

A Lost Lady (1923),[1] like *My Ántonia*, portrays a woman largely through the consciousness of a young man who admires her. The setting is again a little Nebraska town—this time called Sweet Water. The story opens at the end of the last century with a view of the heroine's house on a hill comparable to the gratifying impression a nineteenth-century traveler would have had on arriving into Sweet Water by train. The perspective narrows to that of Niel Herbert, nephew of Judge Pommeroy, who is twelve when the story opens. Marian Ormsby Forrester, the central character, is the wife of the town's "great man" (12), Captain Daniel Forrester, "a railroad man, a contractor, who had built hundreds of miles of road for the Burlington,—over the sage brush and cattle country, and on up into the Black Hills" (10). Twenty-five years younger than the Captain and his second wife, Mrs. Forrester arrives in Sweet Water from California as a vivacious bride, departs a lost lady.

In the early drafts of the novel Niel, like Jim Burden, narrated the story; but in revising Cather modified the point of view in order to vivify the heroine's personality. Edith Lewis tells us that "although *A Lost Lady* has been regarded by many critics as the most perfect in form of all her

1. *A Lost Lady* (New York: Alfred A. Knopf, 1958). All references are to this edition.

novels, Willa Cather had, at the start, more trouble with it than with any of the others."[2] That she should have difficulty comes as no surprise. The subtlety of effect which Cather envisioned challenges critical definition. Willa Cather wanted *A Lost Lady* to have the very feel of life. Simply to define the heroine would not express Cather's aesthetic relationship to her subject, and the pressure of this relationship was too strong to resist. She worked at the book "with some fervor," she told an interviewer:

> I discarded ever so many drafts, and in the beginning wrote it in the first person, speaking as the boy himself. The question was, by what medium could I present her the most vividly, and that, of course, meant the most truly. There was no fun in it unless I could get her just as I remembered her and produce the effect she had on me and the many others who knew her.[3]

The remembrance is vivid enough, as the book shows; but the effect she wanted to reproduce is too indefinite and subjective to serve the reader as a guide to the form of the material. "I wasn't interested in her character when I was little, but in her lovely hair and her laugh which made me happy clear down to my toes."[4] And it is a laugh which is Willa Cather's metaphor explaining the psychological movement the book follows.

The best guide to the novelistic form through which the intended effect is achieved is suggested by a phrase in the book itself, "a suave scale." And an examination of the way Willa Cather develops this figure into form explains the contribution of music to *A Lost Lady*. The pattern of impression is established early in the novel. The action really begins in the third section of Part One when the Forresters spend their first winter in Sweet Water and when Niel encounters Marian Forrester in his uncle's office. She has come to invite Judge Pommeroy and Niel to a dinner party. The meeting is the first important one for Niel. The earlier encounters were in childhood and are rendered from a distance, but Niel's meeting Mrs. Forrester on this particular winter afternoon is up close and memorable. Niel's impression, like Cather's, is essentially auditory.

> Niel, greatly bored with the notes he was copying, was trying to invent an excuse for getting out on the street, when he became aware of light footsteps coming rapidly down the outside corridor. The door of the front

---

2. *Willa Cather Living: A Personal Record* (New York: Alfred A. Knopf, 1953), p. 124.
3. Interview by Flora Merrill, New York *World*, April 19, 1925, quoted in Mildred R. Bennett, *The World of Willa Cather* (Lincoln: University of Nebraska Press, 1961), p. 70.
4. *Ibid.*, p. 69.

office opened, he heard his uncle rise quickly to his feet, and, at the same moment, heard a woman's laugh,—a soft, musical laugh which rose and descended like a suave scale. (34)

Throughout *A Lost Lady* Marian Forrester's "musical laugh" with its variations in mood and range is the notable trait of the lady's charm. So deep is the vocal impression on Niel that her voice grows into a musical symbol of her epoch. The double story of a lady's decline and of an age passing away follows the rhythmic rise and fall of her laugh.

The novel begins in a very general way, not in the middle of things nor at their beginning but at some indefinite time near the end. "Thirty or forty years ago, in one of those grey towns along the Burlington . . ." (9). Gradually the focus sharpens to "a summer morning long ago, when Mrs. Forrester was still a young woman" (14), a morning which Niel recalls spending with friends in the Forresters' beautiful grove. Niel was twelve then; the feeling is still generalized. He knows her simply as "a very special kind of person" (19). In the third chapter Niel is nineteen and more sensitive to what makes her special. He becomes acquainted with the Forresters because they are forced to spend the winter in Sweet Water after the Captain's fall with his horse, the accident which ended his rail-road career. With each encounter he finds Marian Forrester more remark-able and more admirable; with each encounter the theme ascends the suave scale. Her elegance and sophistication invest Lady Forrester's presence with an occult influence which Niel observed only from afar in the lobby of the Brown Palace. Her dinner parties are conducted with the easy formality of an accomplished hostess. Then, as Niel comes to know Captain Forrester and other railroad builders better, Mrs. Forrester is more romantically linked to history. Knowing Marian Forrester personally in turn brings Niel's imagination close to a period of American history which fascinates him. He finds, too, a brilliant sense of life. "The charm of her conversation was not so much in what she said, though she was often witty, but in the quick recognition of her eyes, in the living quality of her voice itself" (70). Around Niel in Sweet Water is decline, and he cannot help but be drawn to the lady who fights the common sense of defeat with a sense of triumph, or whose spirit at least is undaunted by it all. She is known through joy. You "felt you were getting on with her" (71) when she laughed. Sadness is alien to Mrs. Forrester's disposition. The suave scale reaches the highest pitch when Niel prepares a bouquet of roses for "a lovely lady" (85), his offering to Mrs. Forrester who has grown into "an aesthetic ideal" (87) for the young man. The scale graduates no higher. One summer morning, he gathers a bouquet, intending to leave it outside her bedroom window; and at the moment when he is, in effect, leaving an offering on the altar, Niel hears two laughs that tell him Mrs. Forrester has a lover, Frank Ellinger, a guest of the Forresters from Denver. "This day saw the end of that admiration and loyalty that had been like a bloom on his existence. He could never recapture it. It was gone, like the morning freshness of the flowers" (86). As it was sound which attracted him to Mrs. Forrester, it is sound which causes his disaffection. He hears her "soft laughter; impatient, indulgent, teasing, eager. Then another laugh, very different, a man's. And it was fat and lazy,—ended in something like a yawn" (86). Niel discovers Mrs. Forrester's infidelity in June; in August he leaves Sweet Water for college. He defers bidding farewell to the Forresters until the day before departing for Boston. The visit is capped with one of several toasts to ambition, old and new, in the novel— "'Happy days!'" As on similar occasions, the glasses are filled with ceremony. The Forresters' personal interest in his career is flattering, but Niel is disquieted by his awareness that circumstances have domesticated these two admired friends into an old country couple. The Captain has suffered a stroke and has lost his fortune in the failure of a bank of which he was an officer. And there remains the painful knowledge of Ellinger's involvement with the Captain's wife. The account of Niel's departure from the Forrester place at the end of Part One dramatizes the ambivalence of feeling. He is descending the hill, and the downward direction underlines the still greater change in fortune that is forthcoming and the falling course of the suave scale. "He went down the hill touched and happy. As he passed over the bridge his spirits suddenly fell. Would that chilling doubt always lie in wait for him, down there in the mud, where he had thrown his roses one morning?" (100)

Part Two shows the scale's descending order, the fading away of Niel's emotional involvement with Lady Forrester. Two years in Boston allow Niel to recover a more balanced view. Now he is less a devout admirer than a guardian. As Marian Forrester becomes associated with crooked speculations, as she loses her public poise and reputation, and as she places her confidence in Ivy Peters, Sweet Water's roué and specialist in shady deals, she inevitably draws away from Niel whose sympathies are with another social and moral order. Again Niel's investing sounds with psychological meaning gives aural emphasis to his attitude. The lady's laughter is diminished to "something nervous and excited" when, for example, she must respond to Peters' presumptuous, indecent story. And

Ivy's farm-hand "guffaw" (119) reminds Niel of the coarseness engulfing Mrs. Forrester and, naturally, lowers the scale still another tone. In the final chapter Niel, leaving an altogether embarrassing dinner at which Mrs. Forrester has entertained Ivy and his friends, again descends from the Forresters' place. The parallel with his departure two years earlier is clear, as is the sounding of the final note of the falling scale.

> Niel went down the hill. "For the last time," he said, as he crossed the bridge in the evening light, "for the last time." (170)

He leaves Sweet Water with chagrin. Years later, after the wound to his vanity heals, Niel thinks of Marian Forrester with a certain warmth but without passion and not without reference to her husband from whom she now takes identity in Niel's memory. "Daniel Forrester's widow" is but "a bright, impersonal memory" (171). The suave scale returns to its first muted note, struck now in a pitch of nostalgia, not anticipation. *A Lost Lady* ends in the same mood of detachment it started with. As generalized time at the start gradually condenses to the fictive present, the time at the end rapidly skips through the years to widen the narrative range. The effect is to open both ends of the novel. By degrees Niel's attitude grows from disinterested awe to reverence and then diminishes from contempt to disinterest. The mnemonic scale opens softly, rises, falls, vanishes.

The significance of the suave scale is revealed not in the thematic flow but in the function of Niel Herbert as a medium for Cather's own emotion. Her announced intention in *A Lost Lady*, quoted in part at the beginning of this chapter, makes clear that she was principally concerned with an impression and with a suitable refractor for the impression. Character analysis or story in any conventional novelistic sense were outside her plan. The vocal pattern which Niel discerns when he hears her in his uncle's office acts as an aesthetic control to duplicate the effect which the novelist recalls from the past. The portrait of Marian Forrester is synchronized by events which shape Niel's attitude. More than a principal of selection, the suave scale amounts to a metaphor for perception. It is a way, in this instance Willa Cather's true way, of observing the heroine. Again, one recognizes in this metaphor a peculiarly Catherian approach to language and to novelistic form through aural experience. We hear Marian Forrester more than we see her, just as Niel frequently hears more about her than he learns directly when he is with her. But Willa Cather's tendency to order fiction according to a rhythmic design is already familiar. What does require special emphasis is the freshness of form in *A Lost Lady* and the new potentiality which the author's strong music sense opens up.

II

Simply as an organizing principle the scale would tell us more about Cather's conception of *A Lost Lady* than about the book's artistic power. It is typical of the aural participation to which the reader is invited that Cather develops Mrs. Forrester's "musical laugh" into a fading anthem for a lost era. And the subtle musical appeal strongly enhances the verisimilitude which Cather achieves.

There are two worlds, two times and places, in *A Lost Lady*, but we are exposed only to one. The linear action occurs in "the discouraged town of Sweet Water" (144), which in the development of "'our great West'" (10) briefly contributed its energy but failed to live up to its promise. Crop failures broke the farmers' spirit. The town becomes a whistle stop on the Burlington. The only enthusiasm is shown by hustlers like Ivy Peters whose energy builds nothing but greed. To live in Sweet Water is to live in failure.

The other world is known by inference. It is the world of men who dreamed a railroad across half a continent. It belongs to the past. The citizens are mainly railroad aristocrats, men who generated the creative force behind the westward movement. To have lived in this world is to have shared in a dream. Repeatedly Niel refers to the age in phrases which distance it from the fictive present: "then," "those days," "the old days." The separation between the two eras acts as a measurement of the values in both. Niel tests the standards of the present against the values of the past. Hospitality, dress, economics, manners, all of Niel's concerns are judged in this way. We come to know the past as Niel does, indirectly through Captain Forrester's stories and style and through Marian Forrester's voice. Her laugh communicates the vibrant quality of the past, the past "caught in the very behaviour of living" (81). "And never elsewhere had he heard anything like her inviting, musical laugh, that was like the distant measures of dance music, heard through opening and shutting doors" (41–42).

Dance music appropriately represents the beauty and vitality which distinguish Mrs. Forrester from other women. In the society of her natural preference dancing was a grace and a freedom. Complaining to Niel about the stagnation of Sweet Water and about the prospect of spending a winter in Nebraska, she says: "'You see there is nothing for me to do. I get no exercise. I don't skate . . . . I've always danced in the winter, there's plenty of dancing at Colorado Springs'" (77). Even in Sweet Water her elegant dinners include dancing, though again it is part of the antecedent action of the novel, that is, before Niel knew her. When Mr. Dalzell, a railroad tycoon, tries to cheer her with an invitation to "'the Springs, for a change of air'" (96), he gladdens her by saying he will report to her interested friends that even in distress she looks "'like [she] were going to lead the ball tonight'" (96). Two years later she tells Niel that her visit with the Dalzells confirmed her feeling that great experience is still within her range. She measures her capacity for excitement by dancing. "'I could dance all night and not feel tired'" (125). Finally, her rarest trait and strongest determination are synonymous with music. "'I shall dance till I'm eighty . . . . I'll be the waltzing grandmother! It's good for me, I need it'" (77).

Dancing, elegant friends, and activity are alluded to but not dramatized. Instead, Cather portrays the lady who will dance until she is eighty rigidly seated at a table playing whist with the Captain, Judge Pommeroy, and Niel. She certainly has "'come down in the world like the rest'" (104–105). The light, spinning dance steps have stiffened into weighty stasis. The sclerotic effect of Sweet Water which Marian Forrester feels and resists is most evident in her husband. The romantic adventurer "looked like an old tree walking" (115). The less visible form of spiritual stoppage in the town shows up in the moral calcification of Ivy Peters, which does, by the way, affect the lady. A weak person might grow old graciously (as Niel prefers Mrs. Forrester to). In one whose power to savor life has been cultivated, the interdictions of Sweet Water do not arrest the desire to live; they arouse it. Restriction also makes the lady vulnerable to attractions inferior to her nature because little else has any pull. Eventually this spirit within her takes flight; Marian Forrester goes to South America from which reports tell that her laugh "'hadn't changed a particle'" (173).

Niel's curiosity about the lady centers on her tie with history. While she kept faith with the manner of the past, she brought to Niel history in living form. When young, Niel cares very much for Marian Forrester as a person, but essentially he is interested in her because she married one of the men who made history. When that pact with the Captain and history is broken, Niel's attention diminishes. Like her laugh, her personality fades into the silence of indifference. She seems a mere symbol of life, something airy which briefly touched the Nebraska plains. It is the prairie phase of her career which is assigned musical meaning. Music suggests a quality and style of life which remain unspecified, just as the pulse behind the age is not defined; but the music is unmistakable. Niel hears it in the accents of regret after Cyrus Dalzell tells Marian Forrester that winter life in Colorado was dull without her.

> Tears flashed into her eyes. "That's very dear of you. It's sweet to be remembered when one is away." In her voice there was the heartbreaking sweetness one sometimes hears in lovely, gentle old songs. (97)

While her voice is warm and inviting Niel can be confident that some trace of happy days remains and that the dreams which pushed railroads across mountains linger. The young man cannot name what he appreciates. The heroic moment comes to him sensuously in an attitude, a dinner, a dance, a smile. The ineffability of Niel's response accounts for his seizing upon Mrs. Forrester's voice as the telling figure for a dying epoch. Her laughter "often told you a great deal that was both too direct and too elusive for words" (71). Cather wants to stress the sensory pleasure of the experience. Either one encounters such vitality firsthand or one never knows it. What is really interesting about that *esprit* is not known vicariously; the "idea" of that life is meaningless. The feel of it is what counts. And once the original source of appeal is gone, the pleasure of it ends. The conduct of sound acts as a paradigm for Niel's experience. If there is no song, not even an acute inner ear can create the real, living phonic sensation. By calling attention to the final undulating appeal of Mrs. Forrester's voice Cather persuades us of the age's end. "It was already gone, that age; nothing could ever bring it back. The taste and smell and song of it . . ." (169).

Two scenes taken in consort exemplify how music implies a world within a world and marks the sonic rise and fall I have suggested as the novel's form. Both are dinner parties. On the suave scale they are diametric, as they are thematically and pictorially balanced. The first inspires admiration for Mrs. Forrester's talent as hostess. "Niel and his uncle were the only townspeople" (43) asked to the dinner for the Denver people—the Ogdens and Frank Ellinger. Despite several difficulties (Frank Ellinger's furtive purposes, Constance Ogden's fatuity, and Mrs. Ogden's plainness), the party succeeds. One understands Mrs. Forrester's social context in the old days to have been more lively and impressive; but the situation is not so hopeless that people do not enjoy themselves.

The guests are appreciative and they observe a common decorum. But the party is a spectral version of the old fellowship. The diamond necklace against Mrs. Ogden's wrinkled throat and "bluish brown skin" (44) suggests the unstable relationship between the mode of the past and the code of the present. Etiquette is ornament. Also, the presence of Constance, giddy and gauchely flirtatious, and Frank foreshadows ruin and betrayal. Obviously the old order is already substantially weakened and run to seed. The atmosphere has a musical quality appropriate to the bated felicity an aging society can experience. The evening ends with Judge Pommeroy's singing "Auld Lang Syne." Constance was asked by the Captain to sing "'one of the old songs'" (57) he likes to hear. Of course, she cannot sing. "'Ah really haven't any voice.'" Of the old songs the one we hear crowns a rising series of references to the perishing past and death. Not unfittingly, the musical hail to bygone days is drowned out by "the Judge's funeral coach . . . lurching up the hill . . ." (57). Mechanical noise and the group's surface hilarity check the deeply sentimental overtones created by the song, but the meaning of this admixture is not obscured. Mrs. Forrester's party for the Ogdens, who are a representative blend of generations and attitudes, is the cup of kindness raised for auld lang syne.

The other dinner is toward the end of the novel. Ivy Peters and his friends are the guests. If the Ogden dinner was a shadow of the past, this affair is a travesty of it. The more Peters plays the gentleman the more offensive the evening becomes. Fellowship has dwindled to foolishness; food has been pulverized to fodder. Not even the immense social skill of Mrs. Forrester can bring "these stupid boys" (162) to life. As she frequently does when severely critical, Willa Cather exposes loutish people to an atmosphere combining the dullness of each person in the group. Paucity of spirit means paucity of mirth. So the meaning of the last gathering is finally revealed in its silence. Where the earlier party, with all its potential awkwardness, had a moment of song, this party hardly manages articulate sound. Mrs. Forrester "was not eating anything, she was using up all her vitality to electrify these heavy lads into speech" (162). Nothing can charge dumbness. In trying to do so, the lady stoops below Niel's sympathy and steps outside his range of hearing. The final report of her South American venture indicates how distant Marian Forrester has become in the interest she holds for Niel. In Buenos Aires she found, we judge, an atmosphere congenial to her delicate spirit.

CHAPTER NINE

The

Professor's

House

Here on earth have we no continuing
place, howbeit, we seek one to come.
Ein deutsches Requiem
Where am I! What balmy air is this that
now I breathe?
Ah! how bright doth seem the blue of
heaven!
The smooth mirror of yon sunny lake
Doth placidly reflect the outline of the
hills;
A white sail skims the surface of the
waves.
How beauteous is the scene.
Ah, this splendid mansion!
This garden on the hill-side situated;
All this I dimly now recall,
Like to faint mem'ries of one's child-
hood's dreams . . . .
Mignon

From the start, both as reader and artist, Willa Cather believed that
the strength of fiction, at least her kind of personal fiction, derives from
simplicity of form. Perhaps because passion was her first interest in art
(and the strength of her own writing), the need for form was intense in
Willa Cather. Form is, for example, what *My Ántonia* is really all about—
giving shape to the past in order to communicate it. Behind even in the
panoramic fullness of *The Song of the Lark* and the scenic amplitude of *One
of Ours*, to cite the most lengthy and conventional books, the reader
discerns a classical sense of form. What is so interesting about the evolution
of Willa Cather's art is the way her long-standing concern for form takes
hold in the tragic novels of mid-career. This control did not come about
by chance. The way Cather sees things affects her fiction, and as she looked
at life more critically the form of her fiction comes under closer regulation.
Plot, for one thing, contracts. As Cather's optimism diminishes, the reader
feels in her novels what the novelist felt during Olive Fremstad's great
moments: that the essential drama is behind the brows. Characters become fewer in number, all but telling details of setting are excluded, and
allusion becomes important in gaining the suggestive definition Cather

wants. Her most finished art has a simple plot line supported by a depth of submerged meaning.

I would advance the relationship between vision and form as far as possible by suggesting that form becomes a repository for faith when the traditional sources prove inadequate. In *A Lost Lady*, for instance, the contour of the narrator's remembrance is more significant to Niel (and Willa Cather) than the subject of the remembrance because he can trust his impression of "that age" of heroic ambition when the age itself is lost and its admired lady a disappointment. In the succeeding novel, *The Professor's House* (1925), Cather's skepticism is more profound. The novel endorses ideals which are nowhere embodied in the narrative present. The visionary Tom Outland is dead, and Professor St. Peter's great work is behind him. The rest of the characters have not set for themselves any goal which would break the heart if not achieved, so in conception they are unsympathetic. There is the Blue Mesa, the kingdom of the soul, but it has been pillaged and is far away. It is now a place of the mind, beautiful but intangible. Where Willa Cather finds it difficult to express the positive values at the center of the novel through living persons or actual places, she is openly involved with form. Form becomes a value in itself. It appears that Cather's preoccupation with the abstract shape of *The Professor's House* follows in a compensatory way from her seclusiveness and rejection of society and its values.

Whatever else she forsakes, Cather's commitment to music holds. The most inventive of Willa Cather's experiments with fictive form corresponds to her most deliberate and sustained adaptation of musical form. "When I wrote *The Professor's House*," Willa Cather said in a 1938 letter, "I wished to try two experiments in form. The first is the device often used by the early French and Spanish novelists; that of inserting the *Nouvelle* into the *Roman* . . . . But the experiment which interested me was something a little more vague, and was very much akin to the arrangement followed in sonatas in which the academic sonata form was handled somewhat freely."[1] Before finishing the novel, Willa Cather told Elizabeth Sergeant that it "was based on a musical form." Though they do not appear in the book, musical notations were part of the original plan. Miss Sergeant recalls two of the requisite three, *molto moderato* for the first section and *molto appassionata* for the second.[2]

1. *Willa Cather on Writing* (New York: Alfred A. Knopf, 1962), pp. 30–31.
2. *Willa Cather: A Memoir* (Lincoln: University of Nebraska Press, 1963), pp. 203–204.

Precisely what *sonata* signified to Cather is unclear.[3] Like most terms which blanket widely varied artistic practices, it can be taken in many ways; and because the term is at once descriptive and proscriptive, the ambiguity is compounded. Moreover, in the allied forms of the term (sonata-allegro, sonata-form, sonata development, Baroque sonata, Classical sonata), it refers to a genre as well as a development; and within both categories—form and development—*sonata* admits unlimited variety of practical observance. From Willa Cather's language it is possible to show her attitude toward the sonata if not her understanding of it. Phrases like "something a little more vague," "much akin," and "freely" imply that she has no precise formula in mind. Since she does use the term "academic" sonata form, she probably does have in mind shape and principle. Whatever her understanding, the principle of the sonata goes back to a three-part design built on contrast. If multiplicity of understanding confuses, it fortunately checks the impulse to interpret *sonata* according to any inflexible orthodoxy and throws the reader back to the novel itself for a clarification of Willa Cather's use of music.

II

Taking the novel as an illustrative definition of Cather's handling of musical form, rather than squaring the work with musical requirements, one sees that sonata describes the experiment in two ways. The novel's rhythm follows the characteristic development of the sonata—statement, development or fantasia, and restatement. Such an arrangement, more accurately, is called the *sonata-form*. While sonata-form refers to the progress of a single movement, it is also an arrangement in little of an arrangement in large because the sonata-form is frequently used in the slow and final movement as well. Willa Cather employs the sonata in both ways. At the same time that the novel's rhythm corresponds to the organizing principle behind the sonata's dynamic growth, the three books of *The*

3. Edward and Lillian Bloom in *Willa Cather's Gift of Sympathy* (Carbondale: Southern Illinois University Press, 1962) speculate that the novel corresponds to the threefold evolution of sonata development and offer Beethoven's Opus 31, No. 2 as a "suggestive parallel." Another commentator, Joseph X. Brennan, in "Willa Cather and Music," *The University Review*, XXXI (Summer, 1965), 258, takes exception to the Blooms' view because "they have unwittingly confused the three-part structure of the first movement of the sonata, properly called the *sonata-allegro*, with the three movements of the entire sonata." He then correctly argues that Cather meant each book to correspond to a movement of the complete sonata. I suggest that sonata is used both as principle and structure.

Professor's House[4] generally agree with the contrasting moods of the sonata's three movements.

Since the structure of the novel bears closely on the use of music, I want to trace the events of the plot more closely than I usually do. Book I, "The Family," states the central conflict: Professor Godfrey St. Peter finds himself alone in a family—in a world, indeed—whose ultimate values are materialistic. The materialism around him takes two unattractive forms. For those with money—his wife, Lillian, his older daughter, Rosamond, and her husband, Louis Marsellus—it is a matter of acquisitiveness—a relentless collecting of expensive houses, furniture, clothes, trips. For those without money—his younger daughter, Kathleen, and her husband, Scott MacGregor—the mercenary mind shows itself through envy. There are those who collect and there are those who covet and there is the Professor. Everywhere about him St. Peter finds an inordinate interest in property for its own sake and an insensitivity to the ideal which even physical things embody, like the history behind the Spanish furniture which Rosie buys in Chicago, the cultural aspect of the family's trip to Europe, or the scientific idea behind the Outland engine which brought the Marselluses their wealth in the first place.

The theme of new prosperity gradually rises in Book I until it dominates. The Professor's new house becomes his wife's sole interest; the family dinners are occasions for money-talk; Rosamond offers to build the Professor a new study; Scott brags about hack poems and "uplift" editorials which he knocks off and which sell so well; and Lillian's attention shrinks to things of showiness and society. The theme finally reaches a climax in the seventh section where the suppressed resentment, threatening from the start, breaks into a hatred between the two daughters which separates them and gnaws at their father's loyalty. Kathleen says of Rosamond: "'When she comes toward me, I feel hate coming toward me, like a snake's hate!'" (85) The action of the following section (VIII) sustains the theme at its high pitch as Rosamond, accompanied by father, mother, and husband goes on a buying spree in Chicago which is nothing less than "'an orgy of acquisition'" (154), as the Professor calls it. For two chapters the theme diminishes before rising again.

When the theme of money returns, it does so in a different way, in a lower key. It is a variation of family finances. First (in XI), the destructive power of money shows itself in speculation. Augusta, the family

4. *The Professor's House* (New York: Alfred A. Knopf, 1959). All references are to this text.

maid, loses $500 in copper stock; and though the amount is small, we know from St. Peter's sense of obligation to make up the loss that the set-back imposes a hardship on her. Then the theme of money's damage and the need for restitution and justice are echoed in the twelfth and thirteenth chapters as Mrs. Crane asks Professor St. Peter to intercede on her husband's behalf. Professor Crane helped Tom Outland develop the engine, but has not been compensated for his work. Now that the Marselluses are rich, he wants payment. St. Peter comes to see how venality touches even those he thought were immunized by a devotion to scholarship. The corollary theme of restitution leads into the second rise of the money motif just before the end of Book I when the Marselluses take the Professor along to Chicago and indulge in another orgy of acquisition. At this point the theme of worldliness and greed fades. The family now goes about preparing for a summer in Europe. Once they cross the ocean and St. Peter is alone with his thoughts, any reminder of showiness and any jingle of change vanish.

Essentially, the rise and fall of the money motif follow the shifts of family affairs. As these doings occupy only the surface of St. Peter's attention, the money motif underscores only a part of the drama. What puts the conflict in sharp focus is not the rivalry among the family members but a higher code of human conduct, an older and higher devotion to the ideal which is now scandalously unappreciated by anyone save the Professor. Devotion to an ideal is the second of two expository themes in Book I. As those around him contend more bitterly for fortune, big or little, and as the essential destructiveness of money reveals itself to him, St. Peter becomes more aware of the importance of a positive commitment to some ideal.

In Book I this counter-theme is subordinate and never emerges through dramatic action; but within the Professor's mind, where the ideal now resides—and where the final drama occurs—it gradually assumes prominence. The intermittent remembrance of the ideal brings into quiet conflict the recollected world in which the ideal was a way of life and the present world in which the ideal has no influence. The inter-weaving of these two themes and the modulating moods of the Professor mark the novel's sonata rhythm.

Willa Cather introduces this counter-theme at the beginning of Book I. First we hear it in a minor key. There is not a direct reference to Tom Outland whose life embodied the ideal. Instead, the ideal comes in the Professor's recollection of his own youth and his pursuit of the ideal.

As he sits in the study of his old house, the idea of moving his notes and books to the new place disturbs him. To transfer his academic belongings would be to yield the small ground on which he has stood victorious. He appears to have sensed all along that the productive period of his life has ended, so he resists a deposal from his center of operations to avoid admitting the truth of his feeling. He is now a recognized scholar, recipient of the Oxford prize for history, but fame brings only the wish to start again. His ideal has gone. The struggle was the thing. His "golden days" (32) were ones of striving and study. When the eight-volume *Spanish Adventurers in North America* was in progress he too had a bright goal. The task's completion (crowned with money from an award) makes the accomplishment meaningless because he has no higher aspiration to replace the earlier one. The theme of the ideal, then, is softly stated at first. Once stated it fades into the background where it always hovers but is not always heard.

When St. Peter and his wife are in Chicago at the opera, the theme again rises (VIII). While hearing Ambroise Thomas' *Mignon*, St. Peter nostalgically reflects once more on his student days in Paris. This "young mood" (94) sustains itself for a short while. In the ninth chapter, where the Professor is back home in Michigan, the twin expository themes come forth in harmonic balance. The first half of the chapter carries us back to France through St. Peter's mnemonic voyage to his youthful hour in Versailles; and the other half extends this journey theme as the family discusses its elaborate plans for a spree in Europe. Willa Cather's juxtaposition here reveals how adroitly the themes are interwoven. The first part develops through nostalgia, in the key of the ideal, and as the same journey motif returns in the second part, it moves through anticipation of careless spending and self-indulgence, in the louder tonality of materialism.

The theme of past glory rises as the Professor's thoughts turn away from the domestic crises around him to Tom Outland, whose pursuit of the ideal paradoxically brought about the family clash. The tenth part recalls Tom's arrival at Hamilton College and the growth of his acquaintanceship with Professor St. Peter. Remembrances of days past relate Tom's vigor and Tom's dream to the family's lost happiness and, finally, the past painfully reminds the Professor of the unhappy present. All of these conflicting impressions depress the scholar. Now Tom is but "'a glittering idea'" (111), as Scott McGregor describes his impression of Tom; now the days of youthful endeavor are gone. After a visit from

Kathleen, who has once again come to complain about Rosamond's hostility, the Professor stands transfixed in the turmoil of present sorrow as if he were "listening intently, or trying to fasten upon some fugitive idea" (132)—the evanescent love for Tom and what he stood for.

The theme subsides as family quarrels take up the Professor's time, but the "fugitive idea" emerges finally at the end of Book I. The Marselluses have departed for Europe with Mrs. St. Peter and the Professor is alone. He muses peacefully about Tom's last years at Hamilton and settles down to edit Tom's diary, a testament of his dream, of self-sacrifice, and of heroic defeat.

The quietly rising theme of Book I becomes a full flourish in Book II in which Cather tells the history of Tom Outland's life and which celebrates the aspirations that informed it. Book II is at once noticeably different and noticeably similar to Book I, and the relationship between the books shows with what originality Willa Cather has adapted the sonata arrangement to fictive form. "Tom Outland's Story" sings of love and devotion, not strife and greed. With this thematic reversal comes a new mood, a repose quite unlike the turmoil in the earlier book. The rhythm modulates from statement to fantasia.

Technically Cather develops this contrast by taking another point of view and by altering the time. Though ostensibly within the Professor's mind (he is editing the diary), the narrative voice is Tom Outland's. With Tom's autobiography we are removed from the present and returned to the past, to a moment of heroic experience, recorded in the accents of valor. These technical shifts have a strong bearing on the symbolic rhythm of the novel because by vivifying the fugitive idea Cather offers firm testimony of a life inspired by an ideal and gives voice to the higher obligation which St. Peter feels. Again, the shift in time back to the past takes the drama entirely out of a temporal order; and Willa Cather shows that the ideal which stirred Tom Outland endures beyond the historical moment and beyond even the Professor's memory. It persists in the immutable human spirit, where all ideals arise and to which they return.

Book II is not just a *nouvelle* within a novel; it is an abrupt reversal of what precedes it. It is dreamlike, fanciful, romantic, exalted. By comparison to the introspective passages of Book I, the only passages which even hint of Book II's mode, the second book is a free flight of the imagination, not only for Tom Outland as narrator but for Professor St. Peter himself. And to the extent that the sonata analogy applies here,

Book II corresponds to the development or, as I prefer to call it, the fantasia, the middle part of the sonata-form.

The fantasia opens with an echo of the money motif, with a poker game where Tom Outland meets his fellow adventurer, Rodney Blake. They become fast friends and decide to give up their railroad jobs and take to the open range, riding for a cattle company. As they set out for cattle country, the theme of beautiful land and freedom arises. Slowly, as they come to appreciate the tantalizing Blue Mesa near which the cattle graze, the theme swells into a rhapsody in Tom's picturing of the Mesa's architectural beauty and aura of permanence. Their painstaking and reverent excavation of the Cliff City on the Mesa brings Tom's tale to lyrical heights as he describes his infiltration of a civilization's mysterious existence. In the fifth part, the theme of a lost, happy world regained continues—not in the high lyrical tone of intuitive appreciation of beauty but, with Father Duchene's historical deductions from their discoveries, in a more assured, rational tone. The sixth chapter sounds the counter-motif of money. Tom goes to Washington hoping to secure federal funds to preserve the ancient city but finds himself in a world without regard for his relics or his ideal. In the seventh and last chapter the two themes coalesce. Discouraged by Tom's fruitless negotiations in Washington, Rodney sells some of the Indian relics to a foreign art dealer. Tom's hallowed city is profanely sacked. The strident motif drowns out the tender strain of ideal love—the sacred vanquished by the profane—but we do hear a brief closing chord:

> I remember these things, because, in a sense, that was the first night I was ever really on the mesa at all—the first night that all of me was there. This was the first time I ever saw it as a whole. It all came together in my understanding, as a series of experiments do when you begin to see where they are leading. Something had happened in me that made it possible for me to co-ordinate and simplify, and that process, going on in my mind, brought with it great happiness. It was possession . . . . For me the mesa was no longer an adventure, but a religious emotion. I had read of filial piety in the Latin poets, and I knew that was what I felt for this place. It had formerly been mixed up with other motives; but now that they were gone, I had my happiness unalloyed. (250–251)

In sum, the fantasia reiterates the themes of the first movement in a different, higher key. Whereas the profane motif dominates in the first, the sacred prevails in the second. As material desires destroy, the first movement takes place within the great destroyer, Time. As one's devoir to the ideal amounts to a participation in the permanent, the fantasia moves outside of change. And yet, the fantasia does more than develop the two expository themes in a joyful key. This history of "youthful defeat" (176) and lost happiness prophetically anticipates the third movement in which Professor St. Peter's own ideals are shattered. Also, Cather's adoption of first-person point of view functions as a bridge between her more expansive, though limited, perspective in Book I and the tight, strict view from the Professor's consciousness in Book III.

The third book, "The Professor," restates the two themes of Book I in personal terms. The domestic tensions are present but in the background of St. Peter's mental disturbance. What disturbs his peace now is an existential sense of life's meaninglessness. His mood is bitter at the beginning and then eases into impassive resignation. Tom Outland's discovery of a transcendent order in the Southwest reminds St. Peter how shallow his own penetration into the historical spirit of "the great dazzling South-west country" (258) has been. Tom's intimate knowledge of its life gives St. Peter a new standard by which to judge his own scholarship, and his work seems a vicarious experience next to Tom's living grasp of the region. The boy "had in his pocket the secrets which old trails and stones and water-courses tell only to adolescence" (259). St. Peter's family, whose frequent letters about European shopping tours he casts aside unopened, has taken him far away from a natural, youthful desire to know the earth intimately. "He was earth, and would return to earth" (265), St. Peter muses, and reflects that the pressure of professional duty and personal association, except for the rare love for Tom, have scotched his chances to live by the original need of his soul. To all he has achieved and loved St. Peter is now indifferent—not regretful, indifferent. When the wind, always bringing a fresh release from drudgery, accidentally shuts the window and blows out the stove, he eagerly surrenders to the possibility of death. But Augusta, the maid, a mediator between life and death, revives him. She brings him around physically and spiritually as well. She, who seems to have accepted death and life with equal assurance and without sentimentality, becomes a living example of how one can live "without delight," how one can learn to live "without joy, without passionate griefs" (282). Though low-spirited, Godfrey St. Peter does realize that submission to accidental extinction is an extension of his bitterness, not a reversal of it or escape from it. He has, at least, the cold joy which comes with resignation. His family will never understand his apathy, just as Rodney Blake never understood why Tom heartlessly dismissed him on the Blue Mesa. One requites faith and friendship in a different coinage from that in which one makes a payment to the ideal.

Book III is clearly not a restatement of the expository themes in any conventional way. As I said before, the themes of the ideal and the material do meet here, but the dramatic representations of the tension are of secondary importance. We are deep within a psyche in Book III. The symbolic rhythm starts with two themes presented in a standard dramatic manner (Book I), moves into a lyrical, quiet fantasia (Book II), and ends with a startling blend of both real and imaginary worlds (Book III). The novel concludes with St. Peter's bitter resignation to a life without happiness. The arrangement departs from the usual procedure of the sonata-form, and this independence from any rigorous plan only testifies to the inventiveness of Cather's experimentation.

III

In *The Professor's House*, as in the other novels and stories, allusions to music reveal the nature of a character and the intensity of a situation. Here Cather integrates music detail with the larger structural rhythm. Each of the three sections has a dramatic pattern of its own commensurate with the mood and meaning of the movement. And collectively the music references heighten the nostalgic tone of the protagonist's recollection.

In Book I music serves as an ironic comment on the domestic drama. On two occasions the Professor hears bells from the Catholic church across the park from his study in the old house where he works. The first time he hears the bells, they prompt a reflection on the envy and greed which have come between his two daughters:

> He would have an hour on his notes, he told himself, in spite of families and fortunes. And he had it. But when he looked up from his writing as the Angelus was ringing, two faces at once rose in the shadows outside the yellow circle of his lamp: the handsome face of his older daughter, surrounded by violet-dappled fur, with a cruel upper lip and ... Kathleen, her square little chin set so fiercely, her white cheeks actually becoming green under her swollen eyes. He couldn't believe it. He rose quickly and went to his one window, opened it wider, and stood looking at the dark clump of pine-trees that told where the Physics building stood. A sharp pain clutched his heart. Was it for this the light in Outland's laboratory used to burn so far into the night! (89-90)

By juxtaposing the music of the Angelus with St. Peter's reflection, Willa Cather underscores the principal themes, sanctity and profanation. The contrast is implicit but effective. Tom Outland's work in the laboratory was a devotional labor, and this is precisely what the Angelus, coming as it does at the beginning, middle, and end of a day's toil, is meant to remind us: the divine direction which creative human endeavor must have. Tom's discoveries embody the direction in the purely scientific nature of his investigation. He sought a formula, not a fortune. The stern faces of Rosamond and Kathleen recall the commercialization and debasing of the young man's labor. Also, the bells, in punctuating St. Peter's work, suggest the scholar's own commitment to an ideal.

When the church bells ring again in the novel, St. Peter pushes his papers aside and ritualistically dines, much as a worker in the field would pause for the Angelus, then pray and have his repast. For all its simplicity, the Professor's meal, gracious without being fastidious, becomes an important event, a civil ritual. So pleasing is lunch that after his chicken with lettuce leaves, red California grapes, and "two shapely, long-necked russet pears" (102), round cheese and wine, his mind returns to his student days in France.

The Angelus launches a psychic excursion leading back into the past, but elsewhere music more explicitly links the past with the present. When the Professor hears *Mignon* in Chicago, Thomas' overture is, for him, "an expression of youth" (93). The "young mood" (94) recalls his visits to the Opéra Comique in Paris and also his early love for his wife, Lillian, a love which as "the melting music of the tenor's last aria" (95) fore-warns us, is waning. The music reminds him of his emotional condition: "The heart of another is a dark forest, always, no matter how close it has been to one's own" (95). Cather is referring to Wilhelm's third act piece about Mignon's love for him which, as Wilhelm knows because he loves another, is fateful. The air runs:

> Ah! little thought the hapless maid, in innocence arrayed,
> What she in her breast now nurtured, would ardent love become,
> And thus perturb the peaceful current, the current of her life, would
>   ere long disturb the current of her peaceful life ....
> That what she now unwittingly nurtured, would disturb the calm
>   current of her life.
> O balmy April, who to the wither'd flowers restor'st their colors,
> Kiss her fair cheek, and a grateful sigh of love cause to escape.[5]

5. *The Authentic Librettos of the French and German Operas* (New York: Crown Publishers, 1939), p. 347.

Wilhelm's last aria brings to light a weakness in the early love between the Professor and his wife. When their eyes meet at the end of the music, it is with an awareness of the aria's message about a fateful love. The music provides the accompaniment for their tacit, mutual recognition of a love lost caught "in a smile not altogether sad" (95), but sad enough.

Husband and wife are prepared for a perception of separateness in marriage by another air in *Mignon*, "*Connais-tu—le pays*," the soprano's famous song in the first act. It is through the response of St. Peter in particular that Cather connects Ambroise Thomas' music with the main ideas in *The Professor's House*. Mignon's "immortal song" (93) brightens the climate of the scholar's mind into spring, to the season of youth and beauty. The voice transports him to *le pays* of lasting tranquility. In the opera *le pays* is Mignon's homeland from which she is cut off, and for St. Peter it is a remote, imaginative place where he might have found himself at home. And by inference, through the picture submerged in the lyric, the soprano's pure voice provides a musical evocation of Tom Outland's Blue Mesa, which in the novel has a symbolic value comparable to that of Mignon's lost homeland in the opera. Both locales are rendered as a sacred abode for the imagination. Like Mignon, Tom is taken out of his land, the Mesa, for all but a brief time; and the music mingles the feeling St. Peter has of his boyhood days with Mignon's description of immortal beauty. The air offers a generalized musical province for all outlanders cut adrift in the world. It gathers together all the yearnings for one's homeland in the novel. As Tom Outland "can always see two pictures" (252) when he looks into the *Æneid*, "the one on the page, and another behind that," so we are to recognize behind the artistic model the specific, personal version. The celebration of this timeless region in "*Connais-tu—le pays*" runs:

> Hast thou e'er seen the land
>
> .   .   .   .
>
> Where the bounty of Heav'n we on ev'ry side view,
> Where ever reigns the spring where the sky is so blue,
> Ah me! were we to-gether
> Yonder, yonder in that fair land, for which I ever sigh,
> 'Tis there, 'tis there with thee I would wander,
> There love, yes, there love and die . . . .
> Oh! 'tis there.[6]

6. *Ibid.*, p. 328.

Ultimately *Mignon* functions in this novel the way so many music allusions work in Willa Cather's fiction—as counterstatement on the novel's action. Mignon finds her homeland at the end of the opera. She finds her true father and, with Wilhelm Meister, finds true love. At the end she is home, and, fanned by the healing and gentle breezes from her native hills, is able forever to banish memories of her troubled past. She looks forward to future happiness. She has regained what she lost—family, love, and country. *The Professor's House* holds no such promise, offers no such romantic design of human destiny. Godfrey St. Peter and Tom Outland remain strangers without a refuge.

For the most part St. Peter reponds seriously to the family rivalries because these issues touch upon the meaning of his relationship with Tom and of Tom's work. Once, when the Professor is in a jolly mood, he sees the comic dimension of their antics. While dressing for a family dinner, he for once looks forward to what is usually an ordeal; and Cather wittily catches St. Peter's momentary ironic detachment in music as he hums a "favorite air from *Matrimonio Segreto*" (106). Cimarosa's spoof of dowries and titilating pacts has no intimate bearing on the affairs of the novel, as does Thomas' opera; but in a way, if one can look at it from afar, it is all an *opera buffa*, this scrapping for money and attention.

Finally, the former happy years which "were really the best of all" (125) have faint musical associations of their own for St. Peter. When his quarrelsome daughters were lively, loving little girls and when Tom's presence was not a source of envy for Mrs. St. Peter, the atmosphere had a musical ring and a warmth. "Oh," muses the Professor, "there had been fine times in this old house then: family festivals and hospitalities, little girls dancing in and out, Augusta coming and going, gay dresses hanging in his study at night . . . and smothered laughter on the stairs" (125–126). He remembers with pleasure the little girls teaching awkward Tom how to dance, and the enchantment the gay house held for a boy whose life was previously so rough. And above remembered joviality the Professor's inner ear still hears a voice, "that singularly individual voice of Tom's—mature, confident, seldom varying in pitch, but full of slight, very moving modulations" (125).

In Book II the music changes. As we leave the world of human folly, there is no need for ironic statement, no need for a musical reminder of a higher world because we are in a richer world. The shift in point of view, really, usurps music's function as a bridge to the past; and the new perspective also precludes the possibility of any allusion to classical music because such a reference, while in keeping with the Professor's view, would be inappropriate in the diary of a youth who is musically sensitive but not musically knowledgeable.

What music one does hear in "Tom Outland's Story" arises from the eternal sound of nature. At first one hears a caged canary "singing away for dear life" (179). The adventure which follows is, figuratively speaking, an extension of this yearning melody, the release of this "beautiful singer" (180) from his cage. To begin with, the reverberations of natural music are thunderous. On Tom's first view of the Blue Mesa, there are black clouds rolling from behind it which suddenly burst into a "growl" (193); and when this rumble subsides one still hears the echo in the earth as "the mesa went on sounding like a drum, and seemed itself to be muttering and making noises" (193). Still later Tom hears a spring welling out of a rock which seems eternally to utter "a soft trickling sound" (209).

References to the earth's music are largely descriptive. Willa Cather does not develop them into a dramatic pattern as she does in O Pioneers! or Death Comes for the Archbishop. More importantly, she conveys the everlastingness of the Blue Mesa through silence. Silence enhances the gravity of the Mesa and marks the perpetual peace in which it endures. At the end of his tale, when Tom is alone, his surpassing experience of the Mesa's beauty comes in the form of an enveloping quiet. There is a gradual loss of auditory sensation (which is a temporal experience) as he intuitively grasps this world's repose.

The absence of sound and motion on the Blue Mesa is actually another kind of music in the novel. The Mesa and the Cliff City which the Indians built there form a sculptured, visual harmony—"frozen music,"[7] as one critic calls the effect. The phrase is well chosen. Willa Cather does link the spatial and temporal arts, as we can see in a column which reminds her readers of Madame de Staël's saying that architecture is frozen music.[8] Tom says that "happiness is something one can't explain" (253). Speech delimits. So, too, with musical sound as a representation of the Blue Mesa's transcendent existence. Sound and conventional music are bound by time, a dimension from which the towering Blue Mesa breaks free. Tom's "happiness unalloyed" (251) goes beyond desire and struggle to fulfillment, a consciousness expanded to take in the physical blue around him. "For me the mesa was no longer an adventure, but

7. Brennan, "Willa Cather and Music," 260.
8. Journal, January 21, 1894, p. 16; collected in KA, p. 206.

a religious emotion" (251). Such a supreme condition lies outside of Willa Cather's application of music either as metaphor or analogy. Any expansion of Tom's intuitive custody of the world in the directions which music takes her fiction would violate the experience. If the mesa city signifies peace, silence, stasis, it also creates a dynamic joy within Tom. His sensibilities are intensely activated, and therein lies the *appassionata* of this movement.

When we return to the present and to the Professor's consciousness in Book III, the psychic shift from lyrical peace to brooding dejection brings with it a different kind of music. As in the first book, Willa Cather provides a song with words, but in Book III the music comes not with ironic undertones but with dramatic directness. The music is recalled just once. It punctuates St. Peter's mind and heart at the beginning of his reflection on the "tramp boy" (257) and his "fantastic" career, and from that point its somber notes resound to the end. This musical association comes as St. Peter ponders the corruption which Tom's great work unwittingly wrought. He hears within Brahms's *Ein deutsches Requiem*:

> Fantastic, too, that this tramp boy should amass a fortune for someone whose name he had never heard, for "an extravagant and wheeling stranger." The Professor often thought of that curiously bitter burst from the barytone in Brahms' Requiem, attending the words, "*He heapeth up riches and cannot tell who shall scatter them!*" The vehemence of this passage had seemed to him uncalled for until he read it by the light of the history of his own family. (257–258)

The relevance of this musical association to the domestic conflict is clear. The commercial engine which the Professor's family makes of Tom's discovery is a corruption of a scientific truth, an ideal. Or, to relate this music reference to the novel's epigraph, the pristine beauty of a turquoise is tarnished by being placed in a setting of dull silver.

Brahms's *Requiem* forcefully heightens the symbolic rhythm of Book III. Tom's diary brings home to St. Peter a lack in his own experience, for at fifty-two he cannot draw upon an early encounter with "the great dazzling South-west country" (258) although he has written of its adventurous beginnings. Tom held its mysterious secrets in his hand. The Professor did not, and does not now. The lesson of his deficient experience weighs heavily on his mind and finally sinks St. Peter into a psychic death, into taking pleasure in the idea of an easeful death. "Yet when he was confronted by accidental extinction, he had felt no will to resist, but had let chance take its way, as it had done with him so often" (282). When he is saved from asphyxiation, he does not have his will to live, just as he did not consciously use it. "He had let something go—and it was gone: something very precious, that he could not consciously have relinquished, probably" (282). Apathetically resigned to a future without certitude or joy, he has, at least, the fortitude which comes from knowing that his work once aspired toward an ideal even if it did not reach the ideal as did Tom's.

There seems to be a subtle logic behind Willa Cather's choice of *Ein deutsches Requiem* to focus the hero's critique of himself and the world. Cather's habit of mind shows itself in two key passages. To the student who asked about the contribution of science to "'human development'" (67) St. Peter replies with the pronouncement: "'Art and religion (they are the same thing, in the end, of course) have given man the only happiness he has ever had'" (69). Tom, the Professor's spiritual twin, reiterates the idea when he describes his aesthetic appreciation of the Blue Mesa as a "religious emotion." What we have in the *Requiem* is an example of their identification of devotional and artistic feeling. This identification reveals Willa Cather's tendency to voice through her characters her own sense of art as a final repository of emotion. The *Requiem* is a most unconventional service in honor of the dead. It is more aesthetic in tone and text than it is ecclesiastical, suitable more for a concert hall than for a church. The text does not come from the mass; Brahms draws from various Biblical sources without regard for liturgical consistency. He fills his work with artistic emotion, placing the music outside of doctrine. The effect is "a sort of funeral ode" or "a sacred cantata,"[9] as several commentators observe. The music has the kind of religious feeling with an authority independent of creed which is in keeping with Willa Cather's view of the kinship between art and religion as represented through St. Peter and Tom Outland.

The allusion to Brahms's work raises another issue. If Professor St. Peter's intellectual pursuits and hard-won fame as a historian have any lasting meaning at all, the drama of the novel does not reveal it. We of course admire him because he grapples heroically with darkness and because Willa Cather implicitly esteems his struggle; but the novel has nothing specific to correspond to our feeling. The *Requiem* does imply a

9. Edwin Evans, *Handbook to the Vocal Works of Brahms*, vol. I of *Historical, Descriptive and Analytical Account of the Entire Works of Johannes Brahms* (London: Wm. Reeves, 1912), p. 164.

higher vision of human affairs which reconciles, for the reader at least, the anguish which St. Peter feels but cannot fully comprehend. The *Requiem* sets forth the brevity of human life and the hope of immortality, themes very close to St. Peter's concern. But where St. Peter fastens on the solemn verse in the third number, Brahms moves on to celebrate the peace which follows human strife. The seventh and last number of the *Requiem* (taken from *Rev.* xiv, 13) runs:

> Blessed are the dead which die in the Lord from henceforth.
> Sayeth the spirit, that they rest from their labors, and that their works follow after them.[10]

This hope is suggested earlier in the Angelus bells which mark the divine aspect of labor, and it comes in the Professor's asking Augusta about the Magnificat. "'But tell me, what is the Magnificat, then?'" (100). She replies: "'The Magnificat begins, *My soul doth magnify the Lord*; you must know that.'" He does not know it, even though Augusta always thinks of "'Doctor St. Peter'" "'as knowing everything.'" Unlike Augusta who accepts justice intuitively, he cannot appreciate that the spirit will rest from labor and the works of men "follow after them." He hears the bitter outburst of the *Requiem* but not the reassuring conclusion.

Actually, St. Peter does gain psychic composure at the end of the novel, and Willa Cather culls the concept describing his state of mind from the *Requiem*. St. Peter "knew that life is possible, may be even pleasant, without joy, without passionate griefs" (282). Shortly following the verse St. Peter remembers from Brahms's work comes this reply (from *Wisd.* iii, 1): "But the righteous souls are in the hand of God, nor pain, nor grief shall nigh them come."[11] What the *Requiem* hopes for after death St. Peter must have to live out life. So he stands. "At least, he felt the ground under his feet" (283). "Ground" implies "grounds," and St. Peter's philosophical grounds are rocklike and solid, perhaps sacred. He stands, as his name suggests, a St. Peter free of God. To paraphrase an inquiry of St. Paul which Brahms uses in the *Requiem*, St. Peter will never know that it is the ideal which removes Death's sting. In the world of gimcrack vulgarities surrounding the Professor, there is no human pattern, no classical form of order. That world he rejects, and Godfrey St. Peter's comprehensive disaffection leaves him in a state

10. Johannes Brahms, *Ein deutsches Requiem Op. 45* (New York: Broude Brothers, n.d.), p. 3.
11. *Ibid.*

foreshadowed by Wilhelm's third act aria in *Mignon*: now that he has rejected the social self and its complicated commitments which he unwittingly nourished, he is back in the peaceful current of his original being. That current obeys the thing in the earth and pulls, not upward as move the Christian churches of his ancestors, but downward into rock as the sacred kivas of the pueblo Indians yearn for ultimate realities by gravitating downward, downward.

CHAPTER TEN

My Mortal Enemy

The holy rites are ended; and from the
    sacred wood
Let every unbeliever go.
When God, in His dark anger,
Shall demand the Romans' blood,
Then from the Druid temple
My voice shall thunder forth.

Norma

My Mortal Enemy (1926)[1] is Willa Cather's starkest novel. Its form is as austere as the author's pessimism is unalloyed, and in its emphasis on hostility and defeat *My Mortal Enemy* stands unrivalled by Cather's other works. Three novels preceding this one are tragic, each ending with some kind of perdition, but compassion smooths the negative shape of events. *One of Ours*, in which Cather's preoccupation with defeat first reveals itself, solidly affirms the heroic idealism of Claude Wheeler at the same time that it criticizes the checks imposed on his aspirations by a war-filled world. Claude is killed in France, but the eagles of the West fly on. *A Lost Lady* also treats dissolution—through a gradual forfeiture of Marian Forrester's ladyhood and through the breakup of the exciting era she represents; but in the report of her admirer-narrator the heroine leaves a beautiful memory behind her and the great venture of railroading is endowed with historical honors. Even in *The Professor's House*, which urges stoicism with a minimum commitment to life, the author's warm understanding of St. Peter's disillusionment offsets the despair of his condition. We cannot forget that life holds no meaning for Godfrey St.

---

1. *My Mortal Enemy* (Vintage Edition; New York: Alfred A. Knopf, 1961). All references are to this text.

Peter, nor can we miss seeing that success does not bring peace but leaves unprotected a deep spiritual emptiness by taking away an absorbing creative effort; still the very intimacy of Cather's portrait of the scholar gives personal meaning to the psychic subtraction he undergoes and the cultural fragmentation he witnesses. We know the man very well and we sense that Cather offers the security of self against the force of decay. Besides, there were his love for an ideal and his love for the idealist, Tom Outland. *My Mortal Enemy* goes further into the darkness of man's condition, if there is any light left at all when St. Peter closes his eyes to the world. In *My Mortal Enemy*, Willa Cather takes St. Peter's despair of finding peace and appreciation in human relationships and makes of it an almost perverse attack on love, the one sacred emotion left to a skeptic like St. Peter. Suppressing her own affection for the characters, she examines human animosity without concession to weakness and without complaint. It is as though Cather adopts St. Peter's imperative to live "without joy, without passionate griefs" in order to test the way things would appear from such a perspective. They are disagreeable, and the chilly objectivity creates a jarring novel.

Willa Cather withholds from the reader more than authorial sympathy for the characters. She provides the skimpiest details of the heroine's life and no analysis of her rather astonishing actions. There is a reticence in the presentation here which levels willfulness and cruelty to common behavior. In a way *My Mortal Enemy* calls to mind the use of the first-person narrator in *A Lost Lady* to draw a heroine with the least amount of detail, but the resemblance is only technical. The relationship between the narrator and heroine in *My Mortal Enemy* has more fear than fascination coloring it. Where Cather develops the narrator in *A Lost Lady* to a degree that he can assess his idol critically, in *My Mortal Enemy* the narrator consistently falls short in her awareness of a woman whose superior nature retains the advantage. The point-of-view character is a pawn in Willa Cather's strategy to preserve the heroine's mystery and impenetrability. Limiting the narrative purview fits Cather's plan for a novel of structural simplicity and technical economy. But "economy" is too weak a word to use describing this novel because it is spare to the point of frugality or even parsimony. The best description of the form is Cather's own: *My Mortal Enemy* is "the novel *démeublé*."

Her description, which is also the best introduction to a discussion of the novel, is given in one of Willa Cather's theoretical observations on her own craft. She writes of the novel *démeublé* in the 1922 essay of that name that "the higher processes of art are all processes of simplification. The novelist must learn to write, and then he must unlearn it . . . ."[2] By "simplification" she means a discarding of all the unnecessary furnishings which have accrued to the fictive form. The novelist, in order to deal only with "the eternal material of art," must abbreviate the action to its most telling moment, subordinate the minor characters to the central ones, and keep the setting unobtrusive and in "the emotional penumbra of the characters themselves." Cather's dictum for the unfurnished novel, which is something of a rigorous refinement of the Jamesian principle of selectivity, calls for a revelation of characters in their "inexplicable presence." Or, to use a figure which would be suitably pejorative to Cather's mind, the novelist must avoid the senseless industry of a tape recorder—a practice which the naturalistic novel promoted—and give only the salient phrase. In chucking out the standard accouterments of the novel, the artist concentrates on the hovering "verbal mood" by working through the positive "thing not named."

> Whatever is felt upon the page without being specifically named there—that, one might say, is created. It is the inexplicable presence of the thing not named, of the overtone divined by the ear but not heard by it, the verbal mood, the emotional aura of the fact or the thing or the deed, that gives high quality to the novel or the drama, as well as to poetry itself.[3]

My Mortal Enemy incorporates Cather's principles for the novel *démeublé*, and her practice squares with her theory. What is particularly interesting for a study of music in her fiction is the way in which music allusion, both as realistic detail and as motif, is retained while so many other devices which served her well before are left out. Music in *My Mortal Enemy* is a good demonstration of Willa Cather's larger conviction that restraint and simplicity create strength. Music all along has gained the concentration and suggestiveness which she now so urgently calls for. With its invitation to the reader to augment action with a melody which the printed page cannot provide, or to extend a snatch of an aria, or in the case of opera to recall a story besides the one before the eye, music is perhaps the best way of achieving verbal mood and an emotional aura. The unfurnished novel is a memorable phrase for an old idea and an old practice in Cather's fiction.

2. *Willa Cather on Writing* (New York: Alfred A. Knopf, 1962), p. 40.
3. *Ibid.*, pp. 41–42.

An examination of music in *My Mortal Enemy* bears out this assertion and also reveals some of the submerged richness which the novel's strictness conceals. More specifically, music offers insights into the enigmatical protagonist, Myra Henshawe, which the foreshortened characterization lightly touches.

II

The story of *My Mortal Enemy* is plain enough. Myra Driscoll, a young beautiful Irish girl, falls in love with Oswald Henshawe, a "free-thinking" German fellow from the same small town, Parthia, Illinois. Over her rich uncle's protestations, Myra marries Oswald. In disobeying her uncle and following her desire she renounces the fortune she was to inherit. They live in New York and prosper, establishing themselves among the culturally privileged in the city. There are moments during their New York years when Myra does not have all the money she requires for a living congenial to the sense she has of herself, and at such times she betrays a hard and punishing nature; but for the most part, the Henshawes thrive in the East. This is the first half of the novel. In the second half, ten years later, their fortunes are reversed. They live on the west coast in poverty, and Myra, having lost her New York friends, is also losing her health. At fifty-five she has nothing and no one but her husband whose presence becomes a more painful affliction than her incurable illness. Oswald becomes, indeed, her mortal enemy, the embodiment of the desire which took her away from ease and happiness. Finally she dies—alone, just as she wanted it.

The uninvolved story is complicated in two ways. First, in keeping with her notion of the unfurnished novel, Cather refrains from analyzing and offers only suggestions. These are presented obliquely through Nellie Birdseye, the narrator, whose name should be taken to suggest undiscriminating flatness of vision rather than comprehensiveness. For half the book, Nellie is a fifteen-year-old ingénue whose report of life and Myra Henshawe is filled with respect for sophistication of any sort. Nellie's view of Myra allows a gain in suspense and numerous ironies, but her perspective also prevents the reader from knowing Myra very well. We are twice removed from the central character, first by the limited view, second by the myopic focus of the vision, the result of Nellie's immaturity. In the second part of the novel, Nellie, twenty-five and well-educated, is a more reliable spectator. But Myra's mind continues to elude her understanding, and ours.

Nellie's sensibility has a bearing on music's importance in *My Mortal Enemy* because it is she who, in referring to musical events and compositions, controls the motif. Music, actually, exists "in the emotional penumbra" of Nellie's reminiscence of Myra Henshawe.

Though all of the music references are part of Nellie's recollected impression of Myra, some are more integral to the assessment than others. Certain strains of music detail define Myra throughout the book, though the key allusion is to Bellini's *Norma*. There are music details associated with Myra's three lives—her Henshawe life in New York with Oswald which she chose to pursue, her Driscoll life in Parthia with wealth and security which she abandoned and which she eventually reverts to in later years, and the period of poverty on the Pacific coast. On the one hand, music romanticizes Myra's eastern world, giving it and her a glow of aloof elegance and rareness; and on the other hand, music intensifies the inaccessibility of the moneyed midwestern life she left, adding a certain ostentation which impresses Nellie. *Norma* gathers these details together and explains Myra's personality, her tensions, decision, and fate. As will be shown, the music associated with Myra combines the thematic opposition between the Henshawe and Driscoll sides of her personality and resolves it.

Nellie Birdseye has a keen sense for the rhythmic patterns of people's action, of place, and of situation. Frequently she communicates her response through musical figure as when, for example, the graceful spouting of a fountain in Madison Square utters the charm of New York City to her impressionable ears.

> I lingered long by the intermittent fountain. Its rhythmical splash was like the voice of the place. It rose and fell like something taking deep, happy breaths; and the sound was musical, seemed to come from the throat of spring. (25)

Music, as metaphor, topic of conversation, or in any form, to the girl is one of the signal indications of sophistication and excitement, the two things Nellie seeks in life, much in the way that books would suggest intellectual activity to another imagination. When she accompanies Myra on a visit to Anne Aylward, a poet friend, Nellie marvels at the familiarity and agitated conversation between the New Yorkers over seemingly beautiful and recondite subjects.

> Their talk quite took my breath away; they said such exciting, such fantastic things about people, books, music—anything; they seemed to speak together a kind of highly flavoured special language. (42)

Music, musical knowledge, and a "highly flavoured special language" characterize the vivacious world in which Myra lives and which Nellie encounters for the first time. Her attraction to music and enthusiasm for it are Cather's way of expressing Nellie's youthful eagerness and sympathetic nature as well as the intimidating urbanity of Myra's world.

Nellie's ear catches an individual's personality through voice. One reason for her sensitivity is a self-consciousness about her own speech. Myra, in her outspoken haughtiness, has made Nellie aware of her "English." "She hated my careless, slangy, Western speech" (38). It is no wonder that a fifteen-year-old girl with a taste for eastern social life and manners but without the accent to match should take special note and even romanticize the cultivated speech of others—especially Myra's. Thus it is Myra's "bright and gay," "beautiful voice" which Nellie makes the telling quality of her polish. She says admiringly and enviously of the older woman: "When she but mentioned the name of someone whom she admired, one got an instant impression that the person must be wonderful, her voice invested the name with a sort of grace" (43). She notices on her first meeting a "peculiar effect of Myra's look and vocative" (43). Whomever Myra addresses and whatever she speaks of are "more attractive" to the adolescent observer. Nellie's awareness of vocal shading brings her to know the other side of Myra's personality, for this "beautiful voice" is a medium for a stinging invective as well as a prepossessing kindness. "Her sarcasm was so quick, so fine at the point—it was like being touched by a metal so cold that one doesn't know whether one is burned or chilled" (7).

This, then, is the sound of the Henshawe world as voiced by Myra: a "highly flavoured special language" with cultivated accents. It is, though, spoken with a forked tongue, the voice of Myra's spirited self and her moneyed New York world. More accurately, this is a collective voice of persons and places. No music allusion gathers these references together; the voice has a general indefinite flavor of civility. Myra speaks in it, Anne Aylward speaks in it, and so do the numerous other "artistic people— actors, musicians, literary men—" (38) who inhabit this splendid world. In short, all of Myra's friends have this "special language."

There is a more truly musical mark of the language. Music fills the New York air in which Myra lives. Nellie associates life in the big city with the Metropolitan Opera (no specific opera is mentioned) and with the presence of musicians and actors at parties. Artistic company as exemplified by Jean de Reszke, who has just returned to the Met after an illness in London, and Madame Modjeska, who is a leading stage star, excites Nellie by giving her a sense of participation in a "nobler worldliness" denied a sensitive girl in Parthia, Illinois. That Myra Henshawe was once a Parthia girl and now figures in a circle of eastern celebrities makes her all the more fascinating to the young western narrator.

The distinguishing quality of this life is its worldliness. That is its brilliance and charm. Its music, though not defined by a specific composition, corresponds to the abiding values of the society it represents. The music is secular. Art, beauty, reputation, jewelry, gracious apartments, and elegant clothes are the appurtenances. For Myra such material beauty and accomplishment are important. Indeed, they are crucial to her. She relies on them because they signify dignity and happiness, without either of which life would be shabby and meaningless. But Myra is by no means a crass materialist. Goods and style are not ends in themselves. It is part of her unusualness that she conceives of life in grand, spiritual terms. Meanness applies to her dealings with people but does not apply to her vision of man. Myra has a lasting faith in the importance of life from which she cannot be dissuaded. That is why she demands a style high enough to suit life's great worth. Something exists beyond change and physical fact, and that is the object of her seeking and the reason for her attachment to material things which suggest permanence.

In a word, Myra is searching for immortality. A yearning for the immortal is explicit in the second part of the novel when Myra is on the west coast, but we also see the same desire for the imperishable in her eastern life. To start with, her search is hedonistic. First she discovers a secular immortality: famous and fortunate friends and valuable things. Art and, through it, artists do not die for Myra. She says, "'How the great poets do shine on, Nellie! Into all the dark corners of the world. They have no night'" (82). Ten years before she makes this remark, she gave Nellie a volume of Anne Aylward's verse. The young poet is dying, but to Myra's mind art has immortalized the soul of the artist.

Myra's faith is partially confirmed by Nellie's recollection of those friends, for the artists do linger in the narrator's memory. Remembering the Henshawes' New Year's Eve gathering, the narrator observes: "Most of them are dead now, but it was a fine group that stood about the table to drink the New Year in" (45). And Myra herself, though she seems to have her mind's eye fixed on hidden things behind the veil between life and death, does pay careful attention to earthly rituals to honor the memory of dear friends. On the anniversary of Madame Modjeska's death, Myra asks Nellie to arrange for a mass to celebrate "'the spirit of that noble artist, that beautiful and gracious woman'" "'here in heathendom'" (86). A sense of the immortal exercises so persistent an influence on Myra that her commitment to people seems determined by their manifestation of some lasting spirit. And this, I suggest, is one implication of calling Oswald her *mortal* enemy in a terrifying deathbed soliloquy: he not only took her from her natural religious and moneyed affinities but he offers no evidence, to Myra, of such a spirit.

Myra's reference to heathendom comes in the novel's second part, ten years after we see her in New York City, and reflects the spiritual change she undergoes during a fatal illness. In brief, she abandons the secular values of her eastern life and embraces the Catholicism of her youth which has a musical signature, too. "'As we grow old,'" the dying Myra says to Nellie, "'we become more and more the stuff our forebears put into us'" (82). Cather underscores this reversion in the references to Myra's maiden name and by emphasizing her absorption by the idea of immortality. As Myra Henshawe becomes Myra Driscoll, complete with Irish accent, immortality is no longer a matter of fame. It takes on a darker intensity of spiritual desire and search for things beyond the grave, and her speech utters the depth of herself. "I seemed to hear a soul talking" (95), Nellie says. Discounting any justice except personal satisfaction, Myra explains her conversion to Father Fay in this way: "'Religion is different from everything else; *because in religion seeking is finding*'" (94). This unorthodox Catholicism is a construct of her abnormal will and, like money, is made to obey her private demands on the world. All her life Myra has sought something rare and enduring; not having found it, she makes the act of searching an absolute. This consummates her longing. Faith in desire, a feeling she has never been without, consoles her in the desperate last hours when a need for immortality intensifies. As Nellie interprets the mood, the soul is rewarded, spared the end of flesh, in the sharpness of desire itself. Desire gives the woman what life, love, friends did not. Poverty, infirmity, and inescapable rowdy neighbors remove the deceiving comforts of wealth, health, and companionship; and Myra sees life's essential hardness and its eternal dimension—just as Lear's loss of kingship and of filial attention permits a clear vision of his folly and of a world beyond.

This passion for the sacred grips Myra and seizes all her emotional energy and meager financial resources. Her precious, hoarded gold pieces are spent for "'unearthly purposes'" (86). Money buys "'holy words and holy rites'" (85), which mean everything to her now. Artistic companionship and social ritual of her other life are replaced by sacramentals—"an ebony crucifix with an ivory Christ" (92), candles, hallowed phrases, sacred ceremony. Sanctity and yearning for immortality are her only realities. She severs her remaining ties to the physical world which has frustrated her continuously, regarding it all inimical and mortal—mortal enemies all. She chooses to be alone with her immortal friends—sacred objects, memories of those with noble spirits, and her desire.

The complex verbal mood pervading Part II, which recounts Myra's fixation on post-mortal things and her lonely death, is set in a Schubert song mentioned at the beginning of the section. Nellie has arrived at an apartment hotel which, in its oppressive closeness and premature decrepitude, reminds the girl of her own affairs—the family's bad financial luck and the dreary prospect of teaching at an experimental college. Amid this dingy, comfortless milieu rises "a voice humming very low an old German air—yes, Schubert's *Frühlingsglaube*; ta ta te-ta | ta-ta ta-ta ta-ta | ta" (58). She identifies the source as an old man humming away while cleaning some ties with an ugly smelling gasoline. The uneasy combination of her youthful ambition and the old man's resignation to poverty, the architectural mixture of new structure and visible decay, and the general ruin and chaos in the city weigh on Nellie's spirit. Schubert's song objectifies her mood. Like the surrounding conditions, "*Frühlingsglaube*" blends opposite feelings. The melody itself is exceptionally beautiful. The musical line is joyous but touched with a delicate languor. If we consider the words (they are by Ludwig Uhland) which come to Nellie's inner ear but are not given to us on the printed page, we can define the emotional aura in which the action is caught.

> The mild breezes are awake,
> They rustle and stir by day and night,
> They are at work everywhere;
> O fresh scent, o new sound!
> Now, poor heart, be not afraid,
> Now everything must change.
>
> The world grows lovelier every day,
> One cannot tell what yet may happen;
> The flowering will not end;
> The farthest, deepest valley blooms,
> Now, poor heart, forget your pain!
> Now everything must change.[4]

4. *Schubert: 200 Songs*, English Translations and Notes by Gerard Mackworth-Young, Vol. I (New York: International Music Company, 1961), p. xxi.

The persona in the song expresses a faith in the arrival of the joyous season though his heart is burdened with sorrow. With the voice in the song, Nellie can take heart and "forget...pain" because she is young. Around her, however, are signs of irreparable defeat. The song is profoundly ironic. "Now everything must change"; and so it does—for the worse. A more appropriate introduction to the wretched conditions Nellie will encounter would be a lament of winter despair. Immediately after hearing "*Frühlingsglaube*" she meets Oswald Henshawe who incarnates a loss of hope. But for all his physical infirmity, Oswald's decline does not forecast the psychic eclipse of Myra which awaits Nellie. Schubert's lovely song is a motto for all that Myra Driscoll Henshawe has lost. She lies upstairs in shadowy silence.

Willa Cather suggests the nature of Myra's new life in earlier references to the music in her great-uncle's life, a life which Myra reverts to. Like the Henshawe theme, the Driscoll motif has an identifiable quality but is not associated with a specific musical composition. The Driscoll music is marked by wealth, sanctity, death, and Catholicism. Music is one of Driscoll's civic and religious philanthropies. Suiting his display of wealth to Parthia's taste, he supports a local band, just as a more knowledgeable man might endow a symphony orchestra: "He bought silver instruments for the town band, and paid the salary of the bandmaster" (12). In death as in life music attends his opulent presence, endowing it with pomp and religious ritual. Nellie recalls how he was borne to the altar "on a river of colour and incense and organ-tone" (18). Just what final egotistical purpose music fulfills for John Driscoll is clear in his parting admonition to Myra after she speaks of marrying Oswald. "'It's better to be a stray dog in this world than a man without money. I've tried both ways, and I know. A poor man stinks, and God hates him'" (15). He buys music and feels cleansed. Music is a rare commodity which glorifies. Also, it publicizes his spirituality. As further proof of escaping "the end of all flesh" (18), the Driscoll mansion is left to nuns and stands as a monument to his spirit. In the sanctuary one still hears echoes of his music in "chanting and devotions" and "the tinkle of little bells that seemed forever calling the Sisters in to prayers" (17).

In regressing to the person she was before marrying Oswald, Myra, like her uncle, yearns to escape the end of all flesh; but the quest which accompanies her embracing the religion of youth is very different from John Driscoll's. For him immortality is vulgarly purchased and theatrically displayed. He bribes and demands, and he dramatizes. "The church," at last, "went to him" (18). Myra sees into a deeper reality. Experience has shown her the destructability and impermanence of material things. Where he invests death with the trappings of life, she divests death of life's props. The spectacle of life has always been "in her mind" (44), not on stage; and in her mind she achieves immortality. Her uncle departs "on a river of colour and incense and organ-tone." Myra ends life in soundless peace facing "the morning break over the sea" (101)—her ashes cast "'in those vast waters'" (103).

III

Nellie only "began to understand a little" (96) of Myra and what life meant to her. Degeneration of vivacity into debility and misanthropy baffles the narrator. Frustrated in accounting for "violent natures" like Myra's which "sometimes turn against themselves . . . against themselves and all their idolatries," Nellie settles for impressions which stand out in her memory. The tale of the strange Myra Driscoll Henshawe hangs, I think, on an impression shaped by music, a reference to *Norma* in the first part of the book. When all but two guests at the Henshawes' New Year's Eve party have left, Emelia, "a young Polish woman who was singing at the Opera that winter" (46), consents to sing for those remaining. The soprano "went to the piano and commenced the *Casta Diva* aria, which begins so like the quivering of moonbeams on the water" (47). Though Nellie knows the air (it "was the first air on our old music-box at home") this is the first time she hears it sung and has never since heard it done "so beautifully." The impression is fixed as much by abstract meaning as by aesthetic pleasure. After the soprano's reading, Nellie Birdseye, held in the silence of appreciation and recognition, relates Myra to the Bellini aria. Nellie has had great difficulty understanding Myra and explaining her attitude toward her; but now, when she hears the *Casta Diva*, she suddenly discovers what she has sensed all along. Music, in fact, affords Nellie her most penetrating insight into Myra's personality. The passage recalls Cather's language in describing the unnamed things in the unfurnished novel.

> When it stopped, nobody said anything beyond a low good-bye. Modjeska again drew her cloak around her, and Oswald took them down to their carriage. Aunt Lydia and I followed, and as we crossed the Square we saw their cab going up the Avenue. For many years I associated Mrs. Henshawe with that music, thought of that aria as being mysteriously

related to something in her nature that one rarely saw, but nearly always felt; a compelling, passionate, overmastering something for which I had no name, but which was audible, visible in the air that night, as she sat crouching in the shadow. When I wanted to recall powerfully that hidden richness in her, I had only to close my eyes and sing to myself: "*Casta diva, casta diva!*" (48)

Willa Cather evokes the flavor of *Norma* in the fictive setting—what is "visible in the air." Nellie's anticipation of Bellini's music, once Emelia is asked to sing, strongly colors her description of the occasion. She sees Madame Modjeska, the Polish actress, sitting "by the window, half draped in her cloak, the moonlight falling across her knees" (47) and one is reminded of Norma, rising for her divine invocation, also bathed in the sacred moonlight as it comes forth in full effulgence. Even the music's introduction, "like the quivering of moonbeams on the water," has visual associations comparable with the nocturnal setting in the opera. But the analogy goes deeper; as Nellie says, *Norma* "powerfully" recalls "that hidden richness" in Myra Henshawe herself.

Myra is very much a Norma both in temperament and in the division of loyalties with which she must live. Moreover, Cather's novel and Bellini's opera are thematically akin. Both treat a heroine's reconciliation of the opposing obligations of sacred and profane love.

As a Druidical high priestess, Norma has sworn to ignore physical passion and remain chaste. She violates her sacred vows and falls in love with Pollione, the Proconsul of the hostile Roman forces, and has borne him two sons. Because her vows are to the state as well as to a religious ideal, this profane love is a double betrayal. She loves her enemy. Norma struggles to live a double life-in-love. She pays homage to the Druid god and remains loyal to Pollione. But Pollione secretly has fallen in love with a young virgin, Adalgisa, and when the affair is revealed, Norma's relationship with Pollione comes to a crisis. She can live with fear for her enemy's life but she cannot endure his betrayal of her and his corruption of the young girl. Her first impulse is to kill her husband and the two children he fathered, and then allow herself to be burned for the transgression. She softens, however, and tries to arbitrate by offering Pollione safe conduct from her land if he will go without the girl. Pollione refuses. Norma then confesses her guilt to the Druids and surrenders herself to death. This is her sacrifice to duty and love, her atonement. Pollione, stirred by Norma's courage and devotion, asks to die with her; and together they go to the expiating fire.

Bellini's romantic denouement is not Willa Cather's. But the conception of a strong-willed heroine coming to grips with contending forces within herself and a hostile world outside is clearly at the heart of Willa Cather's creation of her protagonist. At the beginning of the second act of *Norma*, the heroine voices the painful ambivalence of her loyalties, an expression which echoes Myra's complaint:

> I do not know;—opposing feelings
> Tear my soul: I love, at the same time,
> I hate . . .[5]

And in the *Casta Diva*, which is specifically linked to Myra's mind, we are given insights into what is rich, powerful, and fearful about Cather's heroine.

As well as being musically compelling, the *Casta Diva* is a masterly bit of duplicity. On the surface it is a prayer to chastity and for peace. All the while Norma reverently invokes the chaste moon and bids the divine rays to penetrate her life, she is herself unchaste.

> Chaste Goddess, chaste Goddess, who gilds
> These sacred, these sacred, these sacred ancient plants,
> Turn your face to us;
>
> . . . .
>
> Bestow that peace on earth
> Which you cause to reign in Heaven.

What starts as a prayer for peace ("*Spargi in terra quella pace*") ends as a cry for vengeance ("*Non isfugga al giusto scempio!*"). Norma finishes the sacred rites by promising to clear the sacred wood of profane intruders ("*dai profani*"). The Druids plead for vengeance against the Roman occupation forces, especially for the death of Pollione, the Roman leader. Assuaging their ire, Norma scornfully claims her personal power to destroy him: "Yes, he shall fall, I can punish him." But in the same breath she tenderly admits that her heart cannot punish the man she loves: "*Ma punirlo il cor non sa.*" ("But my heart cannot punish him.") Torn between sacred duty and physical desire, Norma publicly reasserts her commitment to the sacred, at the same time that she knows she is unable to keep the vow.

Pollione, before Norma learns of his infidelity, means everything to her. He is her country and her heaven, and for that she will deceive

5. For my discussion of Vincenzo Bellini's *Norma* I have used a vocal score published by G. Schirmer (New York, n.d.). The translations are mine.

and fight, for that she allows her heart to control her head. She sings:

> Oh! my faith, beautiful return to me
> In all your first beauty;
> And I shall defend you against
> The whole world.
> Oh! my faith, beautiful return to me
> Your serene ray
> With life inside you
> And I will have a country, and I will have a Heaven,
>   and I will have a Heaven.

But when she is betrayed, she becomes another person. She can unleash limitless cruelty. Her hard self bids for *"Guerra! strage! sterminio!"* ("War! carnage! extermination!"). Then Pollione becomes for Norma what Oroveso, her father, calls him, a *"sacrilego nemico"* ("sacrilegious enemy") for whom she can feel no pity. In the end, however, love transforms the wicked and the profane. Norma and Pollione atone for their sin and *"eterno amor"* begins *"là più santo"* ("there, more blessed above").

Myra's duplicity and fate take different forms. She too falls in love with her enemy when she marries a man who shares little of her spiritual preoccupation. Publicly she shows fidelity to Oswald and privately she clings to beliefs that he has taken her from. She confides to Nellie: "'Yes, I broke with the Church when I broke with everything else and ran away with a German free-thinker; but I believe in holy words and holy rites all the same'" (85). In returning to those holy values she fulfills Norma's threat to purge the sacred wood of sacrilegious enemies and profane intruders. Myra is a Norma made of sterner stuff. That is her claim on our respect, and that is her fearfulness. Nellie "had never heard a human voice utter such a terrible judgment upon all one hopes for" (95). Her mind towers above "'heathendom.'" Again, that is her self-conceived right to immortality, dignity, and admiration. But her total passion for the unearthly makes us dread her. To her penitential rage—"'Why must I die like this, alone with my mortal enemy!'" (105)—one can add, by way of explanation, a threat which Norma makes and Myra fulfills:

> At last I want you to be unhappy
> Just as I am.

In addition to the spiritual kinship between Norma and Myra, there is a stylistic quality about Bellini's music which allows Nellie simply to close her eyes and sing the *Casta Diva* in order "to recall powerfully" the complex personality of Myra. That "overmastering something" in her, Nellie insists, is "audible." The strength of Bellini's manner in *Norma* derives not from contrapuntal and orchestral elaboration but from a simple melodic line. Even the *fioriture*, the vocal colorings, are functional as clues to mood. The opera is passionate but Bellini's music is simple. He deliberately controls the music so emotion arises from the potentiality of a single line. The effect is a purity of expression and regulated intensity. Emotional content is there in a distilled form. Bellini's way of creating emotional strength explains to Nellie her response to Myra. Her directness, too, covers a "hidden richness" and passion which the final years do not fully reveal. One afternoon at the theater, Myra is deeply disturbed by the presence of a man who failed her husband in an important need. Her remarks are direct and sharp, as they usually are. "'I've never forgiven him'" (44). But the bitterness within is much sharper. "The scene on the stage was obliterated for her; the drama was in her mind." Bellini's style, with an emotional richness supporting a simple melody, aurally images Myra Henshawe's temperament. It is, also, a model for Willa Cather's stylistic intention in *My Mortal Enemy*.

"In the old adobe church stands the bell—

. . . .

Death Comes

for the

Archbishop

Strike it now and you shall hear,
Sweet and soft, and silver clear,
Such a note as thrills your heart
With its tender, magic art,
Echoing softly through the gloom
Of that ancient, storied room,
Dying softly, far away,
In the church of Santa Fé."

From *The Life of Archbishop Machbeuf*

The two ideals which Professor Godfrey St. Peter enunciated before his
students, and which he saw laid waste in the career of everyone near him
except Tom Outland, are the very agents which bring Jean Marie Latour's
life to heroic perfection in *Death Comes for the Archbishop* (1927).[1] "'Art
and religion (they are the same thing, in the end, of course),'" argued St.
Peter, "'have given man the only happiness he has ever had.'" In addition
to a sensitive nature and faith, Bishop Latour has an operative will to make
the idealist's vision an actuality. One incident draws attention to the
creative urgency behind his fine feeling. He rides out fifteen miles from
Sante Fe to show his companion, Father Joseph Vaillant, a single yellow
hill among countless green ones. Latour's early desire as a missionary was
to build a cathedral for the diocese of New Mexico, but the plan remained
tentative until he confronted a golden rock. The religious project required
aesthetic sanction in his mind before he could break ground. His taste
was gratified by the color, reminiscent of the colonnade at St. Peter's in
Rome and of his native Clermont in France, and by the topographical
beauty, inimitably of the American Southwest. Cather makes Latour's

1. *Death Comes for the Archbishop* (New York: Alfred A. Knopf, 1959). All references
are to this text.

sense of place as profound as his appreciation of the important human needs which the locale will serve. His double ministry is shown in his hands. He picks up a chip of the golden stone and regards it in his palm. "As he had a very special way of handling objects that were sacred, he extended that manner to things which he considered beautiful" (241). In his reverent, alert touch one sees the itch of a maker, especially when the thumb smooths the bit of rock.

It is not unusual for Willa Cather to have her characters act out or formulate in a novel a problem facing her in her writing. Projection is a way of working out and justifying an idea (and perhaps the habit of fictionalizing an artistic problem is a reason why she did so little theoretical writing in her later years). Latour's need to discover a substance proper to his concept of a cathedral parallels Cather's responsibility to give her narrative a proper shape. Her terms are the Bishop's: Cather must bring a religious story into artistic wholeness. Two French priests, Latour and Joseph Vaillant, fulfill the mission of their church in the Southwest and are themselves converted to the life of the land. And Cather's handling of the story is with a similar double feeling for the sacred and the beautiful. From paintings of the saints and from a ritual of the church, Willa Cather draws her techniques. As Latour molds the gold stone of the American South-west into a religious form, Willa Cather employs principles from the Puvis de Chavannes frescoes of Saint Geneviève and the Angelus bells in constructing an artistic legend. In effect, form seconds meaning: the novelist composes *Death Comes for the Archbishop* into a fictive mimesis of the hero's genius to unite art and religion.

Two perceptive studies of *Death Comes for the Archbishop* demonstrate Willa Cather's formal success with borrowings from the other arts. Clinton Keeler analyzes the way Cather achieved an intention to write "something without accent," something like "the Puvis de Chavannes frescoes of the life of Saint Geneviève."[2] She borrows visual techniques— immobility, flatness, light, and distance—to render history "not as 'actuality,' nor as anarchic forms within the mind, but as events ordered by a tradition."[3] Looking at the novel from another direction, one closer to the focus of this book, Robert L. Gale suggests that the form corresponds to the pattern of the Angelus.[4] As Clinton Keeler has helped to

2. Letter of November 23, 1927, to the editor of the *Commonweal*, reprinted in *Willa Cather on Writing* (New York: Alfred A. Knopf, 1962), p. 9.

3. Clinton Keeler, "Narrative Without Accent: Willa Cather and Puvis de Chavannes," *American Quarterly*, XVII (Spring, 1965), 126.

4. Robert L. Gale, "Cather's *Death Comes for the Archbishop*," *The Explicator*, XXI (May, 1963), item 75.

explain the spatial arrangement of the novel, Mr. Gale has illuminated its temporal progress. His observation is supported by Cather's propensity to employ aural technique in this fashion and by her specific use of the Angelus bells in *The Professor's House* to show the countercondition to Bishop Latour, that of an idealist cut off from the devotion sounded in the bells.

The Angelus rings in the first book of the novel, awakening Father Latour "after his first night in his Episcopal residence" (42). Now that the dispute with the Bishop of Durango is ended and Latour's jurisdiction favorably settled, he can begin putting "'this Augean stable'" (7) of contending diocesan interests in order. "He recovered consciousness slowly, unwilling to let go of a pleasing delusion that he was in Rome. Still half believing that he was lodged near St. John Lateran, he yet heard every stroke of the Ave Maria bell, marvelling to hear it rung correctly (nine quick strokes in all, divided into threes, with an interval between); and from a bell with beautiful tone" (43). The bells which arouse Latour to work also punctuate each major undertaking in bringing the vast territory into the Church. Cather marks nine such steps besides the prologue. Each in its way gives homage to the Virgin Mary under whose patronage Latour conducts his propagation of the faith in New Mexico. Robert Gale suggests a division of the nine books according to the rubric of the devotion to the Virgin, so he separates the triptych into "introductory, laudatory, and finally revelatory." Taking my clue from the orchard Father Latour plants and carefully tends, I would suggest that each third follows the more organic pattern of generation. The diocese, Latour's great garden, develops from seed, to sprout, into bloom.

The tillage in the first three books amounts to Latour's planting episcopal power where it was wanting. First (Book I) he reclaims the territory from the Mexican clergy who refused to recognize his authority. From Durango, the Bishop and his Vicar journey to Mora (Book II) and bring the sacraments to the Spanish-speaking natives of the diocese. Then Latour ventures westward (Book III) "among the old isolated Indian missions" (82), Santo Domingo, Isleta, Laguna, and Ácoma. The three main groups in his pastorate, the Church authority in Mexican hands, the Mexican people, and the Indians, are all brought under his supervision. The second trio of books gauges the reverse pressure, that of native influences on Father Latour. The interplay between provincial American custom and the Frenchman's Continental manner generate the spiritual growth of New Mexico. In Pecos (Book IV) Latour learns that American Indians can be Catholics only on their own terms, with their peculiar superstitions and mysteries. In Taos (Book V) the entrenched corruption of Padre Martínez and the special liberties the Mexicans take with Catholic traditions convince Latour that the Church must accommodate itself to the demonstrative Latin temperament and go along with what to the European intellectual sometimes appears a tasteless show of fervor. Then in Sante Fe (Book VI) Latour realizes that whatever special directions Indian and Mexican customs give Catholicism, his church includes, as it always has included, educated people of the world like the Olivares family. The concluding set of three books pictures the harvest of Latour's garden. Book VII opens in "the month of Mary and the month of May" (200). The two priests are together and have a rare moment "to enjoy the garden they had laid out soon after they first came to Sante Fé" (200). "The apple trees were in blossom, the cherry blooms had gone by." The territory itself has grown enormously by the Gadsden Purchase. The Cathedral is to be built (Book VIII). It is built (Book IX); the garden flourishes with fruit trees and vegetables; the Bishop reflects on the growing things around him; he dies. The bell tolls "just after dark" (299).

So burgeoned the Diocese of New Mexico in nine strokes. The numerous narrative insets of varying mood, pace, and moral suggest the temporal and spiritual formation of an epoch. The technique shows in montages the geographical expanse of the Southwest as well. By striking a note and passing on without holding it, as Cather described her plan,[5] the action is lengthened while vivified.

Having sketched the novel's movement according to the Angelus bells, I want to go on from Robert Gale's insight to examine the total service of music in *Death Comes for the Archbishop*. Besides fashioning the novel to emblematize Latour's creativity and devotion, Cather provides another pattern of music references to figure the result of the Bishop's genius—cultural synthesis. Above all, the novel honors the emergence of a new Southwestern civilization from various lines of influence. The influence of nature and the different human ancestries have distinct symbolic designs. The intricate exchange of place, people, and traditions occurs, among other media, through music, which expresses a common humanity pervading ethnic variety. Fittingly, in her novel about the founding of a culture Willa Cather uses the symbolic reference that she consistently associates with human warmth and achievement and which, in *Death Comes for the Archbishop*, distinguishes the ineffable character of a heterogeneous yet harmonic culture from those which led to it. Music is the beautifully appropriate voice of the Southwest and its colonists.

5. *Willa Cather on Writing*, p. 9.

II

Father Latour's missionary excursion to the New Mexican territory is mythologically a journey back to the origins of life. The adventure partakes of the eternal return to the center of history or, as Bishop Ferrand calls the Southwest, "'the cradle of the Faith in the New World'" (6). As the first leader of the See, Father Latour will "'direct the beginning of momentous things.'" And he is very much aware of being thrust into something new and unessayed. Conditioned by Europe where the traces of humanity are deep and ubiquitous, his mind catches immediately the different sound and shape of a rough, young world nearly untouched by man. The place suggests antediluvian "confusion" (99) to his orderly imagination. Approaching Ácoma, he looks out "over the great plain spotted with mesas and glittering with rain sheets" and visualizes "the first Creation morning." After saying mass for the Ácomas, he retires to "a naked rock in the desert" and homesickness condenses into a meditation on being out of "his own epoch" and back in "the stone age" (103). From Europe and its great past Latour has come to "a country which had no written histories" (152).

But the territory has the makings of a future for someone capable of bringing medley into coherence. That potentiality is heard in an elemental music of nature which first arises back in the mythic sources which made Father Latour feel so out of his own time and place. When he takes refuge from a storm in an ancient, secret cave reserved for Indian ceremonies, he hears nature's physical music:

> Father Latour lay with his ear to this crack for a long while, despite the cold that arose from it. He told himself he was listening to one of the oldest voices of the earth. What he heard was the sound of a great underground river, flowing through a resounding cavern. The water was far, far below, perhaps as deep as the foot of the mountain, a flood moving in utter blackness under ribs of antediluvian rock. It was not a rushing noise, but the sound of a great flood moving with majesty and power. (130)

The experience of the water sound is gradual and is never quite complete because the noise puzzles the priest. Initially he feels a disturbing vibration in the cave, a hum "like a hive of bees, like a heavy roll of distant drums" (129); but when Jacinto digs a hole to satisfy his friend's curiosity and to ease the priest's vague discomfort, Latour senses a terrible, unknown energy in dormancy. He hears in "one of the oldest voices of the earth" (130) the strength of life, life in turbulence as are all things Southwestern, and life in incipience. Figuratively speaking, the sound of water is the mighty note to which the sounds of other life are keyed.

The simplest echo of this primordial note is in the wind. Wind speaks for the air of a place, and air in Cather's fiction always symbolizes, in addition to natural beauty, a moral atmosphere. Her heroes suffocate or draw in free, cool air, depending on whether the emotional climate encourages or suppresses feeling. As one already knows from the refreshing effects on Thea Kronborg and Tom Outland, the air of the Southwest is especially rejuvenating. In *Death Comes for the Archbishop* the bracing airy current whispers a message of its stimulating power. When he eventually retires, Latour chooses to live in New Mexico rather than return to France precisely to inhale the tonic excitement in the air of the Southwest. "In New Mexico he always awoke a young man; not until he rose and began to shave did he realize that he was growing older. His first consciousness was a sense of the light dry wind blowing in through the windows, with the fragrance of hot sun and sage-brush and sweet clover; a wind that made one's body feel light and one's heart cry 'To-day, to-day,' like a child's" (275). He would die in exile for "something soft and wild and free, something that whispered to the ear on the pillow, lightened the heart, softly, softly picked the lock, slid the bolts, and released the prisoned spirit of man into the wind, into the blue and gold, into the morning, into the morning!" (276)

The Indians live by that morning world. The elements are assimilated into their life in a way that enriches an everyday act with spiritual value. They store secrets in the earth, erect pueblos in the sky, maintain an undying fire, and make clay sheaths to hold water, the most precious of the elements. With the Indian, the universal yearning for something permanent finds its utmost expression in mysterious nature ceremonies and in pantheistic symbols. Such an aesthetic unites beauty and function, bringing art and religion into the highest kind of balance by integrating nature with the human need for form. Indian life sanctifies the earth, which is their beginning and end: "it was the Indian's way to pass through a country without disturbing anything; to pass and leave no trace, like fish through the water, or birds through the air" (233).

Accordingly, Indian music is terrestrial, simple, and baffling. Cather keeps Indian music in the background, just as Indian beliefs remain unintelligible to the white mind; but she makes it clear that their special sound modifies the tone of Southwestern culture. The music is grave and faint, it has a drum rhythm like the subterranean stream. There are the religious dances at Laguna which Jacinto attends but says nothing of even to his friend the Bishop. And in "The Legend of Fray Baltazar," which recounts the life and destruction of a decadent seventeenth-century missionary, the Padre, having killed an Indian servant boy by flinging a mug at him for spilling some gravy, becomes alarmed when he hears the "singing murmur" of his potential executioners. He catches the cadence of the pueblo mind but not its ideas. The hum and buzz of the "rhythmical intonation" (112) closes the circuit of communication to other races.

Cather connects the surface rhythm of the Indian spirit with the sound of nature when Latour enters the forbidding Indian cave with Jacinto. A "dizzy noise" (129) envelopes him and stuns him almost to vertigo. Jacinto leads him along a tunnel into the mountain and digs a hole so the white man can hear the underground river. Latour's mythic sense explains "the dizzy noise" as a reverberation of the deep water, but inextricably part of the "extraordinary vibration" (129) is the talismanic rattlesnake which the Indians have hidden. Its frightening sound apparently comes from "the curious hole" (131) which Jacinto "so carefully closed." During the night Latour tries to get another glimpse of the aperture which held his attention, "but there against the wall was his guide, standing on some invisible foothold, his arms outstretched against the rock, his body flattened against it, his ear over that patch of fresh mud, listening; listening with supersensual ear, it seemed, and he looked to be supported against the rock by the intensity of his solicitude" (131–132). The intermingling of water and serpent sound has strong religious overtones. Latour can make "Jacinto repeat a *Pater Noster*" (131) but he cannot separate the Indian from beliefs which are in his blood and ear. Cather wants to emphasize the intimacy the Indian enjoys with nature and she identifies Jacinto's keen auditory sense with a heightened religious perceptivity. "Their country ... was a part of their religion; the two were inseparable" (294). And just as "'the things they value most are worth nothing to us'" (135), so the significance of certain sounds conveying meaning to the Indian will be imperceptible to white ears.

Father Latour hears Indian music in Navajo country during a stopover on his way to Albuquerque. On the way back from a daily walk, he "heard the deep sound of a cottonwood drum, beaten softly" (230). Retracing his path to the settlement, the priest sees Eusabio, another Indian friend, sitting in front of his hogan singing in the Navajo language "and beating softly on one end of his long drum" (231) and two very small Indian boys who are apparently learning a tribal dance. What stirs the priest's interest is the way some inner rhythm seems to take hold of the little boys (they are four and five years old). Without "a word of instruction" they nimbly follow "the irregular and strangely-accented music" through "flowing, supple movements of their arms and shoulders" and with a "sure rhythm" in their tiny feet. Eagle Feather and Medicine Mountain, as the boys are named, have the tempo of nature. A mere tap of Eusabio's finger or a stroke with a stick ignites a sympathetic body beat which, like the Angelus, through sustained movement becomes as much an aesthetic observance as a religious rite.

If the culture developing in the Southwest remains true to its origins, it will inevitably draw from the soft Indian strain. Though the red man is by nature taciturn and unobtrusive, he succeeds in communicating his identification with the earth to a man like Bishop Latour who can appreciate a sensibility very unlike his own. The wooden parrot, for example, which "had always been the bird of wonder and desire" (87) to the pueblo Indians is not reduced to a curio by Latour. Again, the priest comprehends the Ácomas' choice of rock for their sanctuary because he sees it their way as "the highest comparison of loyalty in love and friendship" (97). His sympathy is noticeable in small courtesies. At Jacinto's, Latour shares a supper of "hot corn-bread baked with squash seeds" (121), an Indian delicacy, and later while on the trail Latour divides his provisions, bread and coffee, with Jacinto. Respect for the Indian fashion of doing things is not condescension on Latour's part, nor is it a gambit to win confidence. It is an artistic discrimination among nuances expressive of deep human attitudes. By ear Bishop Latour discerns the delicacy and form of Indian style. "He had noticed how kind the Indian voice could be when it was kind at all; a slight inflection made one feel that one had received a great compliment" (91). The Bishop's understanding of the Indian voice, his esteem for subtle Indian courtesies, in effect preserves the Indian refinement for the larger Southwestern culture and saves the region from being cut off from the rhythm and grace of its oldest life.

If a bass vocal chant and a cottonwood drum represent the trace of Indian tradition in the cultural mixture, then the banjo symbolizes the other vernacular influence, the Mexican heritage. Both musical rhythms are similarly indefinite, spontaneous, and primitive; but where the Indian chant is mysteriously hushed and remote, the Mexican music is imposingly loud and nearly uncontrolled. There are gentle and languid touches in the banjo, but a strident frenzy dominates the music. Bishop Latour himself, whose tastes run toward the ordered and the understated, finds banjo music "more than a little savage" (182). On one occasion while the French cleric is visiting friends, a "strange yellow boy" appears with his banjo to entertain the guests.

> After supper was over and the toasts had been drunk, the boy Pablo was called in to play for the company while the gentlemen smoked. The banjo always remained a foreign instrument to Father Latour; he found it more than a little savage. When this strange yellow boy played it, there was softness and languor in the wire strings—but there was also a kind of madness; the recklessness, the call of wild countries which all these men had felt and followed in one way or another. Through clouds of cigar smoke, the scout and the soldiers, the Mexican *rancheros* and the priests, sat silently watching the bent head and crouching shoulders of the banjo player, and his seesawing yellow hand, which sometimes lost all form and became a mere whirl of matter in motion, like a patch of sand-storm. (182–183)

To Bishop Latour banjo music is very much the spirit of an undiscovered and untamed country. The unrestrained music calls to the missionary's mind the territory's pressing need for discipline and direction. There are great energies and talents in New Mexico, and there is a great need to give its passion a purpose.

Banjo music, then, holds double metaphorical value: it represents New Mexico's attraction for the heroically adventurous and expresses the powerful spirit of its Mexican first-comers. That temperament, as personified in Pablo, "a magician with his instrument" (178), is, again, a musical one. For all its abandon and wildness the Mexican vigor is intensely human—perhaps exhaustingly human—and such a lusty spirit, so distinctly more assertive than the muted Indian strength, strongly colors the popular culture. The Bishop repeatedly finds admirable examples of spiritual fervor and warmth in his Mexican associates.

There are also those of finer musical perceptions in *Death Comes for the Archbishop*, and through their influence Southwestern life is brought in line with the cultural tradition of Europe. The center of this improved sensibility is the Olivares' home in Sante Fe. Their home is "full of light and music" (180). Presiding over the musical and elegant household is Doña Isabella, a former singer and voice teacher in New Orleans, the most gracious, cultivated American in the novel. She "had done much to Europeanize her husband" (176), and she has done even more to refine Sante Fe. "Pretty and accomplished," she introduces a "lavish style" into New Mexican life. "She spoke French well, Spanish lamely, played the harp, and sang agreeably." Her three languages correspond of course to three of the ethnic components in New Mexico, but the special cachet of her style is music. And her harp, the delicate and complex counterpart of the banjo, symbolizes the varied European traditions which meet in her home and which are shaping New Mexican life.

It is at Doña Isabella's home that Bishop Latour hears Pablo play and it is on the occasion of his playing that Father Vaillant, eager to change the key of the evening, leads Señora Olivares to the harp. This evening she sings "La Paloma" (her repertoire consists of songs in three languages), which is her husband's favorite. It is the "last time the Bishop heard her sing" (186) that song. Don Olivares dies a while later, and Doña Isabella silences the harp. Her deliberate abstention from music is Cather's typical gesture of sorrow. It occurs in *My Ántonia* and *One of Ours*, and in *Death Comes for the Archbishop* the silencing of musical expression signifies the same tragic condition which prevails in the earlier books. Where the Olivares household was once so graciously arranged, it is now, after the kind master's death, in sad disarray: "Chairs and window-sills were deep in red dust, the glass panes dirty, and streaked as if by tear-drops. On the writing-table were empty bottles and sticky glasses and cigar ends. In one corner stood the harp in its green cover" (189). When certain ambiguities about the will are clarified and the wealth goes to its proper heirs, the household regains its old hospitable mood and musical air. It sparkles with "the high tinkle" of the harp and with the sweetness of Doña Isabella's voice. The "'little *poésie*'" (192), as Father Joseph calls Doña Isabella's music, of which the Southwesterners have so little returns with all the charm and verve of its maker. Again music articulates a moral atmosphere, here "that simple hospitality of the frontier, where people dwell in exile, far from their kindred, where they lead rough lives and seldom meet together for pleasure" (180).

III

There is in the territory a musical tone higher than the faint utterances in the wind and the crude sounds of a drum and a banjo, finer even than the charming harp-songs of Doña Isabella. It resides in the educated, Continental tastes of Joseph Vaillant and Jean Marie Latour. In *One of Ours* Willa Cather arms the American liberators with a special musical gift for the oppressed French people; now she has two French missionaries return the gesture with a musical *cadeau* for America. To an imperfect young civilization each priest lends a refinement of personality, and that grace of soul manifests itself in musical sensitivity. Besides signalizing the great cultural drama taking place in New Mexico, music exemplifies the individual human aptitude from which culture is born and nourished.

Father Vaillant is the more openly congenial of the two. Energetic and warm, "he added a glow to whatever kind of human society he was dropped down into" (228). Vaillant's paradoxical nature accounts for his adaptability. Physical frailty contradicts indefatigable energy; coarse aspect hides delicate feeling; gusto and delight in things like food conceal a personal asceticism. Vaillant successfully finds his way through whatever "pathless deserts" (41) destiny leads him. In youth he felt disposed toward a secluded, monastic life though "he could not be happy for long without human intercourse" (227). Social dealings he has in unpredictable varieties among maverick adventurers. The faith he plants seems rooted in the rapport Vaillant establishes with people. They feel free to place a confidence in his love, and trust of this kind accounts for his apostolic success. As might be expected in Cather's narrative of one whose *métier* is "'work for the heart'" (208), "music was a passion" (228) with Joseph Vaillant. Cather says of his first assignment in America:

> The ugly conditions of life in Ohio had never troubled Joseph. The hideous houses and churches, the ill-kept farms and gardens, the slovenly, sordid aspect of the towns and country-side, which continually depressed Father Latour, he seemed scarcely to perceive. One would have said he had no feeling for comeliness or grace. Yet music was a passion with him. In Sandusky it had been his delight to spend evening after evening with his German choir-master, training the young people to sing Bach oratorios. (228)

Love of music evinces a spiritual rareness which the eye cannot see. It seems right that Vaillant's accomplishment not be exclusively visible. The "man of inconsistencies" with "a pleasing tenor voice" (177) confers on his mission a particular sympathy, an ardor, detected by feeling and through direct experience, which churches and statistics cannot memorialize. "Perhaps it pleased Him to grace the beginning of a new era and a vast new diocese by a fine personality" (254). His personality gives new life to Christianity in the Southwest. One of Vaillant's first restorative acts in Sante Fe is discovering a big silver bell in the basement of San Miguel and raising it in the courtyard. The bell is very old (fourteenth century); when its sound is reborn, it rings for his work in the present and it rings for the future.

Father Latour endows the epoch with an equally fine yet different personality. He is quiet, introspective, scholarly. Vaillant brings with him a breviary and the ordinary of the mass, but Latour transports "a large and valuable library" (227). His response to music accords with an intellectual cast of mind which inherently moves from a particular thing to the idea behind it. When he hears or thinks of music, the melody occasions a complex mingling of feeling and idea. Latour has a way of savoring the total appeal of music. Ultimately music goes back to religious devotion which is his strongest need and which unifies everything in his life. One early evening during his first days in Sante Fe, for instance, he sees the brilliant glow beneath the evening-star and thinks of another star in "*Ave Maris Stella*, the song which one of his friends at the Seminary used to intone so beautifully . . ." (37). Music suggests Latour's poetic response to nature and implies a psychic peace, the feeling of a man equal to himself and the world. He hums the hymn and returns to his desk. The music running through Jean Latour's memory is that of a plain song, a free rhythm moving within the limited scale of chant. The hymn is characteristic of early Christian church music. As in the setting of the novel (where "the pale blue darkening sky" doubles, as it does elsewhere, as sea), "*Ave Maris Stella*" is sung at vespers. Specifically, the hymn belongs to the Little Office of the Blessed Virgin which a cleric recites on appropriate feast days. In *Death Comes for the Archbishop* the hymn serves to honor the starred ideal in human form which is central to Latour's mission, the Virgin.

Ave, Star of ocean,
Child divine who barest,
Mother, ever Virgin,
Heaven's portal fairest.

Taking that sweet Ave
Erst by Gabriel spoken,
Eva's, name reversing,
Be of peace the token.

Break the sinners' fetters,
Light to blind restoring,
All our ills dispelling,
Every boon imploring.

Show thyself a Mother
In thy supplication;
He will hear who chose thee
At his incarnation.

Maid all maids excelling,
Passing meek and lowly,
Win for sinners pardon,
Make us chaste and holy.

As we onward journey
Aid our weak endeavour,
Till we gaze on Jesus
And rejoice forever.

Father, Son, and Spirit,
Three in One confessing,
Give we equal glory
Equal praise and blessing.[6]

Like the "*Magnificat*" which Augusta explains to Godfrey St. Peter, "*Ave Maris Stella*" sings of a human heart rejoicing in the magnification by an ideal, Willa Cather's triumphant theme.

On that first morning in his official residence when he hears the heavy bell that Father Joseph unearthed, the Bishop's mind is transported farther back than personal history. As the Angelus plays, Latour's historical sense sharpens: "Before the nine strokes were done Rome faded, and behind it he sensed something Eastern, with palm trees,—Jerusalem, perhaps, though he had never been there. Keeping his eyes closed, he cherished for a moment this sudden, pervasive sense of the East" (43). The intuition is altogether subjective, but subsequently he learns that the mental images closely approximated historical fact. Sante Fe, it seems, owns a bell dating back to 1356 which incorporates certain Spanish adaptations of Moorish traditions. Craft is a small part of the bell's story, however. It has been associated with "'heroic undertaking'" (44) from its initial consecration to St. Joseph in the wars with the Moors to its recent transportation from Mexico City by ox cart. Moreover, the Bishop explains, the devotional use of bells in Catholic services originated in Eastern practices. The Templars "'brought the Angelus back from the Crusades, and it is really an adaptation of a Moslem custom'" (45). The bell has history in its tone. Through Vaillant's labor and Latour's sensitive interpretation the bell becomes the living sound of a rich history taking hold in remote Sante Fe. With the enormous bell the American frontier seems

6. *The Roman Breviary*. An Approved English Translation Complete in One Volume from the Official Text of the Breviarium Romanum (New York: Benziger Brothers, 1964), pp. 154–155 in the Common of the Saints.

formally within the jurisdiction of historical record. The bell tolls the beginning of a new cultural order in New Mexico—an order which reaches as far back in time as "this silvery bell note had carried" (43) Father Latour's fancy.

Latour's sixth sense, which detected history in the bell, leads him to an understanding of the function of art which contributes to the success of his mission. Thinking about the handmade wooden statue of the Virgin in his church and the ornate wardrobe and jewelry the Mexicans make for the figure, the priest comes to realize that peasant craft performs the same service of achieved art: it momentarily arrests an ideal thereby making something higher than man and yet intensely human. Art brings to human scale the ideal beyond human reach. Latour's inclusive aesthetic vision enables him to apprehend profundity behind simplicity.

> These poor Mexicans, he reflected, were not the first to pour out their love in this simple fashion. Raphael and Titian had made costumes for Her in their time, and the great masters had made music for Her, and the great architects had built cathedrals for Her. Long before Her years on earth, in the long twilight between the Fall and the Redemption, the pagan sculptors were always trying to achieve the image of a goddess who should yet be a woman. (257)

In seeing the Virgin as a union of humanity and divinity and the art in homage to the Virgin as a bridge to a transcendent order, Latour implicitly joins art, all art, with religion. Both levitate man's spirit. Through art and religion man gives bounty to God, and the gratification in the act derives from the making of "something to fondle and something to adore" (257) whatever the peculiar form it takes.

Bishop Latour's comment on miracles best reveals the aesthetic keenness of his mind. Vaillant takes a miracle to be "'something we can hold in our hands and love'" (50), but the Bishop does not misconstrue tangibility with the miraculous. For him a miracle is "'human vision corrected by divine love.'" It is a vigorous insight into an identity, an illumination. Religion is a way of seeing the world; it is an aesthetic in the root meaning of the word, a *perception*.

> "The Miracles of the Church seem to me to rest not so much upon faces or voices or healing power coming suddenly near to us from afar off, but upon our perceptions being made finer, so that for a moment our eyes can see and our ears can hear what is there about us always."

His use of an aesthetic vocabulary to define a theological matter cancels any possible division between art and religion, the pairing of which evidences a unified sensibility, as we say. Jean Marie Latour's life and ideas can stand, I think, as Willa Cather's final answer to the problem of the status of art because his work verifies what she thought to be true from the time she started to write but for which she had not before been able to create a proper spokesman. "The world was made by an Artist," wrote Cather in 1894, "by the divinity and godhead of art, an Artist of such insatiate love of beauty that He takes all forces, all space, all time to fill them with His universes of beauty; an Artist whose dreams are so intense and real that they, too, love and suffer and have dreams of their own."[7] The universe as scanned by Latour's mind is an orderly progression of divine art. Man's art imitates creation, or the Art of God. Knowing that man re-creates for himself the great art around him, Bishop Latour does not discount the spiritual importance of even the crudest forms of human art.

So it is that Latour can bring together the diversities of New Mexico and can appreciate the often repeated claims of the Southwest to a pluralistic culture. A Mexican boy says to Latour: "'We want our own ways and our own religion'" (27). Padre Martínez, though he takes the view to the schismatic extreme, rightly insists that the Church relate to the peculiarities of New Mexican life. "'We have a living Church here, not a dead arm of the European Church. Our religion grew out of the soil, and has its own roots'" (147). And the Indians are quite as insistent, in their own silent way. No white man could graft "his own memories of European civilization into the Indian mind" (92). The Bishop does not want to. His respect for domestic custom implicitly encourages the people to be themselves. At the end of his career he takes special pleasure in knowing that the growth of the diocese has not been at the expense of local tradition. He "often said that his diocese changed little except in boundaries. The Mexicans were always Mexicans, the Indians were always Indians" (286). The continued strength of old identities pays tribute to the catholicity of Latour's taste. And his success makes us reconsider the question of Cardinal Ferrand in the Prologue which at the time seemed merely captious and patronizing. "'But has your priest a versatile intelligence? Any intelligence in matters of art, for example?'" (11) Aesthetic awareness of Latour's breadth brings about more than a Catholic renaissance in

7. *Journal*, October 7, 1894, p. 13; collected in part in *KA*, p. 178.

New Mexico. The Church is renewed. On the yellow rock, of that yellow rock, stands the Cathedral.

"'I shall die of having lived'" (269), says the old Bishop to a young priest, and Latour has lived by a dream and has seen a dream fulfilled. And one thing more: he has heard a symphonic emergence of a new life— the oldest voice of the earth, a wind's whisper, a cottonwood drum, a chant, a banjo, a harp, a bell tolling the Angelus.

CHAPTER TWELVE

The Shadow
on the Rock

> Day of wrath, upon that day
> The world to ashes melts away,
> As David and the Sibyl say.
>
> *Dies Irae*

Shadows on the Rock (1931)[1] is without a discernible musical design and has relatively few music allusions. Paucity of music in this work comes as something of a surprise since its conception was described in musical terms by an author gifted in using music in her fiction. The most important sound to be heard in Quebec, where the novel takes place, is the bell at the episcopal church. The bell is also the most important music reference in the novel. Though it does not prompt in any of the characters the kind of reflection aroused in Professor St. Peter when he hears the Angelus played at the Catholic church across the park, and though it does not bind the novel structurally as does the very unusual bell of Sante Fe, in *Shadows on the Rock*, as in *The Professor's House* and *Death Comes for the Archbishop*, the bell symbolizes the cycle of human life moving in harmony with a high devotion.

The cycle in *Shadows on the Rock* runs from October of 1697 to November 1698—with an epilogue fifteen years later—and dramatizes Willa Cather's familiar interest in colonial life, this time in French Canada. The novel opens with an October farewell to the French ships returning home and closes with the November death of Count de Frontenac,

1. *Shadows on the Rock* (New York: Alfred A. Knopf, 1955). All references are to this printing.

Governor General of Canada. The events of this year portray one of those crucial, small degrees by which man makes a home for himself in a strange land. As the first and last incidents of the book suggest, the seasonal frame signifies the end and new beginning of things on the Canadian frontier. The transplanting of a culture is seen through the small domestic acts of the Auclair family. Euclide Auclair, a philosopher apothecary, migrated in 1689 from Paris with his wife and four-year-old daughter, Cécile. When the story begins, he is near fifty, Madame Auclair has died, and Cécile is twelve. Like Mr. Shimerda, Auclair is a gentle city man and cuts a strange figure in a pathless place. But Cécile, like Ántonia, has more than her share of vitality and desire. Cécile's giving form to the new France by preserving the custom of the old France tells the story of Quebec. Her marriage to Pierre Charron, a native-born Canadian who "had the good manners of the Old World, the dash and daring of the New" (172), and the birth of their four sons promise a continuation of her beliefs.

Life on the rock progresses according to the bell. Bishop Laval, the strong-willed, aristocratic (and controversial) ecclesiastical leader of the settlement, himself rings the bell, and its sound shepherds the flock, even the strays, together. First, the clangor from the church expresses the tight control of the man. "The Bishop got up at four o'clock every morning, dressed without a fire, went with his lantern into the church, and rang the bell for early mass for the working people. Many good people who did not want to go to mass at all, when they heard that hoarse, frosty bell clanging out under the black sky where there was not yet even a hint of daybreak, groaned and went to the church. Because they thought of the old Bishop at the end of the bell-rope, and because his will was stronger than theirs" (74). Unfailingly the bell tolls each morning, reassuring the two-thousand-odd immigrants on a rock in a wilderness that their hardship and isolation are part of a divine plan. Special occasions in Quebec are holy days which the bell dutifully proclaims for all within its range. It communalizes holidays and sets the tone of life. On All Souls' Day Bishop Laval,

> was at his post at one o'clock in the morning to ring the Cathedral bell, and from then on until early mass he rang it every hour. It called out through the intense silence of streets where there were no vehicles to rumble, but only damp vapours . . . to give it overtones and singular reverberations.
>
> "*Priez pour les Morts,*
> *Vous qui reposez,*
> *Priez pour les tré-pas-sés!*"
>
> it seemed to say, as if the exacting old priest himself were calling. (94)

And when the wandering Bishop, Laval's successor, Saint-Vallier, finally returns to his parish after thirteen years of absence, the church bells welcome him.

The peal heartens the Canadian pioneers. The religious importance is secondary. Antoine Frichette, who has just told Euclide Auclair of a terrible six days in the winter wilderness, explains what the bell symbolizes for people living on the edge of security. "'A man sits here by the warm fire, where he can hear the bell ring for mass every morning and smell bread baked fresh every day, and all that happened out there in the woods seems like a dream'" (145). The sound means strength and comfort to the twelve-year-old Cécile. "The punctual bell and the stern old Bishop who rang it began an orderly procession of activities and held life together on the rock, though the winds lashed it and the billows of snow drove over it" (105). This inhuman instrument undergoes the same cruelties of nature that the people endure, so its sound acquires a peculiar personality. The bell has the very quality of Quebec life, "hoarse" (74 and 243) and has a "heavy, muffled tone" when the Quebec "air was thick with snow" (105). We are meant to take the bell as the Count de Frontenac does while waking from a dream just before he dies—as the unique voice of French Canada.

> The sound of a church-bell rang out hoarse on the still air: yes, that would be the stubborn old man, Bishop Laval, ringing for early mass. He knew that bell like a voice. He was, then, in Canada, in the Château on the rock of Kebec; the St. Lawrence must be flowing seaward beneath his windows. (243)

The bell does speak for Quebec. Climate seasons the sound, giving it a sharp heaviness; and terrain fixes the course and effects of the sound, allowing the bell, situated at the top of the rock, to reverberate freely through the mountainside. Persistence, punctuality, and religious devotion are the human needs the bell spiritually satisfies. Cécile, a founder of Canadian domestic culture, values the bell for the confidence it gives to those who must begin working as the bell does, in darkness. There are bravery and toughness in the bell. And there are shadows on it too.

I have perhaps unduly emphasized the bell symbolism. Actually the bell calls no more attention to itself than do the other details of early Quebec life. Domestic life—cooking, preserving, cleaning—occupies Cather's main interest. The ringing of the cathedral bell inconspicuously passes into the dense background of daily affairs. Little can be taken for granted on the rock. The community's trust in the bell reminds us that civilized life has taken hold here, but the process has not advanced to the point where the settlers have leisure for such a luxury as music. Giorgio, the Count's drummer at the guardhouse, associates music only with moments of celebration. About to walk seven miles in icy conditions to celebrate a family Christmas, he warms himself with the idea of "réveillon,—music and dancing, and a supper with blood sausages and pickled pigs' feet and dainties of that sort" (109). His grandfather, Giorgio tells Cécile, will play his Alpine horn before daybreak, as he always did. Those in Quebec proper are to be treated to Christmas mass with seminarians singing (113). Again, these occasions are mentioned but not dramatized. Music seems to be an indulgence which a new society only rarely can afford.

In June, 1698, after the ice thaws, when five ships arrive from France with provisions and news, for a few days life is "like a continual festival, with sailors overrunning the town, and drinking and singing in the Place half the night" (209). Reunion prompts music. The settlers feel close to the motherland. During the celebration Pierre Charron gives a supper for his friend, Maître Pondaven, captain of one of the French ships. Pondaven's parrot fascinates Jacques and Cécile, and to amuse the children the captain whistles a song for the bird to imitate. It is "A Saint-Malo," an air which Cécile sings for many months after the ships have left. The song has always meant a great deal to French Canadians because Saint-Malo is the ancient port from which many saw France for the last time. "A Saint-Malo" has strong patriotic implications as well. The first time it occurs in Shadows on the Rock (223) the children's amusement and the French captain's nostalgia explain its presence. When Cécile sings it later that November, winter is about to set in and seal Quebec off from the rest of the world; then "A Saint-Malo" takes on psychological importance. Like Mignon's "Connais-tu—le pays" in The Professor's House, "A Saint-Malo" recalls the beauty and surety of home for outlanders. While the ships can come through the seaway with material and spiritual replenishment from France, the settlement is part of the world. When the St. Lawrence is frozen and impassable, however, Quebec is alone. The song bridges the ocean when vessels cannot cross it.

In the Catherian world the heart too has a home. To these French adventurers Quebec is also a state of mind which, Cather says, "for each of us is the only world" (97). So while Cécile thinks of France, her mind is on life in Canada, perhaps all the more fixed because she must make the days for herself. *"A Saint-Malo"* speaks for her commitment to building life against the great odds confronting her.

Though the street outside was wet and the fog brown and the house so quiet, and though the Count was ill up in the Château, she was not feeling dull, but happy and contented. As she knitted and watched the shop, she kept singing over Captain Pondaven's old song, about the three ships that came

A Saint-Malo, beau port de mer,
Chargés d'avoin', chargés de bléd. (251)

The words of the song are trivial, but the melody and spirit are gallant. It goes:

To Saint-Malo, port on the sea
Did come a-sailing vessels three.
　　We're going to glide on the water, water away
　　On the isle, on the isle to play.

Did come a-sailing vessels fleet.
Laden wi' oats and laden wi' wheat.

Laden wi' wheat and laden with oats
Three ladies come to bargain groats.

"Merchant, tell me t' price of your grain."
"Three francs for the oats, and little to gain.

"Six francs for t' wheat, and t' oats are three."
"And even t' half's too dear for me.

"The grain's too dear by more than half."
"If it will not sell, I'll give it like draft.

"And I'll give it like draft, if it will not sell."
"Why, then we'll come to terms right well."[2]

The importance of *"A Saint-Malo"* for Cécile answers the question Father Hector Saint-Cyr poses to himself when he hears sailors singing in the Place and their mates on the ships answering the song with another. "Why should this particular cliff in the wilderness be echoing tonight with French songs, answering to the French tongue?" (225). The imagination requires a world of its own making, distinguished by the daring that goes into its cultivation. Hardship makes the venture all the more worthwhile.

2. Marius and Edward Sapir, *Folk Songs of French Canada* (New Haven: Yale University Press, 1925), p. 124.

By preserving the ideals which formed the imagination, the new country of the mind "will shine with bright incidents, slight, perhaps, but precious, as in life itself . . ." (98).

Very little of what I have attributed to music in *Shadows on the Rock* arises from a music motif. The words of "*A Saint-Malo*," the only specific music allusion, do not bear in an important way on the dramatic substance of the novel. Music belongs to the atmosphere of meaning here. Willa Cather did not want anything "too conclusive" or "too definite." In a 1931 letter to Governor Wilbur Cross of Connecticut, thanking him for his appreciatory review of the book, Willa Cather explains her intention in this way: "It is hard to state that feeling in language; it was more like an old song, incomplete but uncorrupted, than like a legend . . . . I took the incomplete air and tried to give it what would correspond to a sympathetic musical setting; tried to develop it into a prose composition not too conclusive, not too definite . . . ."3 The novelist admired the way Continental customs were naturally reset in Canada and how old habits provided security for men living in a strange, new land. Behind the cultural transfer she divined an attitude about living capable of withstanding differences in time and place because its values are changeless. The constant impress of such a view of life on a formative civilization is the melodic line upon which the full composition was built.

In Willa Cather's fiction, music generally brings action close to the reader, evoking the act of living and the emotional aura of the action. Fiction which is largely mnemonic in impulse, as Cather's is, requires projection from remembrance to the reader's involvement if the drama is to have force and shading. The Canadian novel is a deliberate attempt to retain a distance between action and reader. The kind of scene which music evokes would bring the past near, too near, the reader's participation. The letter to Governor Cross introduces two words which help explain the place of music in *Shadows on the Rock*. Cather tried for "a series of pictures remembered rather than experienced."4 By keeping music as part of the setting, the "remembered" quality is preserved. Possibly Cather's personal feelings at the time she wrote the book account for the limited use of music in the writing of this period. Her father's death in 1928 and her mother's in 1931 saddened her deeply and quickened an escape into art. In fiction she reconstructed what life had torn down, like the family; and through the heroes she tried to work out a way of

3. *Willa Cather on Writing* (New York: Alfred A. Knopf, 1962), p. 15.
4. *Ibid.*

confronting the fact of death from which she could not escape. The restraint on the use of music apparent in *Shadows on the Rock* is more pronounced in *Obscure Destinies* (1932), a collection of three stories which continue the preoccupation with death and a life remembered.

II

Seated on the sidewalk of Singleton, Kansas, with feet touching a dusty road heated well into evening by a hot summer day, the young narrator of "Two Friends" witnesses a unique event in the sky, an occultation of Venus. The bright planet steadily slides to the moon, then totally vanishes into its circumference wherein the bright star remains lost for some time, fifteen minutes or so. A spot appears, briefly, on the opposite rim of the moon. The great evening star sails free of the moon and takes its own course through darkness. That is all—two celestial bodies meet; but to the narrator it seems miraculous that they should come together before one's eyes. Venus and the moon cross each other's path only once in a man's lifetime. Then blue expanse separates satellite and planet.

Obscure Destinies[5] is about eclipses and such things. Each of the three stories reveals a conjunction and a dispersion which characterize the peculiar course of human affairs. Congenial people meet and move on swiftly—and independently—toward death, the eventuality that gives meaning to the passage leading to it. In the stories a ballet-like movement repeats itself. Polly, Anton Rosicky's daughter-in-law, is initially aloof from her father-in-law; but before he dies they are drawn together. Momentarily their hands meet, then are drawn away. Old Mrs. Harris comes forth from the shadows of the Templeton household to ask a favor of Mrs. Rosen and to accept a kiss on the back of a purple-veined hand. Having known love, Mrs. Harris dies. And the two friends, R. E. Dillon and J. H. Trueman, establish a rapport, argue, and move on to die without the friendship of the other. Three times repeated in the book, this conjunctional movement becomes axiomatic of life. Individual lives chart discrete paths, cross, continue hiddenly. It is the law of nature. The exceptional crossings are moments of love.

Each human concurrence is described with a detached wonderment comparable to the feeling the narrator has when seeing Venus' union

5. *Obscure Destinies* (New York: Alfred A. Knopf, 1960). All references are to this printing.

with the moon; in each tale the breaking away is rendered with a subdued, sad understanding. Darkness of several kinds encloses the meetings of man and man. There is the darkness of our perception; we cannot account for the gift of being able to extend one's hand in love. It is also a physical darkness of setting which throws the bright happenings into relief. "One soft, warm moonlight night" (69–70) Dr. Ed Burleigh drives by Rosicky's grave. The full moon reveals the openness of the field with "nothing but the sky overhead" (71), and "Rosicky's life seemed to him complete and beautiful." Old "Mrs. Harris felt that she and her bed were softly sinking, through the darkness to a deeper darkness" (189), but she passed through the brightness of Mrs. Rosen's affection. In the third story the narrator feels a weighty regret over the broken friendship between Dillon and Trueman wherever "there is a smell of dust and dryness in the air and the nights are intense . . ." (229).

Willa Cather's approach to form in *Obscure Destinies* is predominantly visual. The figure of an eclipse and the volume's title imply a visual perception which the technique extends. The mind of the principal characters is opaque to the reader, their future veiled. They go out of sight as they follow the itinerary of whatever is to come after death. According to her biographer, Willa Cather had the paintings of Courbet in mind when she wrote "Two Friends."[6] The other two stories do not offer a single tableau, but they do leave strong pictorial impressions. (Whether they are Courbet-like is a problem for another critic.) Cather gains visual emphasis by deliberately underplaying the aural. In Singleton the "road . . . seemed to drink up the moonlight like folds of velvet. It drank up sound, too; muffled the wagon-wheels and hoof-beats; lay soft and meek like the last residuum of material things,—the soft bottom resting-place" (211–212). Rosicky, Mrs. Harris, and the two friends are old and near death. The first two especially think about their return to the soundless resting place of earth. Those whose minds are fixed on the cause and end of things are quiet. They are quiet but in no way are they morose. Grandmother Harris, for example, "had the kind of gravity that people who take thought of human destiny must have. But even she liked light-heartedness in others; she drudged, indeed, to keep it going" (112). Cather's pictorial conception of form corresponds to and enforces the reposeful temperament of her heroes. These characters are ties to Willa Cather's recollection of "certain unalterable realities, somewhere

6. E. K. Brown, *Willa Cather: A Critical Biography* (New York: Alfred A. Knopf, 1953), p. 292.

at the bottom of things. These anchors may be ideas; but more often they are merely pictures . . ." (193).

Each story has a center of calm occupied by an old hero who is not far from death. Set around this person are people of various ages very much absorbed in the act of living. Each story is like a solar system with the hero as the attracting center around which family members or acquaintances revolve, each in his own orbit, at his own speed, on his own route. The phase is nighttime, when the sun is hidden from sight and when one sees by the moon. Like the sun, the heroes are overshadowed—dying or dead. The center, again, is silent. As the dying hero is defined by the vitalities around him, so the repose of his mind is contrasted against the vibrant sounds circling it.

Without placing more importance on music (rather broadly taken as aural appeal here) than Cather does, we can see how the aural references contribute to Cather's technique in *Obscure Destinies*. "Two Friends" is the most rigorously pictorial and therefore the least aural story. The narrator recalls Dillon's "musical, vibrating voice, and the changeable grey eye that is peculiarly Irish" (195), but these are fleeting sensible qualities which passed from existence with the man. The meaning Dillon holds for the narrator lies behind physical fact—just after "the last residuum of material things"—when he sat with Trueman "on those moonlit summer nights," "two dark masses on the white sidewalk. The brick wall behind them, faded almost pink by the burning of successive summers, took on a carnelian hue at night" (210–211). Sound is part of daytime and the living; the two friends belong to nightfall and memory.

In "Neighbour Rosicky" the contrast between the still center and the bustling outer world is strong. Music calls to mind the past and youth. When Rosicky was young he traveled a great deal, from eastern Europe, to London, to New York, to Nebraska, pursuing man's usual delights, wine, women, and song. In New York he thought everything was fulfilling. "He often stood through an opera on Saturday nights; he could get standing-room for a dollar. Those were the great days of opera in New York, and it gave a fellow something to think about for the rest of the week" (27). With Zichec, a flutist friend, he spent what he imagined to be the richest life. "They were both fond of music and went to the opera together. Rosicky thought he wanted to live like that for ever" (29). He did not really want to live like that forever. The earth holds a stronger attraction. It means freedom and wide horizons. So he tries his luck in Nebraska. As he matures, Rosicky re-establishes the tie with the earth which he made in childhood. He seems energized by growing things—plants, animals, children. When Rosicky realizes just what he wants in life, his course is away from music and urban excitement toward a quiet life. Rosicky's death is described as total stillness. The peace is so "complete and beautiful" because it fulfills perfectly a need of Rosicky's spirit. "He was a very simple man" (32) who belongs to the earth. Death means "rest for vegetation and men and beasts" (19). When Ed Burleigh visits Rosicky's grave, "a sudden hush had fallen on his soul. Everything here seemed strangely moving and significant, though signifying what, he did not know" (70).

Rosicky's desire for quietude and his preoccupation with silence and death are not indicative of spiritual moribundity. He is vital until death and very much alive to the unnoticed needs and virtues of others. "Rosicky had a quick ear" (27–28) for music, Cather observes. As one expects, he has an equally quick ear for people. A confidence in Polly, though she shies away from him as a foreigner and therefore out of the ordinary, is well placed. The girl is city-bred and "musical" (40) and is discontented with rural tasks and uneasy in solitude. The Methodist choir, where she once sang, offered Polly a social expression which household chores lack. Rosicky appreciates her restiveness. Though secure now, he seems never to forget the ache he felt on that Christmas day in London when, so desirous of life, he ran after "'de Christmas singers . . . a good ways, till I got awful hungry'" (52). He is by nature a man of love who can perceive tenderness in others. "It was as if Rosicky had a special gift for loving people, something that was like an ear for music or an eye for colour" (66). His genius is never heard or seen as it would be if he were a musician or painter. "It was quiet, unobtrusive . . ." (66). You felt Rosicky's warmth in his broad, delicate hand.

Mrs. Harris' mind is quieter yet. She is all but obscured by a ceaseless activity of the younger generations around her. The Templetons are filled with life, as brimming with life as the house is with people: Victoria, Mrs. Harris' daughter, is pregnant; Hillary, Victoria's husband, is so naturally cheerful that he can whistle away vexation; Vickie, their daughter, looks forward to university studies and the future; then there are the twins, aged ten, Ronald, six, Hughie, a baby, Mandy, the hired girl, and the cat, Blue Boy, energetic creatures all. The cumulative sound of all this living is profuse. "Shouting and racing" (87) fill the yard; and blended into this din are Hillary's singing, Victoria's pleasantries, Vickie's exuberances and Mrs. Rosen's "quick pleasant chatter" (97). Sound and music (like Planquette's *The Chimes of Normandy*, which the Templetons attend to distract Victoria from her recently discovered and unwelcome pregnancy) mark the characters' expectancy and their involvement in life. Mrs. Harris, like Rosicky, draws pleasure (even identity) from the enveloping vitality but she is near the end of life and seems to live beyond present events. Her knowledge of what all the various concerns about her mean seems beyond speech. She seldom laughs though she is usually content. "She had the kind of quiet, intensely quiet, dignity that comes from complete resignation to the chances of life" (78). She never asks for anything for herself, neither the rubdowns which Mandy performs nor Vickie's confidence. She has a ripeness of knowledge which makes her compassionate. Everything alive must suffer and everything in life suffers change, the old woman realizes, and she does not attach herself to instabilities. Her wisdom is also her courage. "The kitchen was quiet and full of shadow" (93); in its quietest, darkest place rests Mrs. Harris. Once, only once, she speaks to Mrs. Rosen about Vickie's financial problem. Her appeal succeeds, and she advances life at the moment she is to take leave of life. "'*The Lord is my shepherd,*' was comfort enough" (94) for her. Like Lear she seems to be one of God's spies who "take upon's the mystery of things."

The tranquil presence of the heroes in *Obscure Destinies* signifies a refinement of vitality and experience. The many things they have come upon in their long journey through the world—life, death, joy, pain, nobility, grossness—create a spiritual toughness which takes the form of a soft manner, a quiet benevolence, in relations with others. An allusion to the *Dies Irae* in "Old Mrs. Harris" brings these themes together.

The Christian Latin hymn is not used as music, but the association with one of its numerous musical settings is inevitable. In the story Vickie comes upon the hymn in the Rosens' copy of *Faust*, inserted between the two parts. Whoever left the hymn there obviously was caught by Goethe's fragmentary use of the *Dies Irae* and sought out the full text so he could know the words powerful enough to melt Gretchen's "inmost heart." Goethe alternates the choir's chant with Gretchen's complaints to the Evil Spirit. Music warns Gretchen of the pain awaiting her now that she has fallen from honor unless God spares her. The significance of the hymn eludes Vickie, who is translating it, and its meaning escapes Mrs. Rosen, who is listening to her. For them the *Dies Irae* is a test of Vickie's Latin. But for Willa Cather the hymn carries significance beyond the knowledge of the characters. As at the end of *The Professor's*

House when St. Peter's recollection of a verse from Brahms's *Requiem* introduces an eschatological consideration of man's work, so in "Old Mrs. Harris" the *Dies Irae* underscores a deliverance from life for those who are approaching "noble darkness" (41). The *Dies Irae* raises the same question *Obscure Destinies* raises, man's fate. Again like the stories, the hymn begins when the speaker is on the edge of life. Cather emphasizes that Vickie translates the entire hymn, but we are given only the first verses which announce the imminence of the last day.

> "Day of wrath, upon that day
> The world to ashes melts away,
> As David and the Sibyl say." (107)

What follows is a painfully sincere expression of man's fear of divine justice and his hope for mercy. Exposed to its own malevolence the heart rejects itself as unworthy.

> Thou, whom avenging powers obey,
> Cancel my debt (too great to pay)
> Before the sad accounting-day.[7]

The *Dies Irae* springs from the same underlying assumption of man's double nature which gives strength to Rosicky's moral knowledge. There is the self-denial which Grandmother Harris practices. The *Dies Irae* implies a program for life as comprehended with the knowledge of impending death which Rosicky and Mrs. Harris have achieved. They do not anticipate the exact Christian end of the *Dies Irae*, but they act as though justice can be squarely met. Where the hymn has terror, Cather's heroes show stoical resignation. Where the hymn prays for relief, the heroes expect neither grief nor joy. In responding to the distress of mankind they are alike.

> Well may they curse their second breath,
> Who rise to reviving death;
> Thou great Creator of mankind,
> Let guilty man compassion find!

Finally, the *Dies Irae* points to the undisclosed future of man, to his obscure destiny.

7. *A Dictionary of Hymnology*, revised with new supplement, and edited by John Julian (London: John Murray, 1907), lists over a hundred translations of the *Dies Irae*. I used the one by Wentworth Dillon, Earl of Roscommon, which is in common use and recommended by F. J. E. Raby, an authority on Christian-Latin poetry. The text comes from *The Works of the English Poets*, vol. 8, edited by Samuel Johnson (London: C. Whittingham, printer, 1810).

CHAPTER THIRTEEN

My heart sees its own likeness
painted on the sky;
it is nothing but winter,
cold, savage winter.

Die Winterreise

Die

Winterreise

O! come every one that thirsteth, O
come to the waters: come unto Him.
O hear, and your soul shall live for
ever!

Elijah

Willa Cather's taste in music altered in a way familiar to lovers of music. Her preference shifted from the dramatic and symphonic to the more intimate, lyrical forms, from the elaborate to the simple. In later years, even before she established a close friendship with the Menuhin family in the 1930's and attended Yehudi's concerts faithfully, chamber music and recitals interested her more than did the opera. The refinement of taste in music parallels and probably accelerates the radical change that Willa Cather's fiction underwent in the 1920's. Action becomes structured according to a simple musical line which the novelist felt preserved an essential human rhythm: a "suave scale" to capture the impression made by the heroine on the narrator of *A Lost Lady*; a sonata development to catch the mental tempo of Professor St. Peter; and the nine strokes of the Angelus to synchronize the march of culture in *Death Comes for the Archbishop*.

The music used in these novels to shape plot is a melody without words or ideational content. But Willa Cather's predilection is for vocal music. Song is at the core of her involvement with music. In smaller compass than structure, her use of music up to now depends on the words accompanying a melody. Song combines the appeal of melody and story; and because song is music in breathing, human form, it can express many facets of personality. Fred Ottenburg says in *The Song of the Lark* that "'the voice simply is the mind and is the heart.'" The mind and heart, especially the minds and hearts of creative people, are Willa Cather's subject. Interest in that subject deepens as her art matures. What happens to her use of music as her vision broadens can be seen in the preponderance of German *Lieder* over operatic arias in *Lucy Gayheart* (1935),[1] her penultimate novel. The voice—which is the mind and is the heart—moves from where it augments theme to a position of structural importance.

The narrative line of the novel has simplicity characteristic of *Lied*. Lucy Gayheart, daughter of a watchmaker in Haverford, a small Nebraska town, goes to Chicago to study the piano. There she falls in love with a middle-aged singer, Clement Sebastian, for whom she works as a part-time rehearsal pianist. After a few months, Sebastian sails for Europe; in Italy he is drowned in a boating accident. News of his death reaches Lucy in Nebraska where she is spending the summer. Haverford has always been too small for her; now that Sebastian is dead and all her expectation of a future working with him gone, the town is depressing. She overcomes her sadness and decides to return to Chicago, but she dies before she can carry out her plan.

The novelist's turn to *Lied* in *Lucy Gayheart* represents her final and most daring attempt to endow fiction with the levitating power of music —to create a form that can breathe a living soul, Cather would say. Though similarities do suggest themselves, it would burden the argument to urge that Willa Cather's use of *Lieder* shares in the desire of German Romanticism to demonstrate the underlying unity of all arts and then of life and art; *Gesamtkunstwerk* is not Cather's sort of endeavor. Her range is much narrower and more personal. In the *Lied* she finds the fusion of language and music—meaning heightened by melody—which she sought to achieve in her own work in her own way. In its melodic line the *Lied* has the classical simplicity that Cather came to prefer.

A clue to the contribution of *Lieder* to *Lucy Gayheart* occurs early in the novel. The evening of January 3, the day Lucy returns to Chicago from a Christmas vacation in Nebraska, she attends a song recital given by the great baritone Clement Sebastian. The recital alters her life. In part, she is overly receptive to Sebastian, for tomorrow she will start work as his accompanist. (She was engaged before the holidays to substitute for James Mockford, his regular accompanist). Also, she has heard Sebastian

1. *Lucy Gayheart* (New York: Alfred A. Knopf, 1935). All references are to this text.

once before, and on that occasion she felt that he was different from other singers, though she could not tell why. Now she learns the distinguishing quality of his talent. This discovery, the particular music Sebastian sings, and the artistry he brings to it account for the intensity of her response. She hears Franz Schubert's famous song cycle, *Die Winterreise* (*The Winter Journey*). The reading yields an insight into the nature of art:

> She had never heard *Die Winterreise* sung straight through as an integral work. For her it was being sung the first time, something newly created, and she attributed to the artist much that belonged to the composer. She kept feeling that this was not an interpretation, this was the thing itself, with one man and one nature behind every song. The singing was not dramatic, in any way she knew. Sebastian did not identify himself with this melancholy youth; he presented him as if he were a memory, not to be brought too near into the present. One felt a long distance between the singer and the scenes he was recalling, a long perspective. (38)

The "long distance" between singing voice and recollected drama properly serves as an index to Willa Cather's conception of *Lucy Gayheart*. Schubert's devices such as mixing modalities and repetition, which are peculiar to music, obviously offer Cather little technical assistance in composing a novel, and would be only analogues to fictive art. Still, there are many things about *Die Winterreise* which illumine the artistry of *Lucy Gayheart*—for example, Schubert's treatment of the theme which is identical with that of the novel. Beyond analogy and beyond specific theme, in the large area of response where all art meets, one finds a deep similarity between the effects created by both the song cycle and the novel. The tonal pattern of the whole book achieves just such an elevation as that the young Lucy felt in Sebastian's shaping of Schubert. I want to consider *Die Winterreise* more fully than I usually treat the music material bearing on Cather's fiction in order to establish its connections with the novel. A consideration of Cather's handling of music might also help to counter-vail the recurrent disapproval *Lucy Gayheart* has received even from some of the novelist's most admiring critics.

II

The twenty-four songs comprising *Die Winterreise*[2] deal mainly with the painful rejection of love, and the pervasive mood of both the poetic

2. All translations are from *The Penguin Book of Lieder* (Baltimore: Penguin Books, 1964), edited and translated by S. S. Prawer. Unlike most English versions of the poems, Prawer's are literal and are not falsified to match the music.

text and musical setting is melancholic and nostalgic. The narrative line is spare. A luckless lover become a friendless roamer returns in the dead of winter to keen his loss and express his anguish. The emotional curve of the wanderer's lament dips from sadness and rejection to despair with sudden rises of hope in between. Narrow and uneven as is the range of this emotion, it constitutes the central action of the song cycle. There is a hint of physical change in the singer's solitary tracks across the frostbound countryside, but nothing is made of it. And details of the past love affair remain mysterious.

The journey in winter is so indefinite and the lost beloved so impersonalized that the drama of the poem derives not from a falling out of human love but from a disaffection with all life. The singer is rather like a mythic figure, an Adonis, say, searching for the sprouting of new life in the dead land of winter. The maiden personifies spring; the youth voices the hope for rebirth. The absence of detail concerning the wanderer's past emphasizes his large mythic office. What we know of him comes through his soliloquies, with their protests and requests, which form a succession of states of pure emotion, a sequence of highly stylized romantic attitudes, all of which express the need for regeneration. The sequence has no logical development; *Die Winterreise* amounts to a revelation of shifting moods about life from one long enough deprived of life to feel a special need for it.

Structurally the lamentation creates a double drama. The songs utter the youth's awareness of his present situation, of a life without love, his winter isolation, and simultaneously, as he looks back on his life with love, they express a remembrance of May happiness. The sexual distinction between the youth and his beloved, again, is more generic and ceremonial than human. The alternation between the opposing conditions of bloom and deadness, of spring and winter, is musically stated through Schubert's use of major and minor keys. As a critic explains, "the major mode has the principal function of symbolizing the happiness of the past, while the minor represents the darkness of the present."[3] The imbalanced modality of the song cycle darkens the emotional meaning. Of the twenty-four songs, only seven are in the major key; and even in these joy is edged by sorrowful implications. The bright songs intensify the dark ones. The voice, I should think, must catch the breaking sweetness of hope itself. In the poetic text the manner is identifiable as a Wordsworthian modulation between recollection and response.

3. Alfred Einstein, *Schubert, A Musical Portrait* (New York: Oxford University Press, 1951), p. 304.

The first two songs, "Good Night" and "The Weather-Vane," set the place and establish theme and mood. The youth is back to the locale of his love. It is a winter night, but there lingers a memory of the Maytime love and "a nosegay of flowers" which have passed. "The girl spoke of love," but nothing came of it. Now all is drear. The farewell ("Good Night") is really a lead-in to the singer's emotion. The identification of his psychic abandonment is made with the seasonal cold and hardness. The somber landscape becomes a heartscape. Deflected from his intention to bid the girl "Good Night" by the thought of the disturbance the greeting might cause, the singer broods. Then the weather vane on the girl's house inspirits him as it seems to invite him closer. Invitation becomes another rejection; like mistress, like weather vane—both are fickle.

Mocked from without by the indifference of land and house to his plight, the youth turns within. He finds no relief, but he can articulate his emotional state. The third, fourth, and fifth songs release his yearning. "Frozen Tears" questions how tears that well from the fierce heat of the heart can freeze on the cheeks. Nature is cruelly out of step with man's desire. "Frozen Rigidity" attempts spiritually to dig beneath the snow and uncover the "green fields" through which the lovers walked "arm in arm." The land is dead, numb. How, the youth sings, can one retrieve the vitality that is gone? "Is there no keepsake, then, / that I may take from here?" The fifth song, the popular "*Der Lindenbaum*," suggests that peace is found in the carved memory on its bark.

"Friend, come here to me—
Here you will find rest."

The call from the branches beckons to death, not to joyful memory, as the repeated "rest" in the second invitation implies: "'There you would find rest!'"

Snow as external symbol for grief makes more poignant the need for green life. The youth hopes that tears, like snow, will bring forth new life, that joy will rise out of pain. In "Flood" and "On the River" Schubert writes tear music, not water music as suggested by the titles. The frozen crust of the once "clear wild stream" reflects the "cold and motionless" condition of his heart. "Is there a raging torrent / beneath *its* surface too?", as there is in the desire for new life in man? Unaccountably, the youth's mind turns to spring. The icy prospect thaws into a vision of glowing warmth, of flowering lime trees, of fair eyes afire; but this is "A Backward Glance." The answer comes to his query about the way to regain joy: memory alone transforms pain. Memory transforms pain into painful joy. Happiness is known only in retrospect. "Will-o'-the-Wisp" and "Rest" (the ninth and tenth songs) beg for stillness and direction.

"Dream of Spring" shifts to the major key of "*Der Lindenbaum*" and describes "green meadows," "bird-calls," and leaves. These he "dreamt" but does not have. The ineluctable "dismal cloud" shades the world; the searcher stands alone. With the admission of "Loneliness" come three reminders of isolation each of which comprises a song: the mail that brings no letter, the snow that prematurely ages one's head, and the preying crow that awaits to claim a dead body. "The Crow" marks the emotional nadir of this spiritual quest for life; and in Schubert's characteristic rendering of the idea of isolation, the voice sings in stark unison with the piano.[4]

There follows a "Last Hope." A "coloured leaf" may yet be seen on a branch, and on this ephemeral vestige of life hangs hope. Like a thing possessed in dream, it vanishes. The storm tearing the sky flashes the picture of his state. No longer able to find peace and hope of life in dream the youth surrenders to a "Delusion" that bright things are coming. The light dancing before him proves to be a trick which leads eventually, in the twenty-first song, to "The Inn" of death, a graveyard.

The two songs which follow, the twenty-second and twenty-third, are singularly important for *Lucy Gayheart*. They record images and attitudes which clarify Lucy's own search for life. "Courage" (German *Mut*) strikes a new note—defiance, almost cynical defiance. "If the snow flies into my face / I shake it off." The right to life is insistent, as though the expression of one's claim itself could spite the forces operating against joy and life. "If my heart speaks," the youth is determined to sing its music. The voice of death reaches him but he lends no ear. "Let fools lament!" In two stanzas the song moves from confidence to proud disdain of sorrow and of those who bother to mourn aloud. The third stanza intensifies the youth's pluck into a violent, almost hysterical, declaration of a right to life—in the face of a God who has scandalously ignored his need.

> Gaily on into the world,
> braving wind and weather!
> If there is no God on earth,
> we ourselves are gods!

4. Richard Capell, *Schubert's Songs* (rev. ed.; New York: The Macmillan Company, 1957), p. 237.

There is nothing in his previous experience to warrant the outburst of assurance, and there is nothing explicit to endorse this strong surge of belief in man's super-nature; but there is everything in the music to persuade the listener that the claim is valid. The heart says so, and the heart is the final authority on spiritual matters. Schubert in his music seems to agree.

The twenty-third song supplements the bravura of "Courage." In "Phantom Suns" (*Die Nebensonnen*) the youth sees three suns, observes them for a moment, and asserts:

> You are not my suns!
> Go, gaze into other faces!
> Not long ago I had three suns—
> now the two best have gone down.

The concluding couplet argues: "If only the third would follow them—/ I shall feel better in the dark." The two suns that "have gone down" must be his beloved, or Love itself, and hope, which sounded its own end in the sixteenth song, "Last Hope." The third sun, which still shines but shall soon set and leave the youth "in the dark," must be Life. And though he anticipates the end of life as an improvement of his plight ("I shall feel better"), he has really come to kneel before the mystery of life and commit himself to it. Other promises are deceptive, friendly gleams; life, though its source and pattern remain unknown, requires and receives love. The pledge to life justifies the bold self-reliance and is the positive achievement of the journey.

The last song, "The Hurdy-Gurdy Man," associates the youth's destiny with that of a beggar-musician—an apt twinship to suggest expression of emotion and quest for meaning. Both men are numb, the man in his fingers and the youth in his heart; both are surrounded by snarling dogs; both go unheeded by their fellow men. Both depart into the dead, snowy land in psychic and musical unison. "Strange old man— shall I go with you? / Will you grind your music to my songs?"

In résumé, *Die Winterreise* is a spiritual excursion from spring to winter rendered in the psychic death of a rejected lover who is resurrected to re-encounter the dead world in which he suffers. The mind hunts for the secret of Life. He learns that both love and hope deceive and that life alone is worth clinging to. The two suns of love and hope have set on the winter horizon; the third sun, life, is setting at the end of the cycle, as the youth goes off singing to the crank-organ tune of his companion, a beggar.

III

Lucy Gayheart, too, is a *Winterreise*, drawn not as a lyrical sequence of loosely connected emotional states but as the narrative definition of a developing sensibility. In both cases, the focus is on the fate awaiting a romantic personality. Whereas Schubert's song cycle describes a day's return to the region of amorous misfortune, Willa Cather's novel recounts approximately a year's venture from the town of confinement and banality to the city of vitality and love and then the return to the town. The final importance of both journeys is alike: the romantic youth and the romantic young woman each discovers the limitation of human love, and the knowledge leads them to surrender to the secret energy of life for which human love was an impermanent representation. Both acquire a mind of winter. The novel begins during the Christmas holidays in 1901, when Lucy is home vacationing from her music studies, and ends in January, 1903, when, home again, this time to escape the city associated with her dead lover, she meets her own accidental death. Within this short span of time and in those two places Cather gives all there is to know of Lucy Gayheart's life, the significance of which the heroine herself puts in seasonal terms. Rebuffing Harry Gordon, a hometown admirer who thinks of her only in hometown ways and makes his claim for love accordingly, she says: "'Everything has changed this winter'" (110).

Two patterns dramatize Lucy's winter passage. The more conspicuous is the seasonal cycle. Reversing the conventional order, Cather has the romance begin in the dead of winter. In spring love burgeons, in summer the lovers separate, in autumn the lover dies, and in winter the beloved dies. The corresponding geographical movements are a winter journey eastward to love in Chicago and an autumn return westward to Nebraska. The other pattern is in music imagery. In a sense *Lucy Gayheart* is a *musikalische Reise* as well as a *Winterreise*. Lucy leaves Haverford, Nebraska, and goes to Chicago to study the piano, and through her work with music she is initiated into large emotional possibilities. Musical awareness attends a general deepening of her moral vision. The growth of the two is inseparable, especially since music accounts for what is fine in Lucy—spontaneity and a passionate receptivity to life.

The novel acquires serenity in Cather's controlled perspective. The first view of Lucy is so long after her time in Haverford that people "do not talk of her a great deal" (3). The closing view personalizes the memory of Lucy but preserves its distancing silence as Harry Gordon meditates on the great change in the world since her death twenty-five years earlier. The far-off view reveals Lucy in hushed motion, "dancing or skating, or walking swiftly with intense direction, like a bird flying home" (3). Her vigor and grace are literally engraved in Haverford in "three light footprints, running away" (231). The impressions are in a sidewalk in front of the Gayheart house. Lucy made them when she was thirteen while darting over the fresh pavement from a flower garden to greet Harry Gordon. The toe marks go deeper than do those of the heel, which seemingly only grazed the surface. The contour calls to mind "swiftness, mischief, and lightness" (227). After her death, "nothing else seemed to bring her back so vividly into the living world for a moment." Cather vivifies the pictorial images of dynamic pursuit by adding sound—just enough aural vibration to suggest the human pulse behind the memory. Touches like the "very musical bells" (11), which Harry adds to his sleigh to please Lucy, hint of her delight in small matters. The musical bells are intimately associated with her. Just before she drowns in the river, Lucy hears them. She knows that Gordon is approaching and because of the cold decides to ask for a lift toward the stretch of river where she skates. He refuses her. "His sharp-shod horses trotted on, the sleigh-bells singing . . ." (197). That night he encounters the rescue party carrying Lucy's dead body back home. "He took off his sleigh-bells and walked his horses into town after the wagon train" (218).

Motion is therapeutic for Lucy. It gives form to an interior rhythm, a "rhythm that had to do with escape, change, chance, with life hurrying forward" (24). Music realizes this momentum in beautiful form. The first time she hears Sebastian sing at a recital, music sanctions the "joy of saluting what is far above one" (12). Through this confirmation music leads Lucy to reflect on her emotions. She discovers a melancholy and a "profoundly tragic" (30) sense in the baritone's style; he voices a darkness she feels inside. Cather brings the girl's knowledge of the second side of herself to our attention by having Sebastian's last group of songs begin with Schubert's setting of Heine's "Der Doppelgänger." The persona of the poem sees his other self caught in pain from want of love. The reader sees a prophecy in the poetic discovery. Lucy begins to grapple with a dark feeling beneath the sanguine vivacity which usually rules her life.

> You ghostly double, pale companion—
> why do you ape the pain of love
> that tortured me, in this very place,
> so many nights in times gone by?[5]

Of the several nuances of revelation which come through music Cather develops the one explaining the emotional impact of the song on Lucy. "Some peoples' lives are affected by what happens to their person or their property; but for others fate is what happens to their feelings and their thoughts—that and nothing more" (32). For these people, vocal music is the perfect kind of enlightenment because it speaks directly to the heart and the mind. "As she sat listening to this man the outside world seemed to her dark and terrifying, full of fears and dangers that had never come close to her until now" (31). The anticipation of danger recalls the youth in *Die Winterreise* who also can reminisce about the future as "the ravens croaked from the roof-top." Cather's musical prefiguration of disaster is Byron's "When We Two Parted," which is Sebastian's encore at the first of his recitals that Lucy attends. The air also undercuts Lucy's emotional claims since at this point her relationship with the singer is exclusively in her fancy, and it chides her fabrication openly and accurately:

> When we two parted,
>   In silence and tears,
> Half broken-hearted,
>   To sever for years,
>
> Pale grew thy cheek and cold,
>   Colder thy kiss;
> Surely that hour foretold
>   Sorrow to this. (32)

The closer Lucy draws to Sebastian at rehearsals and at concerts the more fully his music influences her heart and, therefore, her fate.

The closer she draws, the more Lucy learns of the way art can meliorate the personal life of the artist, an issue Willa Cather seems inevitably inclined to raise. Here Sebastian is Cather's spokesman: He decries fashion in art which exposes quality to the vagaries of dinner chitchat. Sebastian's aloofness is designed to protect his integrity from

5. Prawer, *The Penguin Book of Lieder*, p. 66.

public whim. Withdrawal affects even the intimate relationships of the artist. The failure of his marriage resulted from the psychological hardening which Cather believed an artist needed to acquire. As the great artist's integrity must be unassailable, so his private life must seem inaccessible to others. But to the romantic heart barriers of this kind actually are inducements. Lucy idolizes Sebastian's isolation. "If you brushed against his life ever so lightly it was like tapping on a deep bell; you felt all that you could not hear" (46). Lucy can hear a good deal, and she feels still more. Sebastian's real self recedes while his professional self appears more clearly to the girl. She is puzzled by his amiability because it betrays her impressions and expectations. Outside the studio he seemed "stern," "forbidding." In the privacy of rehearsals "he met her with a smile, and throughout the morning was friendly and affable. Yet she went away feeling that the other man, whom she used to see secretly, was his real self" (49). She reserves the right to assert feeling over fact whenever the world does not go her way or follow her understanding.

That her feeling has merit even to others is implied in the contrast with her rival at the keyboard, James Mockford, Sebastian's regular accompanist. Mockford is "'not especially good'" interpreting music like that of Mozart and the Italian composers which requires a personal and liberal approach; but "'in the true German Lieder, whatever he does seems to be right'" (56). Precision is his strength. He is haughty and defensive, as lesser talents can be when they sense a professional threat. He deliberately closes the circle of Sebastian's relationships by reminding the easily overawed Nebraska girl that she is an outsider and that Sebastian's situation excludes a personal and professional third party. We see how envious and self-assertive he can be in his calling Sebastian by his first name, accenting it in the French way (Clément), and by his familiar tone— privileges Lucy may not claim. Mockford also is intriguing behind the scene for a more prominent billing than accompanist. Lucy's generosity forbids such machinations.

She also knows her place artistically. She sees that "an inexperienced country girl" (60–61) does not bring the requisite training to the work. Her flattering admiration perhaps serves Sebastian's vanity as much as her playing serves his voice. She accepts this secondary and patronized status because the experience provides rare opportunities for her heart to exploit. If the relationship is false, one-sided, her excitement about his elegant life and music is genuine. Through self-knowledge comes guarded confidence, and confidence depends on whichever truth is trustworthy. To Lucy, truth is beauty and feeling. When her famous employer is on tour, she sits at the piano to play over some songs of *Die schöne Müllerin* (*The Fair Maid of the Mill*), another Schubert song cycle. The gesture is not without its delicate ironies. While the song cycle belongs to Sebastian's concert repertoire, it fits nicely into Lucy's collection of spiritual specialties. Schubert's music bridges the baritone's absence by carrying the girl to the atmosphere of soft, tranquil feelings which his life signifies. The piano music seems to beckon the return of the voice it is meant to accompany in much the same way that Sebastian's presence would complete Lucy's euphoria. And the words, which the allusion invites us to supply, duplicate the circumstance and hope of the voice in the songs—a peasant lover, here a Nebraska girl, calling for a lost beloved. Lucy's thoughts mingle with images from *Die schöne Müllerin* as she plays the music. "She was thinking that he must be already on his way home, settled in his stateroom and rushing through the great snowy country up there . . . full of forests and lakes, she had heard tell" (66).

All her work at the piano is rewarding; music improves the quality of her life. But her involvement in the many messages of love in the music she plays invites a fatal transference of art to life. She expects Sebastian's life to have the romantic intensity of his songs. When she asks if he never got "'any pleasure out of being in love,'" for example, he says: "'N-n-no, not much'" (69). Lucy grasps the dramatic distancing in Sebastian's singing but cannot separate the message in music from the demands of life even though, had she listened carefully to the lyrics, she would never have confused the two. The analogy Cather applies to Lucy's euphoria is Schubert's "*Die Forelle*" ("The Trout"), written to Christian Schubart's poem. In Sebastian's world, irritations are shut out. "Life was resolved into something simple and noble—yes, and joyous; a joyousness which seemed safe from time or change, like that in Schubert's *Die Forelle*, which Sebastian often sang" (76). Later the song of the nimble, jolly trout cheated of its freedom by a fisherman-thief serves as a *leitmotif* for the singer's entire world, which is inseparable from the girl's conception of peace. Permanence and joy exist in Lucy's mind and heart only, of course; Sebastian's world is snuffed out suddenly.

The country girl brings youth and vitality close to Sebastian. His "secret belief" is that he could pick youth up again "somewhere" (77). With Lucy he does. The emotional reciprocation is youth for music. She lives through his singing, he through her vigor. And so they love. In neither case, however, does love halt the onslaught of change (for Lucy) or death (for Sebastian), as each believes it can; love brings a death of its own. Sebastian should be able to see from his broken marriage that the gold sparks in the girl's eyes are momentary flashes. For all his maturity he seems caught in a romantic need almost as sharp as Lucy's. Curiously, his listening to the girl speak recalls Lucy's listening to him sing: "Sebastian was listening not to what she said, but to the rush of feeling in her warm young voice" (85). The expression of their love is as tacit and intuitive as their motives are inexpressible. The English air, "She Never Told Her Love" (94), vows his devotion and her concealment.

This exchange takes place in March. Winter and Lucy's winter journey are nearly over; and both end happily. In January all was inchoate, full of fair chance. "She began a new life on the night when she first heard Clement Sebastian. Until that night she had played with trifles and make-believes" (94). In March, "the happiest month she had ever known" (92), all is realized. Winter has changed everything. In the cruelest month full of twilights, April, Lucy and Sebastian are separated because of his spring concert tour. He has his art; she, her memories. April also brings Haverford and its memories to Chicago in the person of Harry Gordon. The theme changes from ideal love to prosaic love. Cather adjusts the music references accordingly. Instead of tender, lyrical songs we have dramatic operas. For Lucy the conversion is both an emotional lowering and a removal from art—from being a participator she becomes a spectator—which is pretty much the distinction she makes about life with Sebastian or a future with Gordon.

Gordon's visit brings the values of city and town, art and life, feeling and fact, into direct confrontation. The grounds of the old hostility are shifted to a theater and an art museum, placing the town on the defensive. A winter with Sebastian makes the Haverford mentality seem more mundane than it has been for Lucy, and it was tedious enough when she knew only Haverford. So the prospect of a wealthy hometown suitor taking her to a week of opera—a plan which would have pleased her last year—displeases Lucy. All that she likes and dislikes about Harry Gordon is revealed in his voice, just as the voice of most Cather figures speaks for the inner self. Gordon's speech is genial and confidential but it is also at times tinged with an "impersonal cordiality" (149) and a calculated shade of surprise. It is a voice eminently suited for business affairs, cautious, deferential, bland, and altogether wrong for less impersonal transactions. It cannot compete successfully with a famous *Lied* voice for Lucy's affection. But she catches "a good sense of rhythm" (98) when they are dancing and she knows that Gordon has a good, "real voice" (150) beneath the falsetto; unfortunately he cannot undo the emotional training which warns him against using it. Gordon's evenings with Lucy, planned quite deliberately to sweeten the young lady's attitude toward him and yet not to bore the gentleman, are spent at the opera. At every turn his manners serve him well, though ultimately they are self-defeating as all calculated amenities are. For Lucy's sake, he does not overtly ridicule her fidelity to art and artists; but withholding ridicule implies condescension. Lucy's values are "'sentimentally sacred'" (99), properties irrelevant to the business of living. Lucy senses what is in Gordon's mind and rightly feels that an afternoon at Marshall Field's, selecting handkerchiefs and ties for back home, is more profitable than several hours at an art museum.

Had Lucy followed this instinct she would have spared herself unpleasantness. At the Art Institute their temperaments collide. Lucy is receptive to the French Impressionists; Gordon, suspicious of them. Representational art strikes him as more meaningful because it deals with *fact* and the recognizable world. Fact, as Gordon uses the term, excludes everything Lucy prizes. As she responds to the Impressionist works, larger, richer associations of mood, texture, color—feeling, in short—become fact. Gordon's persistent literalism depresses Lucy. His narrowness threatens to drag her back into the dullness she wanted left behind her. Departing from the Art Institute (Gordon had given her the customary weary tap on the elbow), she yearns to flee the confinement of his sensibility and float with the gulls over nearby Lake Michigan.

The division is widened that evening at the opera during *Lohengrin*. The first measures of Wagner's music lift her back into the Sebastian feeling that she tried to regain that morning. By the end of the first act her place is secured in that "invisible, inviolable world" (104) of desire. In constructing a bridge to the kingdom of the soul, music razes the old make-shift links to lesser places. Like Professor St. Peter during *Mignon*, Lucy leans away from her companion. Later that evening the last brace of the bridge falls. Lucy misrepresents her relationship with Sebastian, calling him her lover, and Harry stalks out of the dining room. He takes his stand for fact and truth. His position, if not his conduct, is foretold in his attitude toward music. "'Music doesn't mean much to me without you, except to remind me of you'" (108). To see his circumscribed sympathy for music is to know his limited capacity for the kind of life and love that Lucy seeks. Both Gordon and Lucy remember things through music, but with him the power does not liberate and transform.

Gordon's visit is the first in a series of spring disappointments. Later in April news of Sebastian's European tour terrifies Lucy who must stay behind by herself. The air, "When We Two Parted," returns to her inner ear as a reminder of the hour that "foretold / Sorrow to this." They embrace, and from the moment together Lucy smuggles a phrase which holds the soul of Schubert's love songs. That Sebastian whispers it in German enhances the tone of masculine tenderness which has already captivated the girl: "'*Ein schöner Stern ging auf in meiner Nacht*'" (128). The beautiful star in Lucy's night soon goes out; Sebastian drowns in Lake Como in September. The seasonal cycle and love circle have rounded: from love, through separation, to death.

IV

Book II shows the effect of sorrow on the star that rose in Sebastian's night. Without the setting of his attention, it loses its shine. Lucy, back in Nebraska, lives in real darkness now and is unnerved by it. The natural rhythm of her body is broken. Graceful, energetic swirling spurts into abrupt nervous running. Instead of pursuing a desire, she tries to escape indefinite nuisances. "It used to be as if she were hurrying toward something delightful, and positively could not tarry. Now it was as if she were running away from something, or walking merely to tire herself out" (146). She wants to be alone, so she tells herself. She really wants to escape knowledge of herself, avoid admitting that she has abandoned her most meaningful engagement, music and musical studies. Readjustment to Haverford on any terms, even stoical ones, amounts to a regression for Lucy. Her natural and radiating friendliness gives way to misanthropy and bitterness and the silly trick of trying "accidentally" to revive a relationship with Gordon. It is a life without direction, the way her frequent walks are purposeless; and it is a life without music.

Images of cold contrast the winter journey of last year in Chicago with the one in Haverford. The invigorating wintry cold of Chicago carried Lucy's spirits on lifts of wind, but the psychological frigidity of the small town stings the girl and forces her to bundle up into psychic withdrawal. Unfortunately the cold does not anaesthetize. Her nerves are easily chafed. Lucy's manner becomes acrimonious in a way that her previous good cheer would have made one think impossible. The very idea of paying a short call, of any human intercourse, chills her. "Her throat closed up, and her mind seemed frozen stiff" (148). Sebastian's mementoes, gloves and marked scores which friends packed for Lucy, stay in the bottom of a trunk. Memories hurt Lucy, as they do the youth in *Die Winterreise*. "To have one's heart frozen and one's world destroyed in a moment—that was what it had meant" (156). "Cold and exhausted" (158) from psychic struggling, Lucy can, again like Schubert's youth, find relief in the very source of pain. "She could breathe only in the world she brought back through memory" (156). Music, of course, is the vehicle of memory and the access to a world elsewhere. In the orchard—Willa Cather's recurrent symbol for curative solitude—Lucy can repeat "lines from some of Sebastian's songs, trying to get exactly his way of saying the words, his accent, his phrasing. She tried to sing them a little" (157). The refrain from the first song she played for him haunts her waking and sleeping hours. It expresses the search in every winter journey: "'*Oh that I knew . . . where I might find Him . . .*'" (157). Life is not found in Harry Gordon, as Lucy still mistakenly believes. Restoring the friendship of last year and explaining the falsehood about Sebastian are futile attempts to melt the vanity and moralistic self-righteousness which cramping small-town ways developed in Gordon. His eyes, "as cold as icicles" (149), show that he cannot act; he cannot even be kind, as his true impulses prompt him to be.

Cold depicts Lucy's condition and music measures its intensity. She cannot bring herself to play or teach the piano. The rebuke of silence again is Cather's special gesture of defiance. Music does come into Lucy's life, however, two weeks before Christmas when a traveling opera company performs in Haverford. As a song recital changed her life last winter in Chicago, so an opera is a turning point in Lucy's life this winter. The work is Balfe's *The Bohemian Girl*, an old chestnut even for a 1903 audience in the Platte valley. And that is precisely Cather's point about the musical evening; everything in a sense is a cliché, everything except the human flair behind it. Lucy is alive enough to recognize the subtle excitement. She hears an old, has-been singer with a sweet but "worn" voice, and this sets Lucy wondering what "singing this humdrum music to humdrum people" means: "why was it worth while?" (181). The old singer exemplifies one who has kept high standards of artistic performance though she cannot meet them. It is the pursuit, the desiring, of her art that sustains the soprano in what little talent she has left. Unappreciative listeners do not matter. The importance is in the brain of the performer. Neither hackneyed material nor dull audience tarnish the artist's luster. Fire and integrity like this inspire Lucy.

The second enlightenment from music forces Lucy to see that she must not allow sadness, family, town, or anything to stand in the way of life. She owes allegiance to herself. "She wanted flowers and music and enchantment and love,—all the things she had first known with Sebastian. What did it mean,—that she wanted to go on living again? How could she go on, alone?" (184) The answer is suggested in that "point of silver light" (11) which flashed before Lucy at the beginning of the novel and which became the *schöner Stern* of Sebastian's night. She felt the "joy of saluting what is far above . . . an eternal thing, not merely something that had happened to her ignorance and her foolish heart" (12). Life is the eternal thing. She must live as much as she can.

Hope deepens into self-knowledge and world-knowledge. Borrowing from *Die Winterreise*, one can say that Lucy sees three "phantom suns" in the darkening sky. Lucy might well provide the accompaniment for what the youth sings of these deceptive allurements. "You are not my suns! / Go, gaze into other faces! / Not long ago I had three suns— / now the two best have gone down." Friendship, youth, home, and all the material success that Gordon represents are delusions; romance, enchantment, the city, art, and all that Clement Sebastian meant to Lucy are equally false. Her true love and real sun is Life; Gordon and Sebastian are phantom suns. "What if—what if Life itself were the sweetheart? It was like a lover waiting for her in distant cities—across the sea; drawing her, enticing her, weaving a spell over her" (184). If it is Life she loves, then her kneeling beside the window "to breathe the cold air" of a winter storm is the perfect genuflection. If it is Life, then she must chase the "fugitive gleam" in the eastern sky for "it was there, in the breeze, in the sun . . ." (183). Starting with the sun, Lucy plans to go eastward to Chicago in March. With her firm resolve to get all she can in the world, there comes back to her mind an encouragement from Mendelssohn's *Elijah*: "*If with all your heart you truly seek Him, you shall ever surely find Him*" (185). She knows what Sebastian meant when he sang it for her. Lucy's determination echoes the strong pronouncement in the song cycle: "Gaily on into the world, / braving wind and weather!" But Lucy's plans for March end in January with her going through the ice and drowning. She does not die from having lived, as she had hoped, but from desiring to live. Willa Cather honors desire. The grim point seems clear: in a world more designed to thwart and diminish than to promote, desire must stand for fulfillment. The tenor's concluding air in Mendelssohn's oratorio suggests an aural image beautifully appropriate to the quality of Lucy's agreement with life that Willa Cather honors here. Elijah too commits himself to whatever lies behind the storm of the world. The prophet's music has Lucy's kind of inner strength. The passage is from Isaiah 54 : 10. "For the mountains shall depart, and the hills be removed; but Thy kindness shall not depart from me, neither shall the covenant of Thy peace be removed."[6]

Lucy's second *Winterreise* is counterpointed against the first one. The music pattern changes, too. The first winter journey is heightened by the numerous allusions to song and opera; the second journey, fatal and sad, is almost without music. Music occurs four times during the second winter journey. It exacerbates Lucy's painful awareness of lost joy or it incites a hope which is not fulfilled.

The third and last book of *Lucy Gayheart* skips ahead twenty-five years after Lucy's death to the winter of 1927. It, too, is a *Winterreise*. This time the searcher is Harry Gordon. As in the song cycle, the journey occurs on a single winter night. And like the excursion of both Schubert's hero and Cather's heroine, Gordon's passage takes place in the mind and has the meaning of life as its goal. It begins as his mind reaches back in time to the hour of a love now lost, then wanders through places of death, swerves through places associated with life and love, pauses over pain and joy, and comes upon the understanding that life itself is the great thing about life, at which point the journey ends.

The funeral for Lucy's father introduces the winter journey. The Gayheart story is over. Harry surveys his past in order to see where it has led him. At fifty-five he can look back with a certain satisfaction on a solid record of achievement—like others of his generation he served in the war with an ambulance unit, returned home to prosper in business, and lived a quiet married life. But he has known a brighter ideal than that provided by the Great War, a richer prosperity than financial success, and a deeper love than his wife's. "Lucy was the best thing he had to remember" (223). "She seemed gathered up and sustained by something that never let her drop into the common world" (215). Even at the time he was punishing her by ignoring the note of pleading in her voice, Harry assumed that "he and Lucy Gayheart would be together again" (217). He regrets his meanness, but time has reduced his sense of guilt. Gordon is resigned to live with disappointments and the remembrance of Lucy. Schubert's young man had his beloved's nosegays, Lucy had

6. *Elijah: An Oratorio* (New York: G. Schirmer, n.d.), p. vii.

Sebastian's gloves and musical scores, Harry has three light footprints, running away.

By bringing us into Harry Gordon's mind, Willa Cather allows us to hear the good, real voice that Lucy heard in him. The winter experience he utters proves what Lucy Gayheart knew to be true all along: for those who live by something much stronger than themselves, "fate is what happens to their feelings and their thoughts—that and nothing more." That splendid something can take hold of a prudent, serious man with the force with which it seizes a capricious, impulsive girl. It assumes many forms. Art for some, artists for others. Whatever the shape, it goes back to love, feeling, and youth. For Harry Gordon, it is Lucy. "She has receded to the far horizon line, along with all the fine things of youth, which do not change" (224). For Lucy, it was Sebastian. For the reader, it is a song cycle. *Die Winterreise* assembles the various winter stories of the mind and the heart in a form which affirms their beauty and power against the negations surrounding them.

V

When Willa Cather first wrote about the Virginia she knew as a child in her 1893 story, "The Elopement of Allen Poole,"[7] she made concrete her recollection of Back Creek Valley's natural repose by including details of its physical music. "The red harvest moon was just rising; on one side of the road the tall, green corn stood whispering and rustling in the moonrise, sighing fretfully now and then when the hot south breeze swept over it. . . . From the wavering line of locust trees the song of the whip-poor-will throbbed through the summer night." Cather registers the beauty of the whispering corn and throbbing bird-song in the heart of the tale's hero, Allen Poole, a "big and blue-eyed" moonshiner who is a favorite with the women and a pest to the tax authorities. One moonlit night, when Allen sets out to elope with his beloved Nell, the song in the southern air touches him. "The man's heart went out to the heart of the night, and he broke out into such a passion of music as made the singer in the locusts sick with melody." Allen Poole, as the brief description leads one to suspect, is another of Cather's "lord[s] of so much life." Like the many others of his spiritual rank in the early stories, Allen is "naturally musical." His whiskey and whistle identify him. His music is also his

7. The story is printed in *The Kingdom of Art*, pages 437–441, and is discussed by Miss Slote on pages 104 ff.

undoing. The passion of music which enchants the whippoorwill becomes a tip-off to the revenue officer who shoots Allen. But before death silences him for good, he whistles for his love: "Nelly Bly shuts her eye when she goes to sleep. . . ."

The whippoorwill and the tranquil harmony of the Shenandoah Valley for which it sings reappear in Willa Cather's mature study of Virginia, *Sapphira and the Slave Girl* (1940),[8] but simple mountain people are replaced by antebellum aristocrats and servants. The change, of course, reflects the difference between first and last interests and reminds us of the convolution of Cather's theme. She starts by celebrating the strong, bold qualities in man's blood and finishes by observing the delicate refinements of his manner. The conclusions of "The Elopement of Allen Poole" and *Sapphira and the Slave Girl* illustrate the way Cather's interest developed. Both end with death. In the story, "he drew a long sigh, and the rest was silence." In the novel, we are told of the aged Sapphira's dying "upright in her chair . . . . The strong heart had been overcome at last" (294). Sapphira's sitting in the parlor as though she is still watching "the evening light fade over the white fields and the spruce trees across the creek" accurately captures the novel's meaning and what Cather's concern for the drama in the heart and the mind of man finally brought her to. She treats Allen's death melodramatically and emphasizes the stillness death imposes on his vitality. Sapphira's stillness comes before death and signifies a deep composure. *Sapphira and the Slave Girl* is Willa Cather's ripeness-is-all novel.

The novel defines a number of life-journeys which lead to a readiness for death, but two are especially important. The title tells us whose they are. Sapphira Dodderidge Colbert is the principal figure. When the story begins, she is in her mid-fifties and in a late stage of dropsy. Though immobilized, her presence dominates the life around her, and she maintains the manner of her slave-owning family from Loudoun County even though slavery is alien to Frederick County where she now lives. Her strong mind accounts for her success, and infirmity seems to have quickened her mental powers. One consequence of this sensitivity is a misconstruction of her husband Henry's kindness toward Nancy, the mulatto slave girl. Assuming that there is an affair, Sapphira sets out to ruin Nancy by inviting Martin Colbert, her husband's nephew and an advocate of *le droit de seigneur* in matters concerning attractive slave girls, to visit them

8. *Sapphira and the Slave Girl* (New York: Alfred A. Knopf, 1940). All references are to this text.

and by assigning Nancy to care for Martin's room. The perfect set-up is spoiled when Nancy asks Rachel Blake, Sapphira's daughter, for help. Mrs. Blake, who already disapproves of slavery, arranges for Nancy to ride the underground railway to Canada. There Nancy prospers as house-keeper for a wealthy British family and as mistress of her own household—her husband and three children. An epilogue describes Nancy's return twenty-five years after her escape and recounts the death of Sapphira. *Sapphira and the Slave Girl*, in short, treats issues which Cather has made her own: the spiritual release of youth, the disposition of a dying woman who matches her will against family and fate, and the manner of the past. The novel's distinctive quality is Cather's studious demonstration of how love and duty in small everyday acts create a dignity of mind with which man can confront defeat and destiny. And, as Wallace Stevens observed, the book is composed with an artistry that conceals itself beneath a clear surface.[9]

The meaning of *Sapphira and the Slave Girl* does not depend on music, but music does amplify Cather's theme in an important way. Several references are obviously matters of detail. Nancy, like many Cather figures, is remembered through song. The child narrating the Epilogue knew Nancy through music before actually meeting her: "*Down by de cane-brake, close by de mill, | Dar lived a yaller gal, her name was Nancy Till*" (281). The song earlier catches Martin Colbert's rakish swagger. As he approaches Nancy, who is in a tree picking cherries, he sings gloatingly of "a yaller gal."

One episode also delicately suggests the brutality of slavery through music. Tansy Dave, a Dodderidge slave, fell in love with Susanna, a seamstress owned by a neighbor, Mrs. Morrison. Dave begs Sapphira to buy Susanna, insisting that he "'would run away and foller her if she was took off on the cars'" (206). Moved by Dave's desperation, Mrs. Colbert tries to buy the girl, but Mrs. Morrison refuses and takes the girl to Baltimore. Dave did run after Susanna but returned disheartened and within six years is reduced from a jolly sort to a "half-witted ghost of a man" (205). The loss of Susanna, "a pretty dancer," alienates Dave from the human community. He used to be "very clever with his mouth-

9. See *Letters of Wallace Stevens*, selected and edited by Holly Stevens (New York: Alfred A. Knopf, 1966), p. 381. Stevens writes: "I am also writing to New York today to ask a dealer there to send you a copy of Willa Cather's *Sapphira*. Miss Cather is rather a specialty. You may not like the book; moreover, you may think she is more or less formless. Nevertheless, we have nothing better than she is. She takes so much pains to conceal her sophistication that it is easy to miss her quality."

organ" and play while the slaves danced, but now he lives alone and on scraps of handouts. Cather's outrage is umistakable and the more forceful because it is dramatic rather than polemical. Slavery can kill man's spirit. Her point is extended through music. Cather endows this dark castaway with a compensatory musical gift expressing the intolerable lonesomeness and heartless immensity of self which slavery inflicted on him. His voice echoes the void of the nonhuman world. "Dave could perfectly imitate the call of the wild turkey . . ." (208).

The most important music references in *Sapphira and the Slave Girl* intensify Cather's religious subject. The first occurs at the Easter service of 1856 when the congregation sings "There is a Land of Pure Delight." The novel provides that portion of the hymn which is relevant:

> Could we but stand where Moses stood
> And view the landscape o'er
> Not Jordan's stream nor death's cold flood
> Would fright us from that shore. (79)

The land of pure delight is not only the obscure post-mortal paradise specified in the song but also a place on earth. Most of the characters are outlanders from where they belong or want to be, and that place of desire is for each a land of pure delight. Sapphira belongs on the old estate in Loudoun County; Rachel Blake, her daughter, in Washington where she enjoyed the activity of a congressman's wife; Nancy in Frederick County even though she does well in Montreal; Till, Nancy's mother, in Chestnut Hill among "folks" and not backwoods people; Old Jezebel, Nancy's grandmother, in Guinea where she was born; and Tansy Dave wherever Susanna is. Music is the anthem for the heart's home and a praise of the Pisgah sight which illumines it.

Another hymn echoes the theme of man's need for a place in the world which nourishes hope. Lizzie and Bluebell, two slave women, sing "In the Sweet By and By" at Old Jezebel's funeral. As in "There is a Land of Pure Delight," this hymn implies a special spiritual eye of man which sees a world behind the one in which he lives. The hymn depicts the visionary world of self and induces us to see our spiritual home. The chorus is repeated. The entire hymn runs:

> There's a land that is fairer than day,
> And by faith we can see it afar;
> For the Father waits over the way,
> To prepare us a dwelling place there.

In the sweet by-and-by,
We shall meet on that beautiful shore,
In the sweet by-and-by,
We shall meet on that beautiful shore.

We shall sing on that beautiful shore
The melodious songs of the blest,
And our spirits shall sorrow no more,
Not a sigh for the blessing of rest.

To our bountiful Father above,
We will offer our tribute of praise,
For the glorious gift of His love,
And the blessings that hallow our days.[10]

In the novel, the blessings that hallow our days are habits of body and habits of mind. Doing our tasks with loving duty dignifies life and trains our Pisgah eye to gaze upon the Promised Land with courage. And for this reason Cather is exacting in her account of the small chores and customs on the mill farm.

The music reference carrying the greatest importance is a Scotch hymn, "God Moves in a Mysterious Way." Henry Colbert ponders the question of slavery and its evils, which in turn raises the question of all human life. As he looks into the spring night, his eye takes in the great design beyond physical fact. "He opened his north window and looked out . . . . As he stood there, he repeated to himself some verses of a favourite hymn" (111). Cather gives six lines, the first two and the second quatrain in full, of Cowper's hymn ("Light Shining out of Darkness").

God moves in a mysterious way
    His wonders to perform;
He plants his footsteps in the sea,
    And rides upon the storm.

Deep in unfathomable mines
    Of never-failing skill,
He treasures up His bright designs
    And works His sovereign will.

Ye fearful saints, fresh courage take,
    The clouds ye so much dread
Are big with mercy, and shall break
    In blessings on your head.

10. *Heart Songs* (Boston: The Chapple Publishing Company, Ltd., 1909), p. 485.

Judge not the Lord by feeble sense,
But trust him for his grace:
Behind a frowning providence
He hides a smiling face.

His purposes will ripen fast,
Unfolding every hour;
The bud may have a bitter taste,
But sweet will be the flower.

Blind unbelief is sure to err,
And scan his work in vain:
God is his own interpreter,
And he will make it plain.[11]

The hymn expresses Colbert's equanimity and is of a piece with Willa Cather's metaphoric rendering of faith in the other songs. The believing eye sees; the unbelieving eye is blind. "God Moves in a Mysterious Way" sings of the visionary possession Moses achieved on Mount Pisgah, the bright view asked for in "There is a Land of Pure Delight." Cather duplicates the eye image in Colbert's own response to what he sees in "the air of the soft, still, spring night." "We must rest," the miller says to himself, "on our confidence in His design. . . . Perhaps our bewilderment came from a fault in our perceptions; we could never see what was behind the next turn of the road" (111).

The relevance of the hymns to *Sapphira and the Slave Girl* is unmistakable: ways of seeing are ways of believing and meeting destiny. The conclusion of the novel describing Sapphira's position in death takes on poignancy when considered in the context of the hymns. She died watching the evening light fall over snowy fields. "When Till came in with the lights, she would let her leave only four candles, and they must be set on the tea-table so placed that the candle-flames inside were repeated by the flames out in the snow-covered lilac arbour" (294). More than a treasured contrivance of an aged lady, the flames inside and their double in the lilacs aesthetically right the fault in human perception. The double image brings what is behind the next turn of the road before the eye. The believing eye balances the parts of His bright designs. The image defines a mental composure strong enough to reach out and possess the invisible world of the heart. Taken collectively,

11. William Cowper, *The Poetical Works of William Cowper*, volume III (London: Bell and Dadly, n.d.), p. 38.

"There is a Land of Pure Delight," "In the Sweet By and By," and "God Moves in a Mysterious Way" respond anew to the question of the value of human labor which Willa Cather posed in Brahms's *Requiem* and the songs answer with a knowledge of human affairs voiced in the *Dies Irae*.

VI

The last three published stories of Cather's career, brought together posthumously in *The Old Beauty and Others* (1948),[12] are further studies of a lost era when life had design and beauty. The reader is never in doubt as to Cather's loyalties. The past is poetically recalled as "the deep, claret-coloured closing years of Victoria's reign"; the present is too worthless to be dismissed. "The Old Beauty" (1936),[13] the earliest of the three stories, makes a case for "'the code'" through Gabrielle Longstreet, a lovely woman in the past of whom time has made a "ruin," who dies of having encountered a couple of "'those creatures'" with the impertinent ways of modern society. "The Best Years" (1945)[14] is less argumentative and more nostalgic and it is a fine piece of fiction. Cather speaks for the last century by showing the quiet heroism of a very young country teacher, Lesley Ferguesson, and the benefits of "clan feeling," of being on one's own earth with one's own people. The last story in the collection, "Before Breakfast" (1944),[15] presents the past more psychologically, rather as St. Peter would think of life if he were confident of his place in the world. The mood in "Before Breakfast" is the "glorious loneliness" Cather captures so well, a time to "audit" one's past life. On balance Henry Grenfell finds that his boyhood and youth, his marriage and fatherhood were reasonably fulfilling. Family and fortune satisfied his needs for community, and whenever responsibilities of these sorts threatened to invade his personal privacy or to alter his fundamental nature he resisted them, thereby keeping them from becoming resentments. He still is himself. "Nothing had changed," so he can accept the passing of youth into old age as a natural process, not cruelty. Death is part of the plan. "A man had his little hour, with heat and cold and a time-sense suited to his endurance. If you took that away from him you left him spineless, accidental, unrelated to anything."

12. *The Old Beauty and Others* (New York: Alfred A. Knopf, 1948).
13. *Ibid.*, pp. 3–72.
14. *Ibid.*, pp. 75–138.
15. *Ibid.*, pp. 141–166.

In the three tales the one musical occasion occurs in "The Old Beauty." It counterpoints the rhythms of youth and age. Seabury is having coffee after dinner with the old beauty and her companion, Mrs. Allison, at the Maison des Fleurs watching young people "moving monotonously to monotonous rhythms,—some of them scarcely moving at all." Gabrielle regards them boredly through her lorgnette. They are doing the tango. She finds it motionless, not at all "'spirited'" like the waltz, the dance of her period. Taking up Lady Longstreet's wish to hear a waltz, Seabury arranges for the musicians to play "The Blue Danube," and waltzes with her. The differences in tempo signify deep differences in the quality of two ages. Modern youth has less verve than do two old people. The past had zest—"'open and free,'" like the swirling measure of the waltz, performed "'with the lungs full.'"

> Gabrielle took Mr. Seabury's arm. They passed a dozen couples who were making a sleepy effort and swung into the open square where the line of tables stopped. Seabury had never danced with Gabrielle Longstreet, and he was astonished. She had attack and style, the grand style, slightly military, quite right for her tall, straight figure. He held her hand very high, accordingly. The conductor caught the idea; smartened the tempo slightly, made the accents sharper. One by one the young couples dropped out and sat down to smoke. The two old waltzers were left alone on the floor.

The scene is ambiguous. Its music leaves us suspended between an impatient dismissal of the new world and a wary affirmation of the old one.

Epilogue

That lucid souvenir of the past,
The divertimento;
That airy dream of the future,
The unclouded concerto . . .
The snow is falling.
Strike the piercing chord.

Wallace Stevens

On a train bringing her back to Colorado, Thea Kronborg surveys the familiar flat country of her childhood and senses from the fresh awareness of a year's absence a vital force peculiar to the Great Plains. It is morning as the train crosses the Platte River and a new sun gilds the undersized willows and agitated shoals along the banks and the sandbars. The levelness of the terrain means home, expansive and amiable. The welcome is just tangible enough for Thea to be able to breathe it in. The air vibrates with excitement and cheer and is alive with song, song of the larks and the human heart singing of its arrival home. And "there was a new song in that blue air which never had been sung in the world before. It was hard to tell about it, for it had nothing to do with words; it was like the light of the desert at noon, or the smell of the sagebrush after rain; intangible but powerful." The aesthetic burden of music in Willa Cather's fiction is to express the ineffable, joyous song Thea Kronborg felt in the soil and in the air. But the song is no single thing.

The song Thea hears is first of all primitive and geological. The wide range of music symbolism in Cather's work comes back to its representation of a cadence in elemental life. Creation and the mysterious process of renewal are musical rhythms for Cather. This life-rhythm is most pronounced in the discoverer novels where the struggle for selfhood is inextricably bound to the change in the earth. Not only Alexandra Bergson's heart resides "down there, somewhere, with the quail and the plover and all the little wild things that crooned or buzzed in the sun." Ántonia Shimerda, Thea of course, Tom Outland, and Jean Marie Latour also feel their destiny stirring in the sound of the soil. Their achievement coincides with possession of the life-rhythm. On the Blue Mesa "it was like breathing the sun, breathing the colour of the sky" for Tom. Sky, earth, and man become a single cadence. Latour enters the same blue world the boy inhabits. "The landscape one longed for when one was far away, the thing all about one, the world one actually lived in, was the sky, the sky!" The moving air liberates. The human spirit curvetting to the sky movement penetrates "the root of the matter; Desire under all desires, Truth under all truths." That is how Professor St. Peter expresses the primitive interest in earth and water which seizes him during his summer solitude. St. Peter knew as a Kansas boy what it was like to live by the flow of the earth. In maturity he knows, too, the consequence of losing the vitalizing contact with the earth. Deprived of air, the free air of desire, man chokes. Accidental happenings smother his spirit and inter him in a quietus "without joy, without passionate griefs."

"Kingdom of the soul" is the phrase Willa Cather uses in her 1900 story "Eric Hermannson's Soul" to locate the natural dominion of the heart. Music not only symbolizes man's spiritual estate but also is the agency of transport to the region which encourages emotional and imaginative instincts. For the crude Norwegian, the violin "was his only bridge into the kingdom of the soul." The violin breaks the binding silence and negativism which religion imposes on Eric Hermannson; the dance allows Ántonia to spin physically to an interior excitement; a concerto gives Claude Wheeler a hint of the cultural adventure which he missed but which he was built to enjoy; a song lifts Lucy Gayheart out of dejection and up to the pleasant remembrance of love. Willa Cather treats music as a bridge across all the obstacles to fulfillment—denial, inhibition, suppression, misunderstanding, savagery.

The outcome of the quest for selfhood which the Cather hero undertakes depends on the outcome of his search for a spiritual home. This is the arc of the bridge. The novelist believes that the claims of self are resolved in terms of place. Man may be deprived of complete discovery and assigned to be a chronicler of "my country," like Jim Burden, or he may remain an outlander, in the fellowship of St. Peter, or he may come upon rich soil in an adopted country, like Latour and Ántonia, or he may desire a bizarre other-world, like Myra Henshawe; whatever his final moral status, the ultimate settlement is with *patria*. Mignon's air, "*Connais-tu—le pays*," in *The Professor's House* gathers together the many expressions of desire for "*le pays*" where everything is spring, blue, filled with love, and where one is surrounded by "the bounty of Heav'n." The yearning, the anticipation, the return to one's Far Island repeatedly is linked to man's musical power.

The treasure of man's individual Far Island is a life "Rich in the simple worship of a day," to cite the line of Keats that Willa Cather borrows. As the tempo of a day is rhythmic, and as the desire for its richness expresses itself in song, so Willa Cather identifies the capacity to worship the pleasures of life with musical sensitivity. In *One of Ours* Gladys Farmer, a pianist of modest talent, puts her faith in "love and kindness, leisure and art" because these are the things which humanize and brighten the world. The humanistic bent of Gladys' belief provides the way we are to evaluate Willa Cather's handling of musical sensitivity. Her sympathy cuts across many kinds of musical aptitudes, in the way that her heroes emerge from many social stations. In the end it is never the quality of musicianship or the finish of musical knowledge alone which wins the novelist's favor. For all their technique and precision, the Mockfords bore Cather. "'A voice is personality,'" Fred Ottenburg says. No amount of technical training will compensate for poverty of spirit. Taste one acquires; personality one must be born with. The stronger the soul the more appreciative Willa Cather is of the person's music. Bad high notes, notes skipped, scratchy or hysterical fiddling, gaucheries of many sorts do not count. Inept execution cannot mar the performance of generous and exciting people and cannot obscure the intention of their music. Describing Blind d'Arnault, Willa Cather makes a crucial distinction between interpretation and aspiration. "As piano-playing, it was perhaps abominable, but as music it was something real, vitalized by a sense of rhythm that was stronger than his other physical senses . . . ." Cather does not always use the term "music" in so special a sense as to make accurate presentation irrelevant to musical art. With professional musicians she makes no concession to sloppy reading. Correctness is minimal expectation. But the amateur musician requires other, broader standards. Clumsy in expression, he may in the profession of living execute his task with singular artistry, and to Willa Cather making and fulfilling the day is the highest art. Being alive to music indicates the presence of the gift for living.

The community of men eager for delight, not ashamed by joy, fulfills itself in song. The song can be the beginning or the end of the spiritual meeting; a telling snatch can become an anthem. Claude Wheeler could never have foreseen how love and kindness, leisure and art become virtues of living—not just abstractions or desires—until he shared in the musicales at the Lincoln home of the Erlichs. Not until Claude hears David Gerhardt play Saint-Saëns's violin concerto could he salute ideals as "real sources of power among men." Indivisible from Jim Burden's recollection of childhood happiness on the lonely Nebraska prairie is the friendly Harling household where informal Saturday night gatherings were made festive occasions by the playing of the old operas. As frequent as salutations and more dramatic than songs of communal jollity are the farewell songs in Willa Cather's fiction. Orpheus' lament from Gluck's opera is Professor Wunsch's adieu to music; Sebastian's singing the English air "When We Two Parted" formally opens and closes his affair with Lucy Gayheart; "Auld Lang Syne" draws the curtain on the heroic hour of railroading in American history.

Willa Cather's habit of highlighting an event with music goes back, I think, to a common instinct among people who are involved with music to celebrate an occasion in a particular way. Special occasion requires special dress, special audience, special music. It may be that music lovers naturally favor sentiment. It may be that after Wagner's exaltation of music no other service seems to revere human affairs quite so well. Whatever the reason, music solemnizes and toasts an occasion memorably. The professional musician carries this propensity even further. A singer selects a valedictory performance very carefully, with an eye to his individual contributions to art. The opening of a season or a new opera house calls for appropriate music, perhaps a new work. In closing an old house music lovers will want somehow to venerate the great tradition the edifice stood for, as when the Metropolitan opened its last season in the Thirty-ninth Street building with *Faust*, the first opera sung there. Willa Cather's use of music shows the same attention to ceremonial detail. Speaking of ritual, Professor St. Peter says near the end of his attack on science: "'It makes us happy to surround our creature needs and bodily instincts with as much pomp and circumstance as possible.'" The total effect of music is a fictive restoration of the drama which has been taken away from modern man.

In the main, Willa Cather defines a moral atmosphere through music. Where man breaks into song, there emotions are respected and people liberal. The condition of giving is raised to its highest power in art which endows feeling with communicable form. The most direct appeal feeling can make is through musical art. We see the great spiritual reach of music at the end of *The Song of the Lark* when Thea Kronborg's voice skips social and artistic distinctions and unites illiterate and sophisticate in a fellowship of the soul. The opera is *Die Walküre*; and the sequence Cather singles out, Sieglinde's discovery that Siegmund is her brother, crystalizes what is taking place on a large scale between singer and audience. The bridge of music is a linking, a union of a spiritual family. Willa Cather's conviction that art spans the many gaps among men to touch an inner sense and her constant reliance on music to dramatize this meeting make the choice of lyric singer as prototypal artist consonant with her vision and sensibility.

Vocal music speaks for desire in living human form. For Willa Cather, singing is the highest musical emanation. She defines personality through voice and in *A Lost Lady* and more complexly in *Lucy Gayheart* shapes her narrative through vocal patterns. Song, which has words to tell a story and melody to convey a feeling, represents a condition of artistic form toward which Cather's fiction aspires. Her admiration for the voice shows itself throughout her writing, but one uncollected story, "Double Birthday" (1929),[1] catches that wonderment particularly well. Doctor Engelhardt was a throat specialist before his retirement. "He had been a medical student in New York while Patti was still singing; his biography fell into chapters of great voices as a turfman's falls into chapters of fast horses." More than the pleasure of being near singers and providing medical aid, Engelhardt's practice was devoted to a lifetime dream of finding "a glorious voice, backed by a rich vitality." By chance, he hears Marguerite Thiesinger rehearsing for Class Day exercises at her high school and discovers such a voice. Marguerite's career provides the greatest chapter in his biography.

The meaning of that chapter is a tragic one. With Engelhardt's backing, Marguerite progresses rapidly, but she dies at twenty-six of a malignant growth in her throat. The physician is baffled by her death. "Youth, art, love, dreams, true-heartedness—why must they go out of the summer world into darkness? *Warum, warum?*" The singing voice not only prompts questions concerning human life but answers them. Life, like song, is beautiful and brief. The song which Engelhardt first heard

1. *Forum*, LXXI (February, 1929).

Marguerite sing is Carl Böhm's "*Still wie die Nacht.*" It begins tranquilly and becomes slightly animated. The lyric articulates Engelhardt's passion for the voice in a way that conveys the sense of the contingency of life itself:

> Still as the night, deep as the sea,
> Should love, thy love, ere be!
> Still as the night—and deep as the sea,
> Should love, thy love, should love, should love—ere be,
>
> If thou love me, as I love thee,
> I will thine own—aye be.
> Glowing as steel,—as rock firm and free,
> Should love, thy love, should love, thy love—aye be.
> Should love, thy love—aye be.[2]

The great voice in Willa Cather's fiction belongs to Thea Kronborg. The spiritual identity Thea comes into when singing Sieglinde is rooted, as she says, in the rocks and waters of the Southwest; and the covenant between man and place involves a compact between man and time as well. Willa Cather regards time as an unbroken sequence. The greatest and most discernible embodiment of the continuum is nature, with a pattern of unimpeded change and cyclical renewal. Man, whose relationship to time is that of a part to the whole, establishes his link to time through nature. Willa Cather represents many different kinds of bonds with nature— from Alexandra's physical resuscitation of the soil to Thea's catching the intervals of "life hurrying past" on her breath—each of which gives man, a particle of time, a particular identity. Willa Cather does not romanticize this tentative catching of a moment and project a family or a reputation into immortality. Rather, she emphasizes the brevity of life and urges that man seize all he can of the moment. What redeems the life of each man is history, time made human. Willa Cather's preoccupation with culture balances the outrage man feels when he sees his transience and the excitement he feels from aspiring toward an ideal. Culture preserves the identity of men after they cease to be. Now music is time formed, formed most beautifully when expressing human desire. The common heritage of man's achieved desire, his artistic contribution, is realized most fully in

2. *The International Library of Music,* volume I (New York: The University Society, 1935), pp. 122–125.

music which, as in the orchestrated ethnic strains in *Death Comes for the Archbishop*, is of a time and a place and a man.

Looking at the music material from another direction, one can see that a great deal of what has been said about Willa Cather's use of music in her fiction implicitly applies to the place of music in her mind. I would add several observations. It is difficult to think of a writer whose work reminds us more strongly that art is the child of memory. Mythology honors Mnemosyne because she bore the nine muses. Long before Willa Cather's announced decision in favor of the anterior half of the war-divided world, which was made at the age of fifty, she had sided with things as they had been. The best way back into the mind and manner of "the precious, the incommunicable past" was something itself precious and fleeting, and something itself supersensory. Music for Cather had everything to do with the form of passion and nothing to do with words which delimit and devitalize feeling. Music is the substance and conductor of remembering. She knew that music is essentially mental; her phrase is "a notable emotional language." The ear only picks up sound; the brain provides the sensitive associations which compose meaning. The meaning which music evokes preserves suggestion and the feel of things. Suggestion became the novelist's re-creation of what was as she felt it to be. Willa Cather's mind trusted music as "That lucid souvenir of the past, / The divertimento." When she found the world depleted of moral values, music was one of the things to which she could give unqualified assent. When she sought to cleanse her artistic manner of inessentials, she not only retained music but deepened its importance. The sonata-form of *The Professor's House* and the use of Bellini's opera in her novel *démeublé*, *My Mortal Enemy*, measure the profundity of Cather's faith in music. The few articles of faith she offered come most consistently through music.

"Uncle Valentine," a novella published in 1925,[3] gives us a character, Charlotte Waterford, whose relation to music seconds Willa Cather's. Aunt Charlotte is one of Cather's most reassuring and winsome ladies. Her psychological and aesthetic treasures are abundant. "Whatever it is that enables us to make our peace with life, she had found it." Her moral armistice would be incomplete without the fortification of music which she prizes above "anything else in the world" because it teaches her to enjoy art and life. Charlotte Waterford is an aristocratized Ántonia Shimerda, a democratized Thea Kronborg, which is another way of

3. *Woman's Home Companion*, LII (February, March, 1925).

saying that she is an idealized Willa Cather. We have only to reverse the initials of Charlotte Waterford's name to see the portrait as an ego ideal, and we have only to note the description of her attitude toward music to know the essence of Willa Cather's own: "She played the piano extremely well; it was not an accomplishment with her, but a way of living." As a way of living, music implies passionate involvement, strong pleasure, following bright happening after bright happening as life creates it. Music is the way of Willa Cather's credo.

Bibliography of Works Cited

WORKS OF WILLA CATHER

NOVELS AND COLLECTIONS

Alexander's Bridge. New edition with preface. Boston: Houghton Mifflin, 1912 and 1922.

Death Comes for the Archbishop. New York: Alfred A. Knopf, 1959.

The Kingdom of Art: Willa Cather's First Principles and Critical Statements, 1893–1896. Selected and edited with a commentary and two essays by Bernice Slote. Lincoln: University of Nebraska Press, 1966.

A Lost Lady. New York: Alfred A. Knopf, 1958.

Lucy Gayheart. New York: Alfred A. Knopf, 1935.

My Ántonia. Sentry Edition. Boston: Houghton Mifflin, 1961.

My Mortal Enemy. Vintage Edition. New York: Alfred A. Knopf, 1961.

Not Under Forty. New York: Alfred A. Knopf, 1936.

Obscure Destinies. New York: Alfred A. Knopf, 1960.

The Old Beauty and Others. New York: Alfred A. Knopf, 1948.

One of Ours. New York: Alfred A. Knopf, 1922.

O Pioneers! Sentry Edition. Boston: Houghton Mifflin, 1962.

The Professor's House. New York: Alfred A. Knopf, 1959.

Sapphira and the Slave Girl. New York: Alfred A. Knopf, 1940.

Shadows on the Rock. New York: Alfred A. Knopf, 1955.

The Song of the Lark. Sentry Edition. Boston: Houghton Mifflin, 1963.

Willa Cather on Writing. New York: Alfred A. Knopf, 1962.

Willa Cather's Collected Short Fiction, 1892–1912. With an introduction by Mildred R. Bennett. Lincoln: University of Nebraska Press, 1965.

Youth and the Bright Medusa. New York: Alfred A. Knopf, 1920.

UNCOLLECTED WRITINGS

"Double Birthday," *Forum,* LXXXI (February 1929), 78–82, 124–128.

"Preface," *The Wagnerian Romances,* Gertrude Hall. New York: Alfred A. Knopf, 1925.

"Three American Singers," *McClure's,* XLII (December 1913), 33–48.

"Uncle Valentine," *Woman's Home Companion*, LII (February, March 1925), 7–9, 86, 89–90; 15–16, 75–76, 79–80.

WRITINGS ABOUT WILLA CATHER

BOOKS

Bennett, Mildred R. *The World of Willa Cather*. New edition with notes and index. Lincoln: University of Nebraska Press, 1961.

Bloom, Edward, and Lillian Bloom. *Willa Cather's Gift of Sympathy*. Carbondale: Southern Illinois University Press, 1962.

Brown, E. K. *Willa Cather: A Critical Biography*. Completed by Leon Edel. New York: Alfred A. Knopf, 1953.

Lewis, Edith. *Willa Cather Living: A Personal Record*. New York: Alfred A. Knopf, 1953.

Sergeant, Elizabeth Shepley. *Willa Cather: A Memoir*. Lincoln: University of Nebraska Press, 1963.

ARTICLES

Brennan, Joseph X. "Willa Cather and Music," *The University Review*, XXXI (Spring 1965), 257–264; (Summer 1965), 175–183.

Gale, Robert L. "Cather's *Death Comes for the Archbishop*," *The Explicator*, XXI (May 1963), item 75.

Keeler, Clinton. "Narrative Without Accent: Willa Cather and Puvis de Chavannes," *American Quarterly*, XVII (Spring 1965), 119–126.

Seibel, George. "Miss Willa Cather from Nebraska," *New Colophon*, II, Part 7 (1949), 195–208.

OTHER SOURCES CITED

BOOKS

The Authentic Librettos of the French and German Operas. New York: Crown Publishers, 1939.

The Authentic Librettos of the Wagner Operas. New York: Crown Publishers, 1938.

Balfe, Michael. *The Bohemian Girl*. Libretto by A. Bunn. New York: Corlyn, 1854.

Bellini, Vincenzo. *Norma*. Libretto by Felice Romani. New York: G. Schirmer, n.d.

Bradbury, William B. *Esther, The Beautiful Queen*. Words by C. M. Cady. New York: Mason Brothers, 1856.

Brahms, Johannes. *Ein Deutsches Requiem Op. 45*. New York: Broude Brothers, n.d.

Capell, Richard. *Schubert's Songs.* Revised Edition. New York: The Macmillan Company, 1957.

Carlyle, Thomas. *Heroes and Hero-Worship.* Centenary Edition, V. New York: Charles Scribner's Sons, 1897.

Cowper, William. *The Poetical Works of William Cowper.* Volume III. London: Bell and Daldy, n.d.

A Dictionary of Hymnology. Revised with new supplement. Edited by John Julian. London: John Murray, 1907.

Dies Irae. Translated by Wentworth Dillon, Earl of Roscommon. *The Works of the English Poets.* Vol. 8. Edited by Samuel Johnson. London: C. Whittingham, printer, 1810.

Einstein, Alfred. *Schubert, A Musical Portrait.* New York: Oxford University Press, 1951.

Evans, Edwin. *Handbook to the Vocal Works of Brahms.* Vol. I of *Historical, Descriptive and Analytical Account of the Entire Works of Johannes Brahms.* London: Wm. Reeves, 1912.

Franklin Square Song Collection. Selected by J. P. McCaskey. New York: Harper and Brothers, 1881.

Gluck, Christoph Willibald. Libretto by Raniero da Calzabigi. *Orpheus and Eurydice. Metropolitan Opera House Libretto.* New York: n.d.

Heart Songs. Boston: The Chapple Publishing Company, Ltd. 1909.

International Library of Music. Volume I. New York: The University Society, 1935.

Mendelssohn, Felix. *Elijah: An Oratorio.* New York: G. Schirmer, n.d.

Moore, Thomas. *The Complete Poetical Works of Thomas Moore.* New York: Thomas Y. Crowell, 1895.

The Penguin Book of Lieder. Edited and translated by S. S. Prawer. Baltimore: Penguin Books, 1964.

Poirier, Richard. *A World Elsewhere: The Place of Style in American Literature.* New York: Oxford University Press, 1966.

The Roman Breviary. An Approved English Translation Complete in One Volume from the Official Text of the Breviarium Romanum. New York: Benziger Brothers, 1964.

Sachs, Curt. *Geist und Werden der Musikinstrumente.* Berlin: Dietrich Reimer, 1929.

———. *The History of Musical Instruments.* New York: W. W. Norton & Company, 1940.

Sapir, Marius, and Edward Sapir. *Folk Songs of French Canada.* New Haven: Yale University Press, 1925.

Schubert, Franz. *200 Songs.* English Translations and Notes by Gerard Mackworth-Young. Volume I. New York: International Music Company, 1961.

Letters of Wallace Stevens. Selected and Edited by Holly Stevens. New York: Alfred A. Knopf, 1966.

Welch, Christopher. *Six Lectures on the Recorder.* London: Oxford University Press, 1911.

NEWSPAPERS

The Commercial Advertiser. Red Cloud, Nebraska.

Lincoln *Courier.* Lincoln, Nebraska.

Nebraska State Journal. Lincoln, Nebraska.

New York *Herald.* New York, New York.

Index

✳   ✳   ✳

This index is divided into two parts. The first is an index to Willa Cather titles; the second is a general index. The italicized numbers in the first part indicate extended analysis or pointed discussion.

Part I

Part II

INDEX